Imagery

Bradford Books

Edward C. T. Walker, Editor. *Explorations in* THE BIOLOGY OF LANGUAGE. 1979. The M.I.T. Work Group in the Biology of Language: Noam Chomsky, Salvador Luria, *et alia.*

Daniel C. Dennett. BRAINSTORMS: *Philosophical Essays on Mind and Psychology.* 1979.

Charles E. Marks. COMMISSUROTOMY, CONSCIOUSNESS AND UNITY OF MIND. 1980.

John Haugeland. MIND DESIGN. 1981.

Fred I. Dretske. KNOWLEDGE AND THE FLOW OF INFORMATION. 1981.

Jerry A. Fodor. REPRESENTATIONS: *Philosophical Essays on the Foundations of Cognitive Science.* 1981.

Ned Block. IMAGERY. 1981.

IMAGERY

EDITED BY

Ned Block

A Bradford Book

The MIT Press
Cambridge, Massachusetts
London, England

Printed in the United States of America

Library of Congress Cataloging in Publication Data

Main entry under title:

Imagery.

   CONTENTS: Brown, R. and Herrnstein, R. J. Icons and
images.—Dennett, D. The nature of images and the
introspective trap.—Fodor, J. Imagistic representation.—Dennett, D. Two approaches to mental
images.—[etc.]
   1. Imagery (Psychology)—Addresses, essays, lectures.
I. Block, Ned Joel, 1942–
BF367.I45   153.3'2   81–24732
ISBN hardcover   0-262-02168-4
ISBN paperback   0-262-52072-9

CONTENTS

Imagery

INTRODUCTION
What Is the Issue?

Ned Block

After fifty years of neglect during the heyday of behaviorism, mental imagery is once again a topic of research in psychology. Indeed, with the emergence of a truly spectacular body of experiments, imagery is one of the hottest topics in cognitive science. There is even a journal entirely devoted to it. The chapters in this book are about issues raised by a particularly fascinating (though oddly elusive) set of imagery experiments. Chapter 1, "Icons and Images," describes Shepard's experiments, in which people seem to rotate mental images (and at a measurable angular velocity). Chapter 6, "On the Demystification of Mental Imagery," tells us that mental images can be scanned; that smaller mental images are harder to see; that when mental images are expanded, they eventually overflow, and what they overflow from has a determinable shape: roughly elliptical; and finally, that images subtend a measurable visual angle, which at the point of overflow can be regarded as the angle of vision of the mind's eye (which turns out to be roughly 20°). Chapter 1 and most of Chapter 6 are about imagery experiments, but the focus of the book is the debate about what the experiments *show*.

The observations that motivate these claims about images cry out for explanation. If a Martian who knew nothing of the insides of people came to earth and was shown these experiments, it would not be unreasonable for him to hypothesize that subjects use some sort of internal pictures in these experiments. But no one writing in this book (nor any of the other serious participants in the debate) thinks that people can literally see and manipulate real internal pictures. Brain scientists have found no pictures in the brain and even if they had, the presence of pictures wouldn't explain the phenomena unless the brain also contained an internal eye to view them and an internal flashlight and internal hands to manipulate them etc. (And even if we postulate an internal eye, would there be still another eye in that eye's brain?) So we have a problem: the obvious explanation of the observations is blocked.

It is worth mentioning that the heart of the problem just described has been around far longer than the experiments. People (some people anyway) have long talked naturally and spontaneously of pictures in their heads. Our Martian would find some reason to postulate pictures in the head just on the basis of what people *say*. More importantly, many of us (those who are doing the saying) find it impossible *not* to think of our imagery experience in terms of internal pictures. Chapter 2, "The Nature of Images and the Introspective Trap," antedates most of the experimental literature discussed in the other chapters, yet the basic issue in this chapter is the same as in the others. As has so often happened in philosophy of psychology, the experiments do not bring up totally new issues, but rather put old ones in a new light.

Thus far I have mentioned a problem arising from experiments on imagery and from introspection—that is, we have reason to think we have internal pictures. But we find none in the brain; so what do we make of our reasons to think there are internal pictures? This problem generates the dispute that this book is about. One side, the *pictorialist* side, takes the naive response to the experimental and introspective evidence to lead us in the right direction. The pictorialists agree that we don't literally have pictures in our brains, but they insist nevertheless that our mental images represent in roughly the way that pictures represent. The other side, the *descriptionalist* side, regards the introspective and experimental evidence mentioned as misleading. On their view we should think of mental images as representing in the manner of some non-imagistic representations—namely, in the manner of language rather than pictures.

In sum, the sentence "John is bald" represents John's being bald. The same possible state of affairs can also be represented by a painting or a statue of a bald John. What the dispute is about, roughly, is whether a mental image of a bald John represents in the first way (pictorially) or the second way (descriptionally). In this volume Dennett and Pylyshyn are descriptionalists, and Fodor and Kosslyn et al. are pictorialists.[1] (Neither Brown and Herrnstein, Chapter 1, nor Schwartz, Chapter 5, take sides. The former chapter is concerned mainly with the evidence, and the latter makes conceptual points about the dispute.) Both the pictorialists and the descriptionalists agree that there are mental representations, but the descriptionalists think that all mental representations are descriptional, while the pictorialists think that at least some mental representations, mental images, are pictorial. All the major pictorialists are willing to allow that there are descriptional representations, and thus they hold that there are (at least) two kinds of mental representations. Now as the reader will see, it is not easy to grasp what is really at stake in this dispute between the pictorialists and the descriptionalists. Though these are among the best articles on the subject, they are all elusive on at least some matters, often even precisely what they are arguing for.

One question arises immediately when one recalls that the pictorialists do not claim that mental images are literally pictures in the head. What the pictorialists claim is that mental images are *like* pictures in their mode of representation (and also in the way they are used or processed)[2] —that is, they represent (and are processed) in ways *like* the ways pictures represent (and are used or processed). This is what the descriptionalists deny. But likeness in *what respect?* Unless we are told, we can't even rule out the possibility that the relevant respect of likeness is one for which mental images are *both* descriptional and pictorial, just as an average person is similar in height to both a giant and a midget.

The question whether the representations of imagery are pictorial or descriptional is not straightforwardly empirical but is one of those problems where everything is up for grabs, including precisely what the problem is. (That is one reason why it calls for philosophic attention.) Given the obscurity of the issue, it is fair to ask why it is worthy of our attention. First, though we have only a vague idea of what the pictorial/descriptional distinction comes to,[3] still I doubt that anyone could read these papers at all sympathetically without being inclined to suppose that there probably is a genuine bone of contention here that is of considerable *intrinsic* interest. Second, the bone is important in many areas of cognitive psychology. For example, it is widely held that "prototypes" play a considerable role in thought. Rosch's work (see Mervis and Rosch, 1981 for a recent review) supports the idea that in reasoning about (say) birds, people deploy a representation of a prototypical bird, such as a sparrow. It is often supposed (see Rosch, 1975 for some experimental support) that such a representation of a prototypical bird is the same sort of entity as a mental image. If prototypes are in the same natural kind as mental images, and if prototypes are as important in thinking as now appears to be the case, then the issue of the nature of mental images is closely connected to the question of the nature of human thought. Finally, if the pictorialist view is right, then the human brain deploys representations (and processes operating over them) of a sort not found in digital computers (whose representations are paradigms of descriptional representations). So digital computers would not be able to process information in the manner of humans (though of course they might nonetheless be able to *simulate* human information processing).

Let us proceed, then, to examine the controversy, but with the understanding that this introduction will not provide an analysis of what the controversy comes to, but will instead make a number of conceptual points intended to help the reader understand the controversy. I shall begin by describing three false candidates for the issue at stake.

Do Images Exist?

Much of the current literature (see, for example, Rey, 1981) gives the impression that the issue is whether mental images exist.

In Chapter 2, Dennett recommends "abandoning mental images," and he even worries that the reader will "doubt that mental images are still taken seriously," and thus think that he is beating a dead horse in arguing that mental images don't exist. Fodor argues against Dennett that images do exist (or, as he sometimes says, that images are psychologically real). He says, in introducing the experiments he discusses, that they "seem to argue forcibly for the psychological reality of images."

What Dennett in fact ends up arguing for—and Fodor against—is the claim that mental images are descriptional rather than pictorial. Dennett asks whether mental images "represent in virtue of resembling what they represent and thus deserve to be called images." Fodor says the data suggest that "what goes on in imagery is very like picturing and very unlike describing." To be fair to Dennett and Fodor, there is a rationale for seeing the descriptional/pictorial controversy as being about the existence of mental images. If it is an analytic truth that what does not represent pictorially is not an image, then if all our mental representations are descriptional rather than pictorial, there are no mental images. But even if we ignore the usual doubts about analyticity, this line is implausible. Our use of the word "image" is grounded in talk of after-images and other mental images as well as in talk of paintings and statues.

My own view is that "the issue of whether mental images exist" is a conflation of several issues, none of which involves imagery in any important way. The culprit is ambiguity or vagueness in the term "mental image". One can take "mental image" to denote experiences, or internal (neural) representations, or even intentional objects. On each of these interpretations, whatever controversies there may be about existence could proceed just as well without mentioning mental images at all. For example, many philosophers and psychologists are skeptical about the coherence of the notion of internal representation because they think that familiar *external* representations such as the ones you are now reading represent only because of the intentions with which they are made and/or used. Since the internal representations cognitive psychologists talk about are not claimed to be made or used intentionally in anything like the same way (indeed it is not even obvious that *we* are the *users* of our own internal representations), the skeptic denies that this notion of internal representation makes sense. I don't propose to try to answer this objection here;[4] rather, I only want to point out that the objection applies equally well to descriptional and pictorial internal representations, and would be as troublesome to friends of internal representation even if mental imagery were ignored.

Are Images Epiphenomenal?

Pictorialists often talk as if the issue between them and their opponents is whether mental images are *epiphenomenal*. Kosslyn begins his (1978) discussion with: "The most fundamental issue in the study of imagery probably is whether the experienced image is functional or epiphenomenal (see Kosslyn and Pomerantz, 1977 vs. Pylyshyn, 1973)."

Shepard (1978) argues against the view that "mental images are at most subjective epiphenomena that play little or no functional role in significant processes of human thought, as some articulate commentators such as Pylyshyn (1973) have been suggesting" (p. 125).

According to the standard jargon of philosophers, to say that mental images are epiphenomena is to say they are just effects (of brain states) and never causes of anything. The usage among psychologists is slightly different, as the contrast with "functional" in the quotations indicates. According to psychologists' usage, epiphenomena can have extraneous effects (e.g., an epiphenomenal bit of brain-writing can affect a neurophysiologist who looks at it), but what makes an epiphenomenon epiphenomenal is that it plays no causal role in the brain's information processing. Thought, reasoning, etc. would go on just as they would if the epiphenomena were not present (see Dennett, Chapter 4, "Two Approaches to Mental Images," note 2). Thus, Kosslyn, describing the version of epiphenomenalism about images that he opposes, says:

> On this view, then, the image representations are merely "along for the ride", and themselves play no part in cognitive processing.

Whether or not we experience images, then, is beside the point. Images could be analogous to the lights flashing on the outside of a computer while it is adding. There is a systematic relation between the mental operations and the flashing lights, all right, but one could smash the bulbs and the computer would happily go adding along. [Kosslyn, 1980, p. 29]

Pictorialists argue against epiphenomenalism by citing *data.* For example, Kosslyn, et al. (Chapter 6) cite experiments on mental rotation, scanning, image size, and overflow. Shepard (1978) describes a series of cases in which scientists claim that their images led to their discoveries.

I shall argue that the epiphenomenalism issue is a red herring: on some interpretations, it just doesn't come to anything that disputants about imagery really disagree about; in another, it reduces to the very descriptionalism/pictorialism controversy that I have been concerned with. The culprit in the confusion is again ambiguity or vagueness in the term "mental image."

To begin with, take "mental image" to denote certain kinds of subjective experiences. If images are experiences, the evidence that pictorialists cite is certainly irrelevant. The experiments on mental rotation, scanning, etc., certainly show (for anyone who doubted it) that *something* having to do with imagery has a causal role in information-processing. But the experiments certainly do not show that what has the causal role is any kind of *experience.* The experiments cast no light at all on whether the experiences are epiphenomenal accompaniments of representations in the brain that are the real causes. Furthermore, Kekule's conviction that images of snakes swallowing their tails helped him win his Nobel Prize (one of the examples in Shepard, 1978) is also irrelevant. Kekule's conviction is on a par with the ordinary conviction that it is our pain that causes us to groan. On a par, that is, in failing to pose any challenge to epiphenomenalism. The traditional epiphenomenalist claims that a brain state causes *both* the pain and the groan. He does not deny the commonplace that experiences often *seem* to cause groans. Similarly, anyone who wanted to defend the view that image-experiences do not play a role in information-processing could allow that they *seem* to play a role. Such an epiphenomenal-ist should say that a third item (a brain state) caused both Kekule's image experience *and* his formulating the idea of the benzene ring. Since the latter occurred after the former, it seemed to Kekule that the latter was caused by the former. The debate here is basically the same as the traditional philosophical debate about epiphenomalism. The claim that image-experiences are epiphenomenal rather than functional is no more challenged by Kosslyn's and Shepard's empirical data than traditional epiphenomenalism is challenged by the fact that pains are followed by groans and seem to be caused by them.

Now take "mental image" to denote certain abstract entities (sample abstract entities: the number *3* or the property of being virtuous). Perhaps they are intentional objects, as Dennett considers in Chapter 4. On that interpretation, mental images can't be epiphenomenal, since they could not be *effects* of any causes. Abstract objects are not spatiotemporal; hence they have no causal commerce of *any* kind. On this meaning of "mental image," the pictorialists' evidence would again be irrelevant.

Finally, take "mental image" to denote the internal (neural) representations involved in imagery. Then mental images play a causal role in information-processing—but who could disagree? Certainly not Pylyshyn in the 1973 article referred to by Kosslyn and Shepard? Why should anyone who believes in internal representations suppose that the brain has a whole set of representations—the representations involved in imagery—that are entirely wasted, playing no causal role in what the brain does.

In fairness to the pictorialists, I should point out that there is one construal of their attacks on epiphenomenalism in which they are not tilting at windmills. In denying epiphenomenalism and emphasizing the role of mental images in information-processing, they perhaps intend to assert that the *pictorial properties* of mental images have effects.[5] If this is what they mean, then some of the experiments they cite are indeed relevant, but now—since only if mental images *have* pictorial properties can these properties have effects—the heart of the issue comes down to the very pictorial/descriptional controversy this book is about. The opponents of the pictorialists claim that images *don't have* pictorial properties, not that they *do* have *ineffective* pictorial properties.

The confusions surrounding the issue of the existence of mental images and the issue of whether they are epiphenomenal turn on the vagueness or ambiguity of "mental image". I suggest that we can avoid confusion by simply adopting the convention of using "mental image" to denote the internal representations involved in mental imagery. Since both sides accept the notion of internal representation, we introduce no bias with this convention. Those who dislike this convention can translate talk of whether mental images are pictorial or descriptional into talk of whether the internal representations involved in mental imagery are pictorial or descriptional.

Imagery and Perception

Are the mental representations involved in imagery similar to the mental representations involved in perception? This is too often taken to be the main issue raised by experiments on imagery. Similarity of representations of imagery and perception has long seemed introspectively plausible to many people, and it is supported by Perky's (1910) demonstration that people could confuse imaging with perceiving (see Brown and Herrnstein, Chapter 1). Recent experimentation by Shepard and Finke and others has shown that imagery and perception share much of the same physiological machinery, and we are increasingly able to specify mechanisms common to imaging and perceiving.

One impressive experiment exploits the well known McCollough Effect. Subjects are shown patterns of black and red vertical stripes and black and green horizontal stripes (see the cover of this book). After looking at these patterns alternately for 10 minutes, subjects are then presented with test patterns (such as the one on the back cover) of black and *white* horizontal and vertical stripes (see Favreau and Corballis 1976 for discussion). Subjects report seeing green on the vertical white stripes and red on the horizontal white stripes. Finke and Schmidt (1977, 1978) showed subjects red and green patches and asked them to *imagine* black vertical stripes on the red patch and to imagine black horizontal stripes on the green patch. When they showed these subjects the black and white test pattern, they found that subjects tended to see the same colors in the white spaces as in the original McCollough Effect (except that the reports were generally of "faint" colors and the tendency to report colors and reported vividness of the colors was related to results on a standard questionnaire for determining vividness of imagery).

Another striking effect of this sort is described by Kosslyn in Chapter 8. It is known that visual acuity for vertical stripes is better than for oblique stripes. If subjects are asked to say when the stripes blur as the experimenter moves them farther away, they report being able to distinguish stripes when they are farther away for vertical than for oblique stripes. Pennington and Kosslyn found amazingly that this effect occurs with imaginary stripes as well. An impressive variety of results pointing to similar conclusions is summarized in Shepard (1978) and Finke (1980).

Although the experimental literature does not clearly distinguish the effects of representations from the effects of the processes that manipulate representations, the evidence to date points to the conclusion that the representations of imaging and perceiving must be treated together as either both pictorial or both descriptional. However, that does not settle the issue of pictorialism vs. descriptionalism since we can still ask of *both* the representations of imagery and perception whether they are descriptional or pictorial. The same problem arises in both cases, and the most we gain by lumping the representations of imagery and perception together is to have one problem instead of two. It's nice to have fewer problems, but we are still left with the fundamental problem whether the representations of imagery (*and* perception) are pictorial or descriptional.

When I've made this point, I'm often told that any evidence to the effect that the representations of imagery and perception are of the same sort must be evidence that both are pictorial, since "if the representations of perception aren't pictorial, what are?" The reasoning behind this objection seems to amount to this: "A good picture of Reagan gives me an experience like that I get from seeing Reagan himself. Now if my experience on seeing Reagan himself is mediated by a representation, what could the representation be like if not like a picture of Reagan?" This reasoning invokes the false principle "Like effects, like causes". The reasoning assumes that if a picture of Reagan and the representation involved in perceiving Reagan himself give us similar experiences, then the picture and the representation must be similar. However, since Reagan himself causes the same sort of Reaganish experience that his picture causes, the principle would support the existence of an internal *Reagan* as well as it does an internal picture of Reagan! The principle is just false. A fire can be caused by bad wiring, lightning or careless smoking. Similar effects have different causes. So the reasoning casts no doubt on the descriptionalist claim that our internal perceptual representation of Reagan is descriptional rather than pictorial, yet causes the same sort of experience as a photo of Reagan.

The Photographic Fallacy

Thus far I have described the dispute between pictorialists and descriptionalists and distinguished it from three other issues that are sometimes confused with it—namely, whether mental images exist, whether they are epiphenomenal, and whether and in what respects the representations of imagery are like the representations of perception. I have also flagged one difficulty in defining the issue as a question whether images represent like pictures or like descriptions; the difficulty is in the *respects* in which mental images are supposed to represent like pictures or like descriptions. I now want to mention another difficulty in this way of thinking about the issue—it presupposes that there is a *single* kind of pictorial representation. This presupposition is false and can lead to fallacy. The fallacy I have in mind is this: there are a variety of types of pictorial representations that differ from one another in the ways in which (or extent to which) they involve "conventions." Compare photographs and stick figures, for example. The descriptionalist forces often ascribe a straw-man position to the pictorialists (one that sophisticated pictorialists would reject): namely, that mental images must represent in the manner of photographs rather than in the manner of stick figures or other pictures that use nonphotographic conventions.

Dennett claims that picturing differs from describing in that picturing forces one either to go into details or else to be explicitly noncommittal. In describing, on the other hand, one has an extra option: one can be *inexplicitly noncommittal*. Dennett says:

> If . . . I were to draw a picture of this man, I would have to go into details. I can make the picture fuzzy or in silhouette, but unless something positive is drawn in where the hat should be, obscuring that area, the man in the picture must either have a hat or not . . . If I write down a description of a person, it would be absurd for anyone to say that my description cannot fail to mention whether or not the man is wearing a hat. The description can be as brief or as undetailed as I like.

Regimenting somewhat (and switching the example from a hat to shoes), I would put Dennett's point as follows:

> The difference between pictorial and descriptional representation is this: In pictorial representation we have three choices: (1) We can represent a man as having shoes, (2) we can represent the man as having no shoes, (3) We can be explicitly noncommittal about whether he has shoes, e.g. by picturing his feet as obscured, so that one cannot see whether shoes are present or not. In descriptional representation we have these options too. We can say that the man has shoes, we can say he does not have shoes, or we can say that we are not going to say whether he has shoes. But in descriptional representation, we have another option not available in pictorial representation: we can simply not go into it; for example, we can say "The man rode a horse." This is not a matter of being explicitly noncommittal, but rather a matter of not going into it—that is, being *in*explicitly noncommittal.

In order for this account of the pictorial/descriptional distinction to be even prima facie plausible, it must be limited to certain properties. Obviously, no picture need go into details about temperature of depicted skin or specific gravity of a depicted hat. What Dennett seems to have in mind is a limitation to certain visual properties, such as shape. (I will ignore the issue of whether an appropriate notion of visual property can be found, since I think there is a more serious difficulty).

Anyway, the crux of Dennett's argument is that imaging is like describing rather than picturing in that in imaging one can be *inex*plicitly noncommittal:

> We can and usually do imagine things without going into great detail. If I imagine a tall man with a wooden leg, I need not also have imagined him as having hair of a certain color, dressed in any particular clothes, having or not having a hat . . . As Shorter points out, my not going into details about hair color in my imagining does not mean that his hair is colored "vague" in my imagining; his hair is simply not "mentioned" in my imagining at all. This is quite unlike drawing a picture that is deliberately ambiguous as one can readily see by first imagining a tall man with a wooden leg and then imagining a tall man with a wooden leg who maybe does and maybe does not have blond hair, and comparing the results.
>
> If I write down a description of a person, it would be absurd for anyone to say that my description cannot fail to mention whether or not the man is wearing a hat . . . Similarly, it would be absurd to insist that one's imagining someone must go into the question of his wearing a hat. It is one thing to imagine a man wearing a hat, another to imagine him not wearing a hat, a third to imagine his head so obscured you can't tell, and a fourth to imagine him without going into the matter of headgear at all. Imagining is depictional or descriptional, not pictorial . . .

My criticism is that Dennett's way of drawing the distinction between pictorial and descriptional representation is faulty because at least some kinds of pictorial representations *do* have the option

Figure 1.

he reserves for descriptional representation, namely the option of not going into it. Consider Figure 1 (a stick figure). Figure 1 does not depict a naked person; rather it does not go into the matter of clothing at all, just as "The man stood on the corner" does not go into the matter of clothing. Our conventions for understanding stick figures allow them to be noncommittal with respect to clothes (except perhaps hats, which is my main reason for changing the example).[6] Even if there is a class of visual properties which a photograph cannot fail to specify (which I highly doubt), the same is not true of all pictorial representation.

In sum, some pictures are unlike (certain sorts of) photographs in being noncommittal about whether the depicted person is wearing shoes. Descriptionalists sometimes neglect this sort of point, thereby being unfair to pictorialists. (Though I've dubbed the mistake "the photographic fallacy," I don't want this title to commit me to the idea that photographs cannot be inexplicitly noncommittal about many properties that could reasonably be termed "visual".)

One final remark on this matter. Dennett has another descriptionalist argument: a picture of a tiger must have a determinate number of stripes, while a mental image of a tiger need not have a determinate number of stripes; so a mental image of the tiger does not represent the tiger pictorially. This "striped tiger" argument is actually quite different from the "man with a hat" argument, as can be seen by noticing that my method of disposing of the latter does not apply to the former. Dennett could concede that a picture can be inexplicitly noncommittal about whether the represented person has a hat or shoes or about the number of stripes on the represented tiger, but he could insist, nonetheless, that there must be a *determinate number of stripes on the picture itself.* (Note that a picture that represents someone as having shoes or a hat normally does not itself have shoes or a hat; however, when a picture represents something as striped, the picture normally must have stripes too.) Fodor argues persuasively in his article in this book (Chapter 3) that there need not be a determinate number of pictured stripes (but see Rey, 1981). Fodor points out that while a printed page normally has a determinate number of letters, an out-of-focus photograph of the page can adequately represent print even if there is no determinate number of image letters.

Obscurity of the Controversy

Earlier, I mentioned one difficulty in understanding the pictorial/descriptional controversy. Without a specification of an aspect of similarity, what is one to make of a claim that mental images are like pictures or like language in mode of representation? The discussion of the photographic fallacy adds some good news and some bad news. The good news is that a rough intuitive appreciation of what respect of similarity might be meant seems to allow some sensible discussion of at least some arguments against pictorialism. One doesn't need much knowledge of the relevant respect of similarity to see that pictorialists needn't adopt a conception of pictorial representation so narrow as to rule out uncontroversial pictures such as stick figures.

The bad news is that now that we have acknowledged different types of pictorial representation, we have to face the possibility that the differences among them are so great as to leave no single respect in which *any* representation (let alone a mental image) could be very similar to all pictorial representations. In order to clarify the pictorial/descriptional debate, we shall have to think about the various ways in which pictures can represent.

A similar point holds with respect to descriptional representations. If mental images are descriptions in a natural language, one would expect "order of report" asymmetries that one would not expect if mental images are pictorial. As Fodor points out, if a subject who was shown a red triangle stored a pictorial representation, one would expect him to answer the questions "Was it red?" and "Was it triangular?" with the same speed. If, however, he stored a natural language description (such as "red triangle"), we would expect one question to be answered faster than the other, since in "reading" a natural language phrase, one reads the first word first and the last word last.

My point is that there are types of descriptional representations that are not like natural languages in this respect. In the English phrase "red triangle," the words have a definite order (and the same is true of phrases in all everyday versions of spoken and written natural languages). But in computer data structures, the elements of what corresponds to phrases need have no order. One can "enter" a net at a "triangle" node (a register that contains the word "triangle") and traverse an "is modified by" link to a "red" node, but one can equally well enter the net at the latter node and go to the former one. So failure to find order-of-report symmetries gives one no reason to favor pictorialism over certain brands of descriptionalism.

So there are different types of descriptional representations as well as different types of pictorial representations. Moreover, as Fodor points out, many representations have elements of both. Maps represent shapes pictorially, but often represent altitudes descriptionally. A better understanding of what types of representation are possible may be what is needed for real progress in our understanding of mental imagery. And in the light of such understanding, the pictorial/descriptional controversy may dissolve.

I hope my comments have set the stage for the debate to follow. Though the debate itself will give the reader an idea of what can be said for and against the opposed positions, it should be clear by now that it is too early in the debate to expect a definitive resolution of the matter. [7]

Notes

1. Though the work of Roger Shepard (and his colleagues) on imagery is seminal, I have not included any of his papers, because he has mainly been concerned with the similarity of imagery and perception (a topic discussed in this Introduction) rather than the pictorial/descriptional dispute. Shepard's notion of second-order isomorphism *is* relevant, however, and it is discussed in note 3 below as well as in Chapter 1, "Icons and Images."

2. How a representation represents, and how it is processed (used) are inextricably entwined (see Chapter 5, "Imagery—There's More to It than Meets the Eye") but only the former is addressed here.

3. An interesting proposal for how to make the pictorial/descriptional distinction can be extracted from Shepard's notion of second-order isomorphism (Shepard and Chipman, 1970). In Shepard's terminology our internal representation of a square is first-order isomorphic to a square if (for example), it consists of neural structures that are themselves arranged in a square in the brain. Second-order isomorphism, by contrast, "should be sought—not in the first order relation between (a) an individual object, and (b) its corresponding internal representation—but in the second order relation between (a) the relations among alternative external objects, and (b) the relations among their corresponding internal representations. Thus, although the internal representation for a square need not itself be square, it should (whatever it is) at least have a closer functional relation to the internal representations for a rectangle than to that, say, for a green flash or the taste of persimmon." (p. 2). Though Shepard does not suggest it, pictorialists may propose that what makes representations pictorial is being a part of a system of representations and processes such that there is a second-order isomorphism between the representations and aspects of the world (see also Palmer, 1978).

Other proposals are discussed at several points in this book. Dennett (Chapter 2, "The Nature of Images and the Introspective Trap") says that in order to be pictorial, an image has to resemble what it represents in shape, color, or form (this condition would, of course, be unacceptable to sophisticated pictorialists, since it would commit them to genuine pictures in the head). Kosslyn et al. (Chapter 6, "On the Demystification of Mental Imagery") and Kosslyn (Chapter 8) combine a proposal like Shepard's, with the idea that parts of a pictorial representation should represent parts of the thing represented by the whole representation. A discussion of these proposals is beyond the scope of this introduction. Though Shepard does not suggest it, pictorialists may propose that what makes representations pictorial is being a part of a system of representations and processes such that there is a second-order isomorphism between the representations and aspects of the world (see also Palmer, 1978).

4. Not to keep the reader in suspense, the answer is: mental representations

represent in virtue of their causal role. See Harman (1975) and Field (1977) for defenses of this idea.

5. That Kosslyn et al. are moving in this direction is suggested when one notes that the first of the following pairs of sentences appeared in their original version (Chapter 6) but was replaced by the second in the version revised for this book: "None of the models of imagery based on artifical intelligence research treats the images that people report experiencing as functional representations." "None of the models of imagery based on Artificial Intelligence research treats the quasipictorial properties of images that people report when introspecting as functional properties of the representation."

6. Dennett could not legitimately object to the change from hat to shoes without finding an independently motivated characterization of "visual property" on which having a hat is a visual property, while having shoes is not.

7. I am indebted to Jerry Fodor for discussion of these issues and to Sylvain Bromberger for comments on an earlier draft.

ICONS AND IMAGES

1

Roger Brown and
Richard J. Herrnstein

The evidence from reaction times is necessarily indirect. It tells us simply that various stimulus-response sequences occur more or less rapidly. But then, if the times add up in a reasonably coherent and orderly way, we infer a hidden mental process. The argument presupposes that the hidden mental operations belong in the world of natural events, where 0.1 second plus 0.1 second equals 0.2 second, or where 0.2 second minus 0.1 second equals 0.1 second, and so on. At the beginning stages of an empirical science an assumption of orderliness can be a large step forward. To consider the subject at hand, it was a substantial advance in knowledge to discover that thought is sometimes serial, sometimes parallel. Though substantial, such findings have not shown the mental work itself, but only the traces it leaves in time. Reaction times are only a shadow of the mental work they record. Other lines of evidence must also be followed if we are to get at the mental work itself.

The Icon

A monograph published in 1960 (Sperling, 1960) uncovered a vital fact about the first few moments after the arrival of a complex stimulus. People looked at an array of letters or digits. The various configurations are illustrated in Figure 1. The stimulus array was

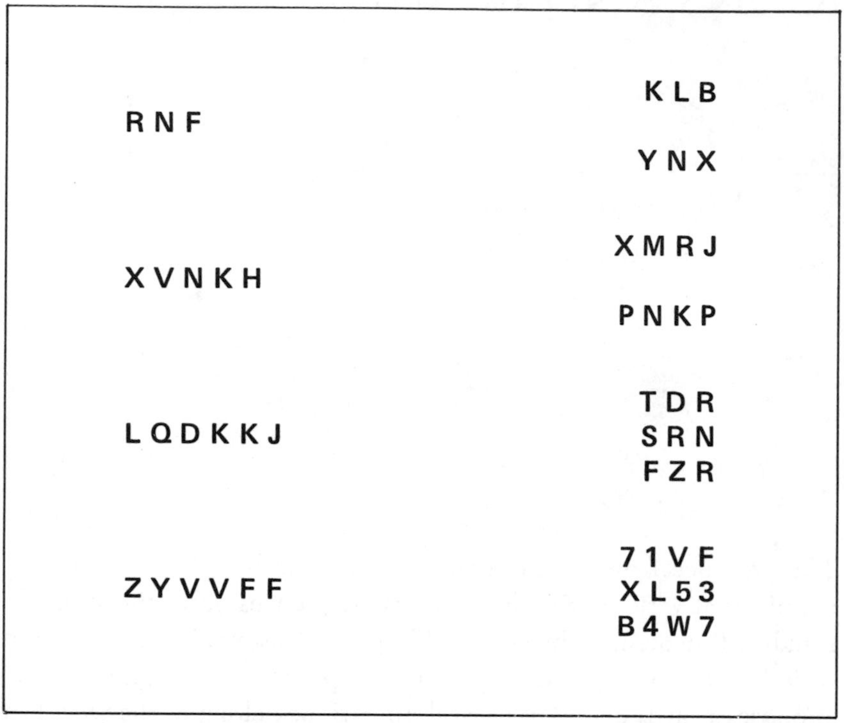

```
                                              K L B
              R N F
                                              Y N X


                                              X M R J
              X V N K H
                                              P N K P


                                              T D R
              L Q D K K J                     S R N
                                              F Z R


                                              7 1 V F
              Z Y V V F F                     X L 5 3
                                              B 4 W 7
```

Figure 1. Each group of characters is an example of the stimuli flashed on a screen for 50 milliseconds. The subject then tries to recall as many as he can. Without extra help, most people can name about five or six characters at best.

presented for a brief interval of time, 50 milliseconds to be exact. The brief exposure prevented systematic eye movements while the stimulus was showing. It is often important in experiments on cognition to present the stimulus just momentarily, to separate what happens while the stimulus is physically present from what happens afterward. That is why the instrument for flashing visual stimuli briefly—called a *tachistoscope*—has long been a standard fixture of the psychological laboratory.

The subjects in Sperling's experiment saw 50-millisecond flashes of letters or digits (black on white) and were expected to recall as many as possible immediately afterward. The bottom curve in Figure 2 shows a typical performance for one subject with stimulus

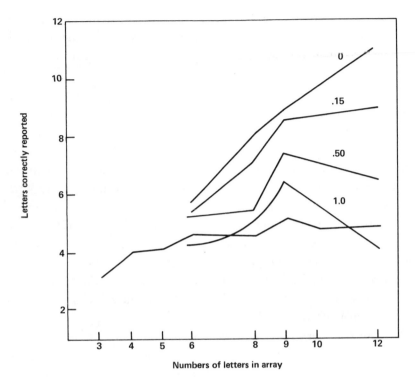

Figure 2. The line at the bottom shows how many characters (letters in this case) a typical subject recalled as a function of the size of the stimulus array. The other lines show recall when a high, medium, or low tone instructs the subject to recall only the top, middle, or bottom row of characters in an array (see Figure 8-2). The labels on the curves give the time interval (in seconds) between shutting off the stimulus array and the tone.

arrays containing from three to twelve characters. The immediate memory span usually ranges between five and nine elements: this subject falls just short of the lower figure. (But that could be because the experimental conditions, particularly the very brief exposure, were not conducive to full capacity.) The subject can retain about as many items from an array of six as from an array of twelve, or so the data suggested up to this point.

Sperling's ingenious next procedure proved that this conclusion needs to be qualified. *After* the subject saw six, eight, nine, or twelve characters, he heard a brief tone. If the tone was high-pitched, he was supposed to recall only the elements in the top row; if low-pitched, the letters in the bottom row; if medium-pitched, the letters in the middle row. He did not know which tone was coming, but his task was simplified because no row contained more than five characters.

Consider first the curve labeled "0." The subject could recall almost perfectly the equivalent of six, eight, or nine characters when he had a tone to guide him. He did not recall eight or nine characters on any single trial because each now had no more than five characters, but he showed that he could recall any letter in the arrays as long as he did not try to recite them all in one trial. With the twelve-character array, he recalled the equivalent of about eleven. But the tone came on just as the letters vanished from the screen. The guide entered as the array left. The other curves in Figure 2 show what happened as the interval between array and tone was stretched from 0.15 second to 1 second. With the one-second gap between the two, the tone lost its value, and performance went back to its original level.

Sperling's experiment and others like it (e.g., Averbach and Coriell, 1961) prove that after the physical stimulus is removed the information in it lingers briefly. For a moment, we can survey a stimulus that is just a psychological phantom of the physical event, or an *icon* as Neisser (1967) aptly named it. We usually cannot recover all, or nearly all, of the contents of the icon. The act of recalling takes time, so that even as a person tries to report what he still sees, it is fading. And the act of recalling may disrupt the icon more directly. Sperling's procedure freezes the fading icon and shows that the earliest levels of perception contain unsuspected capacity.

Sperling's discovery fits into a broader pattern of findings. It had been known for decades that the experience of a visual stimulus could be altered by a second stimulus arriving soon afterward (see Alpern, 1953). For example, a flash of light looks dimmer if it is quickly followed by another flash of light nearby on the retina. If the two flashes had come at the same time, the effect would just be *contrast.* But when the inhibiting stimulus comes later, the phenomenon is called *metacontrast.* In metacontrast, a stimulus affects the perception of an icon, rather than the perception of another stimulus, and that is why we must consider it part of the mental work that goes on in cognition. By studying the interactions of visual stimuli and icons, the experimenter can reconstruct much of the first few instants in the evolution of a fully experienced visual perception (see Kolers, 1962; Kahneman, 1968; and Weisstein, 1968, for a description of this reconstruction).

Attention and the Icon

If Sperling's experiment had presented the tone *before* flashing the letters, his results would have attracted much less interest. If you know ahead of time that you will be asked about the top row or the bottom row of letters, you can do a better job than if you have no advance clue. And this is so even barring eye movements; it is not just a matter of looking in the right direction.

The point can be clarified by a familiar example from heard instead of seen stimuli. Suppose you are about to listen to a piece of music played by an orchestra. If you decide to concentrate on the violins, the violins will stand out. You can train your attention on a component of a sound, even though there is no movement, no pricking of the ears comparable to pointing your eyes. That much is familiar and commonplace. The contribution of Sperling's experiment and the many others that have confirmed it was to hint that you might be able to tune in the violins *after* the fact, our of the auditory *icon* instead of the auditory *stimulus*.

The auditory evidence is consistent with the visual (see Moray, 1970), though it has not yet been developed to the same extent. The "icon" for hearing has naturally been called an *echo* instead (or an "echoic memory," Neisser, 1967). We will return to the auditory mode later, for at this point, we wish to extend the discovery that attention can be directed at parts of the icon, rather than at parts of the stimulus. Or, to put it another way, the evidence suggests that the icon is a much more complete picture of the stimulus than a person's description of it would suggest. The question is, How complete is the icon?

A limited amount of data leaves open the possibility (Shiffrin and Geisler, 1973) that the icon is the next thing to a virtual snapshot of the stimulus. If you glance, for example, at a full page of seven-place logarithms, the resulting icon may contain *every* number on the page in its proper place. Needless to say, you cannot recite all of them. You may recite about six or seven digits in place and then start faltering, but that limited performance may reflect constraints further along in the process. The icon itself may be teeming with information that slips quickly away.

Experiments have clearly hinted at an unsuspected richness of the icon (Eriksen and Spencer, 1969; Crowder and Morton, 1969; Shiffrin and Geisler, 1973). We will describe just one of them in detail (Shiffrin and Gardner, 1972). A subject looks at the face of a cathode-ray tube (in effect, much like a television screen) and briefly sees arrays of letters like the ones in Figure 3. The subject's task is to say whether an *F* or a *T* has been shown. The whole array is present for only 50 milliseconds, much too briefly for eye movements to scan through the four positions. The array must be taken in all at once, and then the subject has only his icon to examine.

In a second procedure, the letters (or hybrids) come one at a time, rather than all at once. For 50 milliseconds, the subject is shown just the character at the upper left, then for another 50 milliseconds the character at the upper right, and so on clockwise through the two lower positions. Instead of a total 50 milliseconds to soak up the stimulus, the subject has four times that—one-fifth second. If the icon were a virtual snapshot, it should make no difference whether the characters came one at a time or all at once. Either way, the subject would be examining an icon to decide whether it contains an *F* or a *T*. But if you need to attend to a stimulus to extract an icon, then the second procedure has a clear advantage. Here, the stimuli come one at a time, so that the subject can devote attention fully to each character in turn. The second procedure spreads out the presentation time to one-fifth second, a leisurely pace by the standards of these experiments.

The results, averaged for six subjects, are shown in Table 1. Performance was about 13 percent better when the alternative to *T*

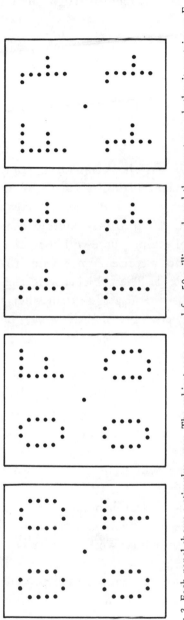

Figure 3. Each panel shows a stimulus array. The subject sees a panel for 50 milliseconds and then must say whether it contains an F, a T, or neither.

Table 1. Effect of Attention on an Icon

	Percentage of Letters Detected	
	Presented Simultaneously	Presented One at a Time
Display with O	82	79
Display with hybrids	68	67

or *F* was the letter *O,* as compared to the hybrid alternative. A glance at Figure 3 will dispel any doubt you may have about that much of the outcome. It takes more information about an *F* or a *T* to tell it from a hybrid character than from an *O,* hence in a brief sample there will be more errors with the hybrids.

The surprise comes from the other comparison contained in Table 1. The subjects were clearly no better when the characters came one at a time than when they came all at once. In fact, the subjects were slightly worse, but the difference is statistically insignificant. The experiment says that 50 milliseconds gives as good an icon of *four* characters as of *one.* But so would a camera, which is the interpretation of perception favored by the results. Other studies (Eriksen and Spencer, 1969) extend the generalization up to ten or so, and no studies have yet set any ceiling to the richness of the icon. Similar conclusions have turned up with other sorts of visual stimuli besides letters (Shiffrin et al., 1973) and in other senses—hearing (Crowder and Morton, 1969) and touch (Shiffrin et al., 1973).

This research points to a level of sensory processing prior to the selective effects of attention, a level where input is automatic and unconscious. We have referred to this level as the "icon," following the lead of Neisser (1967). A person can focus on fragments or sections of the icon by directing attention one way or the other. Directing attention is hidden; it is not overt behavior, like turning your head or reaching out your hand to touch something. Nevertheless, the physical stimulus is momentarily transformed into a sensory icon, and attention, rehearsal, scanning, and so on, seem to act upon it much the way overt behavior acts upon an external stimulus.

We have used the metaphor of a snapshot to characterize the icon. Now we must, finally, note two potential sources of misunderstanding. First, not all the data are visual, though most are. The "snapshot" may be auditory, tactual, and so forth. Second, the icon is not really a snapshot, not really a true copy of the physical stimulus. Our sense organs impose themselves on the stimulus as does every level of the nervous system; we transform the physical stimulus by our makeup. The snapshot analogy means that the early levels transform the stimulus automatically, without varying selectivity. At one stage in perception the amount of information extracted about an item seems, at least partly, to be unaffected by the number of other items also being processed.

Filtering

If we do not want to see something, we can close our eyes or turn our heads. We can shut off part of the sound around us by clamping our hands over our ears or by screeching so loud that the unwanted message is masked. An unwelcome taste may lead to spitting; an unpleasant smell may lead to pinching the nostrils with the fingers.

Obviously, many kinds of behavior promote or inhibit stimulation. You may crane your neck to see something interesting, bring an attractive new food or a brandy snifter within range of smell, turn an ear toward a soft sound, and so on. We take for granted our frequent regulation of sensory input. When the regulation is mental rather than behavioral, or hidden rather than overt, we call it paying attention. We call it attention when we listen for the violins in the orchestra, but not when we turn up the treble register on the audio system. A similar contrast was noted earlier—arithmetic on an abacus and arithmetic in the head. When selectivity in perception is covert, hidden from immediate view, it is defined as mental. Selectivity may be just as orderly and regular when it is hidden as when it is behavioral, though it is harder to study objectively.

One of the central issues in the study of attention has been discussed in the preceding section. Selectivity operates at the first level of experience: we open or close our eyes, pick something up to bring it close to nose, mouth, or ear, and so on. It also operates at a much later level, as when we rehearse an experience mentally. Thinking about an experience may get its traces into long-term memory. But does deliberate selectivity occur at every stage? Are some levels of experience totally passive, as the reviewed experiments seem to say?

The natural metaphor for selectivity is a filter (Broadbent, 1958). Where in the chain of perceptual events can we find filtering, so that some elements are passed along and others are not? How close to the immediate sensory input is selectivity optional, like turning the radio up or down, but still hidden, so that it qualifies as mental? Swets (1963) has reviewed evidence that we can "tune" our ears for a particular sound. If we expect a certain pitch, we hear it at a lower intensity than if we are listening for just any pitch. At a noisy cocktail party, we can follow a single conversation, even when it is across the room or behind us. To do so obviously requires the ability to suppress competing percepts at some level.

A productive technique for studying the selectivity of hearing is *shadowing* (Cherry, 1953; Poulton, 1953). A person wearing earphones is asked to repeat a message as he is hearing it. With a little practice, he usually has no problem. But now suppose the left ear receives the message to be repeated, while another message is coming in through the right. Most people can manage even this more demanding task, but at the cost of apparently blocking off the input to the right ear (see Moray, 1970, for summary). The message in the right ear can change from English to French and back or to German or Latin, and subjects keep shadowing the left-ear message without noting the goings-on at the right ear. Even English played backward passes unnoticed. Reading a list of seven words to the unattended-to ear thirty-five times in a single session makes no lasting impression (Moray, 1959), for the subjects recognize none of the words in a test given a few moments later.

It looks at first as if the filter of selective attention can operate at the immediate sensory level, as if we can somehow shut off an ear the way we can shut off a radio. This would contradict the idea of the icon as a virtual snapshot, but it is not quite right. The unattended stream of stimulation is obscured but not completely suppressed. If the right ear suddenly receives the subject's name or if the voice changes sex, the subject will usually notice it. If the two messages are suddenly made the same, with the shadowed one leading by a few seconds, subjects notice that the other is a repetition. They do so even when one message is in English and the other is its translation into French—but only if they are bilinguals (Treisman, 1964a). When it is English and French and the subject speaks only English, the French is rejected as usual.

The filter is not absolute, as black glasses or ear plugs are. You may think you have not heard what you were not listening for, but experiments prove that the signal has risen quite high in the perceptual process—up to at least the level of language comprehension. If you had not "understood" the rejected message, you could not have discovered that it was the shadowed message in French or that it said your name. Yet the messages are often rejected in some sense, never reaching the point of full awareness. By "full awareness," we mean that the message is sustained in your short-term memory by rehearsal and analysis. By paying attention, you sustain one incoming message, and by the lack of attention you do not sustain the other. The rejected message fades rapidly (Norman, 1969), starved for attention.

Icons as Images

Some of the experiments described earlier focused on the ground floor of perception, prior to attention or other "control processes" (Atkinson and Shiffrin, 1968). The upshot was that there is an icon which is somewhat analogous to the physical stimulus itself. In an older vocabulary, based on personal experience rather than experimentation, we might have said that the data suggest a mental image of the physical stimulus. Common sense has always believed in a "mind's eye" in addition to the physical events in our sense organs. In that respect the research has just confirmed what people already knew. But psychology often advances by converting subjective impressions into objective data. With something as fundamental as the mind's eye, we do not think it necessary to apologize for the work it takes to demonstrate objectively what people supposed they already knew.

People also believe they can conjure up mental images in their mind's eye. An image of your aunt, wearing a straw hat you saw on someone else, can float through your mind, or so it may seem. Can it really? And how could you prove it?

It is so hard to find out anything about how a person manipulates his own subjective images that the problem was almost legislated out of existence. Many psychologists and philosophers in the past fifty years have argued that the right way to deal with mental images is to deny them or to hand the problem over to physiologists (who are generally as stymied as psychologists). Fortunately, not everyone was convinced that the subject was scientifically hopeless, for recent research proves it is not.

A remarkable series of experiments by R. N. Shepard and his associates has displaced a tradition of philosophical skepticism with an extraordinarily vivid glimpse through the mind's eye. You could always look through your own, but Shepard has begun to look through others' by shrewd experiments. In one study (Shepard and Metzler, 1971), subjects saw pairs of line drawings like the ones in Figure 4. They looked at 1600 such pairs, which were constructed according to three different rules, corresponding to *A, B,* and *C* in Figure 4.

A. Here the two drawings are identical except that they are pasted on the page at different angles. It would also be correct to say that the two drawings show the result of a rotation on the plane defined by the surface of the page.

B. These two drawings are two-dimensional perspective projections of the same three-dimensional structure; that is, the two drawings show the result of rotation of the same object in the third dimension.

C. Though the two drawings look similar, they are basically

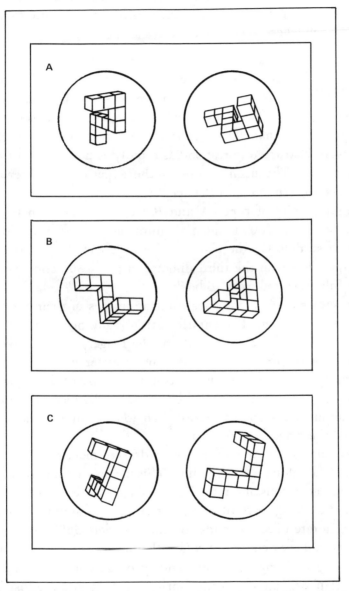

Figure 4. Subjects looked at pairs of perspective drawings like these and had to say whether they were rotations of each other. Each drawing consists of 10 little cubes forming a structure with three right angles. The A pair is a rotation on the plane of the page; the B pair is a rotation in the third dimension, perpendicular to the page; the C pair cannot be made to match by any rotation. Subjects looked at 1,600 different pairs.

different. They cannot be rotated either on the plane of the page or in the third dimension to be brought into exact correspondence.

The subject's task with each pair of drawings, which appeared on a screen while the subject's head was kept still, was to indicate whether they were the "same," in the sense of *A* and *B* above, or "different," in the sense of *C*. With a bit of practice, the subjects averaged more than 95 percent correct responses, even though they were instructed to respond as rapidly as possible while retaining accuracy. The main datum of the experiment, however, was the speed of response, not the accuracy.

Stimulus pairs of types *A* and *B* were rotated from 0° up to 180°. Note that 180° is the maximum angular difference for both types of stimuli. On the plane of the page (*A*), 180° corresponds to upside-down; in the third dimension (*B*), 180° corresponds to being fully reversed front to back.

The subjects felt themselves rotating images in their minds. The data bear them out. If mental rotation really occurred we would expect that the larger the rotation, the longer it would take us to decide that the drawings are the same or different. Figure 5 shows the average reaction times in relation to the size of the angle of rotation for types *A* and *B*. For both types, the reaction time rose from about one second to more than four seconds as the rotation covered the range from 0° to 180°.

Two further features of Figure 5 deserve mention. First of all, the data fall along a straight line. This means that mental rotation proceeds at a constant rate. For the eight subjects in the experiment, the average rate of mental rotation was about 60° per second, or a rate of six seconds for one complete 360° rotation. The subjects said they could not rotate the images any quicker without destroying their rigidity. The rigidity of an image is a peculiarly apt metaphor, suitable for a fabrication that you are just barely holding together.

The two straight lines in Figure 5 have just about the same slope, which means that the subjects rotated the mental images at the

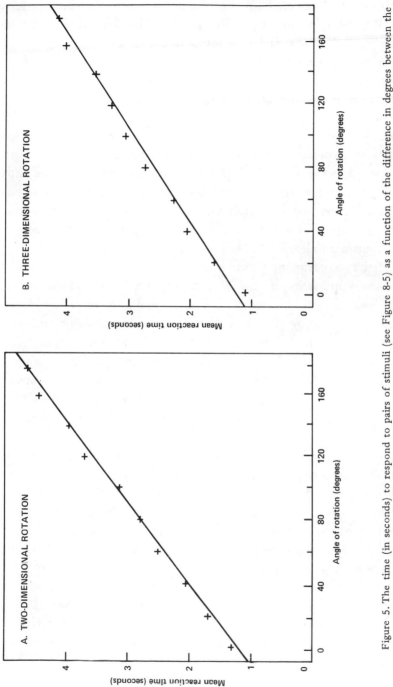

Figure 5. The time (in seconds) to respond to pairs of stimuli (see Figure 8-5) as a function of the difference in degrees between the members of a pair. The maximum possible angular difference is 180°. The left graph is for stimuli rotated on the plane of the page (A in Figure 8-4); the right graph, for stimuli rotated in the third dimension (B in Figure 8-4).

same rate whether on the plane of the page or in the third dimension. Rotation in the third dimension is by far more complex geometrically because it would result in changes in perspective and relative size, yet the subjects handled both tasks with equal speed and facility.

Why should the mental process take equal times for A and B? The two tasks have little in common from the standpoint of the geometry in two dimensions of the line drawings. Only when we accept the experiment's premises do the results make sense. The main premises are, first of all, that *mental rotation* is involved and, second, that the rotation is somehow *three-dimensional.* Even people who believe without question in a mind's eye might be surprised to learn that it can see things spinning in three dimensions. The experiment clearly goes beyond common sense.

A further experiment (Cooper and Shepard, 1973) drew out additional components of mental rotation. The central idea was to compel subjects to rotate an icon of a character to tell if it was backward. The subjects saw printed letters or numerals and said whether or not they were backward, but the judgment was made more or less difficult by presenting the character at various angles from the vertical. The judgment took more or less time as experimental conditions varied, allowing the experimenter to reconstruct things about the subjects' minds' eyes that the subjects themselves barely knew.

Figure 6 shows six orientations for the backward and normal letter R, adding up to 12 distinct stimuli. The five other characters used in the experiment also could turn up as 12 different stimuli. The subjects reported being conscious of something like a mental rotation when they saw the characters out of normal vertical position, especially when the deviation was between 120°–240°. When the character was nearly vertical, it seemed possible to give an answer about its backwardness without mental movement. Note that the need for mental rotation arises only because we usually look at letters and numbers right side up. With enough practice as a subject in an experiment like this, a person would learn which letters are backward and which are not, without having to flip

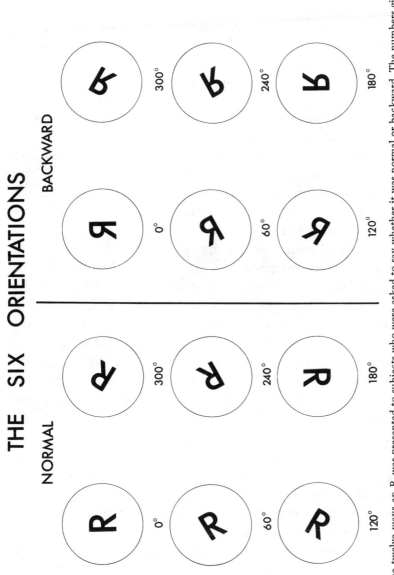

THE SIX ORIENTATIONS

NORMAL   BACKWARD

Figure 6. The twelve ways an R was presented to subjects who were asked to say whether it was normal or backward. The numbers give the deviation from upright in degrees. The other letters and numbers used in the experiment, such as J, G, 2, 5, and 7, were also asymmetrical vertically or laterally. Along with R, these letters and numbers look different when turned upside down or backward.

them upright in his mind. The subjects here did not get enough practice to make mental rotation unnecessary.

The first finding of the experiment is that reaction time depends on the deviation from the vertical. Reaction time was about half a second when the character was upright. The average for eight subjects is shown in Figure 7. Upside-down characters, at 180°, take the longest to decide about, i.e. about 1,100 milliseconds or 1.1 seconds. The subject presumably spins the icon until it is upright enough to decide about; the more nearly upside down it is, the longer it takes. The backward characters reliably took about 0.1 second longer to respond to, independent of orientation angle, for reasons we will return to later. We will also return later to the question of why the function is curved, rather than linear like the data for the three-dimensional drawings in Figure 5.

The procedural variations are shown in Figure 8. *Condition N* is the one we have described: the subject sees a blank screen for two seconds (2,000 milliseconds) and then a character at an angle comes on until the subject responds. In *condition I,* the subject first sees an outline sketch of the letter or number upright and not backward for two seconds. Then the same character comes at an angle and perhaps backward. This variation of the basic procedure tells us the value of knowing beforehand what the character will be. Similarly, *condition O* shows the subject ahead of time how the character will be tilted, without saying which character it will be or, naturally, whether it will be backward.

The most significant procedural variation is *condition B.* Here, the subject first sees the character upright and not backward for two seconds, then an arrow showing the tilt. The orientation arrow could last for either 100, 400, 700, or 1,000 milliseconds before the character to respond to comes on. With this advance information, a subject should generate an internal icon and rotate it into position. Then, when the stimulus comes, all he has to do is note whether it is the same as the already rotated icon. If it is, then the stimulus is not backward; if not, then the stimulus must be backward. The time saved by advance rotation would be subtracted from the reaction time, if this reasoning is correct.

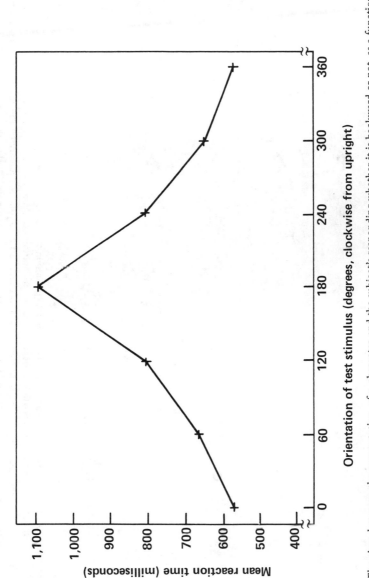

Orientation of test stimulus (degrees, clockwise from upright)

Mean reaction time (milliseconds)

Figure 7. The time between the presentation of a character and the subject's responding whether it is backward or not, as a function of the character's orientation. 0° is upright; 180° is upside down, and 360° is just 0° replotted for symmetry's sake. Responses to backward and normal stimuli have been averaged together.

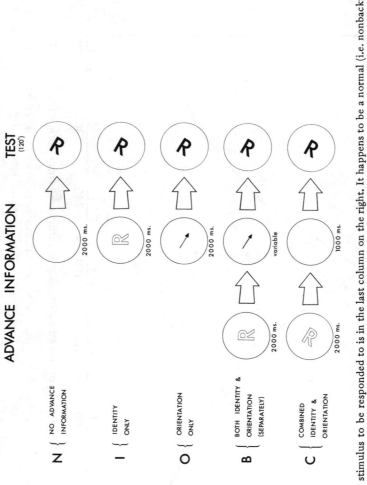

Figure 8. An example of a stimulus to be responded to is in the last column on the right. It happens to be a normal (i.e. nonbackward) R rotated 120°. On other trials, the subject says other characters in other orientations, backward as often as not. The other columns show the variations in the experimental procedure. Sometimes there was no advance information (N); sometimes the advance information was about the identity of the coming stimulus, (I), its orientation (O), or both (B). On some trials (C), the subject saw the rotated character ahead of time, but always in normal view, whereas the stimulus itself could be backward or not.

The final *condition C* presents the subject with the character fully rotated in advance. Then, one second later, comes the stimulus. The subject has to decide only whether it is the same or different. If the same, then the stimulus is not backward; if different, then the stimulus must be backward. The difference between this condition and condition *B* is that the subject must rotate his own icon in *B* while an already rotated stimulus is given in *C*. The question is whether the difference affects the reaction time.

Figure 9 shows some of the relevant findings. They answer a number of questions about mental images. By knowing in advance *either* which character is coming or how it is tilted, but not both, the subject can reduce the reaction time by about 0.1 second (100 milliseconds). This suggests that the subject otherwise spends about that much time figuring out what the letter is and which way it is pointing. You can tell that a character is an *R* or a *5* however it is pointing, but doing it takes about 100 milliseconds. If you see a *5* upside down, it takes about 100 milliseconds to find out where its top is (which may mean nothing more than discovering that it is, in fact a 5). The two kinds of advance information appear to save just about the same amount of time, though we cannot be sure that different characters would not have turned up a difference between tilt and identity.

Even when the subject knows the character's identity or angle in advance, reaction is still much quicker for the upright characters than for the rotated ones. Advance information about identity and tilt does not save the subject the time it takes to rotate the icon produced by the stimulus, and the time taken depends on the tilt. Hence the curves for conditions *I* and *O* are sharply graded. But the curve for *C* is flat, the result of sparing the subject the chore of mental rotation. For condition *C* (see Figure 8) the character is presented ahead of time in its rotated orientation. The subject simply notes whether the stimulus matches the advance information. If not, it must be backward.

The low, flat line for condition *C* is good evidence that mental rotation is an important part of what goes on in conditions *N*, *I*, and *O*, just because it is so different. The clincher, however, is

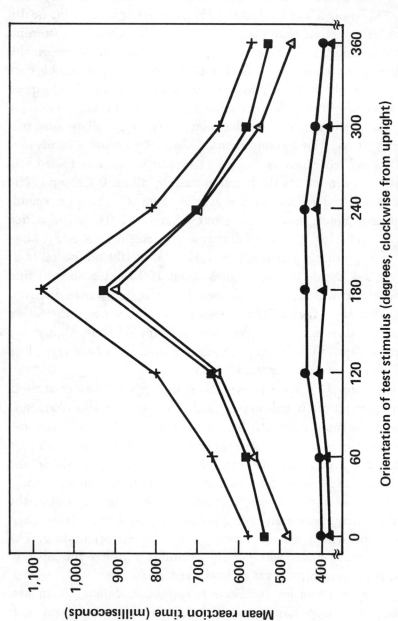

Figure 9. The curve from Figure 7 is replotted, along with the results of the procedural variations summarized in Figure 8. Advance information reduces the reaction time most when it provides a rotated mental image before the actual stimulus arrives.

condition *B*. Here, as you should recall (or remind yourself by looking at Figure 8 one more time), the subject gets advance information about *both* identity and tilt. Then he sees the stimulus itself. When he had the tilt arrow for a full second (1,000 milliseconds), reaction time was quick and almost independent of the orientation of the stimulus (see Figure 9), almost like condition *C*. The plausible interpretation, the one offered by the subjects themselves, is that in condition *B*, advance information permitted a self-generated icon of the character, which was rotated to the proper angle. When the real stimulus came on, the response depended on whether it was the same or different from the icon. Condition *B* reduced itself to condition *C*, except that the subject manufactured his own icon.

Since mental rotation takes time, the duration of the tilt arrow should have been crucial. The subject needs enough time to generate the right icon and to spin it into position. The further he needs to spin it, the more time is required. Figure 10 shows the relevant data. With advance information about tilt lasting only 100 milliseconds, reaction times are just like those when the subject knows only what character is coming, not how it will point. One-tenth of a second is apparently not enough time to get the icon generated *and* spinning. A full second is enough, or almost enough, for the entire internal job. In between fall the curves for 400 to 700 milliseconds, which show progressively greater savings in reaction time.

Cooper and Shepard showed that the icon rotated at about the same speed whether it was internally generally or the residue of an actual stimulus. Concretely, this means that the rotation inferred in condition *B* was not significantly different from that in conditions *N*, *I*, and *O*. The speed of rotation varied between 164° and 800° per second among the eight subjects. The subjects were consistent—as fast, slow, or moderate icon rotators—but they differed sharply from each other. It could well be that the speed of mental rotation is a significant dimension of variation from person to person. Nevertheless, mental rotation in this experiment was much quicker than in the experiment in which icons were rotated in three dimensions instead of two. The difference may be caused by

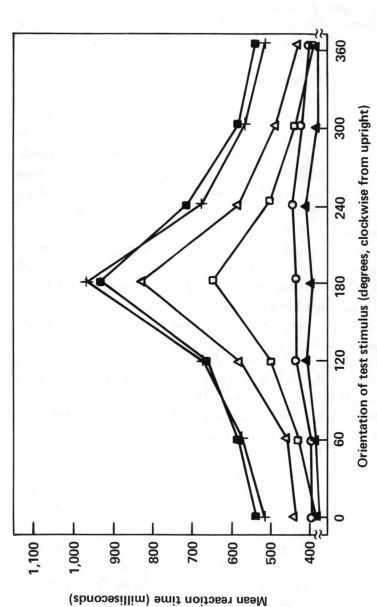

Figure 10. Reaction times in all the procedures in which the subjects knew before hand at least the identity of the forthcoming stimulus. In addition, they also knew the orientation of the stimulus for all conditions but one ("identity information"). The times given in the key tell how far in advance the orientation information came (see B in Figure 8-8). When the information was "combined," it came 2,000 milliseconds before the stimulus (C in Figure 8-8).

using three dimensions instead of two, or it may simply be caused by the familiarity of letters and numbers as compared to perspective line drawings of meaningless forms.

To complete our summary of results, we must take up two remaining features. First, there was the roughly 0.1 second delay in response to backward letters as compared to normal ones, independent of angle of orientation. The best guess is that the subject is prepared for a normal letter and that the rejection of this alternative adds a small increment of time. Second, there was the nonlinearity of the curves in Figures 9 and 10. Earlier experiments had suggested that mental rotation occurs at a steady rate, which would give a linear curve. Cooper and Shepard offer several plausible alternatives to explain this one apparent discrepancy. If we do not need to see a character or its icon fully upright to decide if it is backward, then the angle of mental rotation is actually somewhat smaller than the angle from the true vertical, although we do not know how much less. If you subtract a constant angle from each value of the horizontal axis in Figures 9 and 10, and you pick the right angle to subtract, you will get rid of most of the curvature.

The results of the experiment fit together like the pieces of a jigsaw puzzle, but only if we accept the idea that people generate internally something like the aftereffects of an actual stimulus, what we have been calling an icon. We should clarify our terminology, however. The icon, as we used the word earlier, referred to a virtual snapshot of a physical stimulus. Its most conspicuous property in that context was that it could contain far more detail than a person would be able to hang on to. But that is not necessarily the case. An icon of a simple, familiar stimulus, like an isosceles right triangle, may contain little that fades. It can be continuously reconstructed or restored by information that we carry around more or less permanently. Perhaps we should reserve the word "icon" for the passive, preselective stage of perception, in which case it would be wrong to speak of icons rotating or being generated internally. *Image* would be the obvious candidate to to succeed "icon" in the sequence, but word usage in this newly revived field of study is still highly idiosyncratic.

Long-term memory continuously interacts with the fleeting slice of time that we experience as the present. Here, the same point arises again. An icon internally generated can obviously have no more detail than a subject carries in his long-term storage. But it may have less. If necessary, you can conjure up an italic R or a roman R, upper-case (R) or lower-case (r), and so on. You *may* be able to conjure up all sorts of details, but do you? Unlike ordinary letters printed on a page, an imagined one can be incomplete and still be adequate for the purpose at hand. You can perhaps rotate a mental R without deciding whether it is italic or roman. But perhaps not. We do not know how much detail was necessary in the icon for this experiment, except that the subject needed to know it was an R in order to start rotating it. He could not rotate an abstraction like "any letter or number," but a lesser abstraction like any capital R may do. The answer may, in fact, vary from person to person. Research has made a good case for icons or images in the mind's eye, but it has not quite made them visible to anyone but their possessors—at least not yet.

Isomorphism

The most interesting findings in the experiment on mentally rotating letters and numbers is the similarity of mental work to ordinary, observable behavior. If something is upside-down, then turning it upright is hardly noteworthy. But when it is an icon that is upside-down, then evidence of rotation is noteworthy indeed. Objective evidence of any mental process has been extraordinarily scarce and is consequently in high demand. When the objective evidence seems, furthermore, to be saying that the inner world mirrors the outer (and vice versa, as we shall shortly explain), a profound and ancient gap in knowledge may finally be closing.

The parallel between inner and outer worlds has been traced further in other experiments. One example (Shepard and Chipman, 1970) required subjects to compare pairs of American states for geometric similarity. Is the shape of Alabama more or less similar to that of Idaho than Maine is to Colorado? Fifteen states were chosen, to represent a variety of shapes. There are 105 possible pairs of 15 different states, and the subjects were asked to set them in rank order, from the most similar pair to the most different. The subjects were, in fact, asked to do the ranking twice. First, they were given 105 index cards with the 105 pairs of state *names* printed on them. After these were ranked, another deck of 105 cards was given. These showed the 105 pairs in outline *pictures,* with no names printed on them.

The subjects found both tasks difficult, as well they might. There are more than 10^{168} possible rankings of 105 items, an astronomical number from which the subject felt as if he was trying to choose just one. Nevertheless, the subjects ranked the two stacks of cards in about an hour. The ranks were similar, whether the subjects worked with the names of the states or the pictures. Colorado and Oregon, for example, were judged most similar in both rankings. Oregon and West Virginia were judged least similar for the name cards and nearly the least similar for the pictures. A detailed analysis of the two rankings confirmed that the pairs turned up at comparable points in the two rankings. The mental comparisons were not obviously different from the external ones, except that some subjects seemed a bit unsure of the shapes of certain states, given just their names. The experiment suggests that one can make new sensory judgments about things in their absence. It is unlikely that the subjects had ever asked themselves if Alabama is shaped more like Idaho than Maine is to Colorado. Yet they could easily answer the question when, externally, all they had was index cards with names typed on them. But what did they have *internally* that allowed them to do as well as they did?

Once you get the idea, you can easily think of any number of other examples of evaluating mental representations. People will, for example, say that a harp sounds more like a guitar than a bassoon. They do not need to be listening to the actual instruments when they make the judgment. It seems unlikely that everyone who can perform this simple mental judgment on request has at some time in his life made the judgment while listening to the actual instruments. The mental judgment appears to require some current representation of the sounds, rather than a memory of an earlier judgment. Similarly, you can compare the tastes of steak and eggs, oranges and rice, etc., with no great strain and with nothing in your mouth. In short, some part, or reconstruction, of your past experience is always accessible, and the evidence suggests that what is reconstructed has some important correspondence with external stimuli. More accurately, what is reconstructed corresponds to what we experience in the presence of an external stimulus.

We cannot ever experience the objective stimulus itself, even when it is right there. We experience its transformation by our sensory and perceptual machinery. When we call forth images or icons, the result is to some extent a representation of the original icon or percept, not the original *stimulus*. In that sense, we experience a similar world whether the stimulus is present or not. The physical properties of a tennis ball influence what we see without fully accounting for it. What we see is also an expression of ourselves, our sensory processes and our past experience. When the stimulus is absent, a reconstructed percept (the icon) turns out to have much in common with the original. This correspondence is called an *isomorphism*, which means, etymologically if not actually, "same shape."

The isomorphism between original and reconstructed icon must be qualified a bit further. It does not mean that the two are identical in every respect, for if they were, we would have no way to tell them apart. People who routinely confuse their self-generated icons with external stimuli are suffering from hallucinations, one of the surest signs of major psychosis. Normal people occasionally make the mistake. In our dreams we are likely to be fully deceived by our own icons. Waking, too, we are sometimes deceived, as some old experiments showed.

The experiments were conducted during the first decade of the century (Perky, 1910) at Cornell University, which had one of the few psychological laboratories of the time. Perky's subjects were schoolchildren, college students, and members of the laboratory staff. One at a time, they were brought into a well-illuminated room and seated in a chair facing a smoked-glass screen on the wall. Next to the subject sat the experimenter. The experimenter told the subject to look at the screen and imagine a certain colored object, such as a red tomato, a yellow banana, a green leaf, and so on. The subject then reported what he "saw." In point of fact we should *not* have put the quotation marks around "saw," for behind the screen was another room where two quietly busy accomplices were projecting the very pictures on the screen that the subject was trying to imagine. Preliminary work had established how bright the pictures had to be in order to be actually visible, and the pictures projected during a session fell above and below this threshold region. To make the actual picture a realistic copy of a mental image, its edges were deliberately fuzzy and it was moved around slightly in a random manner.

Almost every subject reported seeing a mental image of the called-for object. But they did so only when the physical intensity of the stimulus was *above* the threshold value. They were, in short, seeing a picture and calling it an image. The experimenter asked probing questions to find out what the subjects thought they were seeing. In every case the answer left no doubt that the experiment succeeded in passing off stimuli as images without the subject's awareness. The experiment produced the inverse of dreams, in which images are taken as stimuli. To take illusion as reality is the other side of the coin from taking reality as illusion. Both arise from the isomorphism of original and reconstructed icon.

Shepard (1968; Shepard and Chipman, 1970) discusses *second-order isomorphism* as a further extension of this correspondence. If there is a certain relation between ordinary objects (or our perception of them), then there may be a comparable relation among the icons representing them. It takes longer to turn a real card 180° than to turn it 90°; it also takes longer to turn an icon of the card the greater amount. A drawing of Oregon looks similar to a drawing of Colorado, and so do the icons. The taste of steak has more in common with that of eggs than with the taste of lemon, and so does our recollection of that taste.

Second-order isomorphism does not mean that the reconstructed icons (any more than the original ones) have the physical properties themselves. An imagined banana is not itself yellow, soft, sweet, etc. Rather, it shares properties with icons of similar objects. It resembles icons of things that resemble bananas, which is not quite the same as resembling the things themselves. The distinction is subtle but vital. We do not have the stimuli in our heads, but we do have a psychological representation of them whether elicited by the objects themselves or by imagination. The "psychological representation" is itself subject to physiological analysis, but that is beside the point. The point here is that objective evidence has uncovered a level of experience where stimulus input and imagined output meet and have common characteristics.

The objective evidence also says that the banana seen (as distinguished from the physical banana) can be acted upon as if it were a real banana. When a person imagines something in response to verbal instructions, like a rotating letter, the result has properties not explicitly requested in the instructions. The obvious example is the relation of the speed of the mental rotation to the size of the angle. The orderly and physically sensible data in Shepard's experiments are part of the evidence for isomorphism. Looking at a card spinning and "seeing" its icon spinning have something in common. The operations we perform on our icons often reveal the same fine detail as we would find if we were operating on the objects themselves.

The principle of isomorphism does not mean, however, that icons are as limited as the corresponding physical objects are. You, yourself, can walk or run, for example. But in your fantasy you may fly, or you may even make the trip to Paris instantaneously. The world of physical objects limits us with its weight, solidity, inaccessibility, and so forth. In the mind you can walk through walls. One reason dreams are so revealing is that in them we encounter a person's psychological productions unfettered by the physical limitations of the world of objects. A feather in a dream is not lighter *physically* than a cannon ball. If it is lighter psychologically, then the dreamer imagined it that way. In dreams we show which icons we are disposed to generate. The world we create is not lawless or capricious, but the laws and regularities are those of psychology, not physics. That is why dreams say so much about us, if we know how to read them.

Perhaps not accidentally, the most convincing experiments on the properties of imagery have usually been visual. Even when stimuli are presented orally, subjects may conjure up a visual icon if the heard stimulus has an obvious visual translation like the name of a friend or of a letter. The visual mode is clearly dominant for some people, if not for all. Nevertheless, there are icons from all the senses at some level.

THE NATURE OF IMAGES
AND THE INTROSPECTIVE TRAP

2

Daniel C. Dennett

The view of awareness or consciousness developed in the last two chapters [of *Content and Consciousness,* 1969—Ed.] makes it quite clear that we are not aware (in any sense of the word) of mental *pictures,* and although few philosophers these days will express outright allegiance to the doctrine of mental imagery, these ghostly snapshots have not yet been completely exorcized from current thinking. Introspection is often held to tell us that consciousness is filled with a variety of peculiar objects and qualities that cannot be accounted for by a purely physical theory of mind, and this chapter is devoted to demolishing this view. The imagistic view of consciousness has been in the past a prolific source of confusions, such as the perennial problems of hallucinations, 'perceptual spaces' and color qualities, to name a few. Once the distinction between the personal and sub-personal level is made clear and mental images are abandoned these problems vanish.

Although the myth of mental imagery is beginning to lose its grip on thinkers in the field, it is still worth a direct examination and critique.[1] I shall restrict the examination to visual perception and mental imagery, since the results obtained there can be applied directly to the other sense modalities. We are less inclined to strike up the little band in the brain for auditory perception than we are to set up the movie screen, so if images can be eliminated, mental noises, smells, feels, and tastes will go quietly.

The difficulty with mental images has always been that they are not very much like physical images—paintings and photographs, for example. The concept of a mental image must always be hedged in a variety of ways: mental images are in a different space, do not have dimensions, are subjective, are Intentional, or even, in the end, just quasi-images. Once mental images have been so qualified, in what respects are they *like* physical images at all? Paintings and photographs are our exemplary images, and if mental images are not like them, our use of the word "image" is systematically misleading, regardless of how well entrenched it is in our ordinary way of speaking.

Let me propose an acid test for images. An image is a *representation* of something, but what sets it aside from other representations is that an image represents something else always in virtue of having at least one quality or characteristic of shape, form or color in common with what it represents. Images can be in two or three dimensions, can be manufactured or natural, permanent or fleeting, but they must *resemble* what they represent and not merely represent it by playing a role—symbolic, conventional or functional—in some system. Thus an image of an orange need not be orange (e.g., it could be a black-and-white photograph), but something hard, square and black just cannot be an image of something soft, round and white. It might be intended as a *symbol* of something soft, round, and white, and—given the temper of contemporary art—might even be labelled a *portrait* of something soft, round and white, but it would not be an image. Now I take the important question about mental images to be: are there elements in perception that represent in virtue of resembling what they represent and hence deserve to be called images?

First let us attack this question from the point of view of a subpersonal account of perception. Consider how images *work*. It is one thing just to be an image—e.g., a reflection in a pool in the wilderness—and another to function as an image, to be taken as an image, to be used as an image. For an image to work as an image there must be a person (or an analogue of a person) to see or observe it, to recognize or ascertain the qualities in virtue of which it is an image of something. Imagine a fool putting a television camera on his car and connecting it to a small receiver under the bonnet so the engine could 'see where it is going'. The madness in this is that although an image has been provided, no provision has been made for anyone or anything analogous to a perceiver to watch the image. This makes it clear that if an image is to function as an element in *perception,* it will have to function as the raw material and not the end product, for if we suppose that the product of the perceptual process is an image, we shall have to design a perceiver-analogue to sit in front of the image, and yet another to sit in front of the image which is the end product of perception in the perceiver-analogue and so forth *ad infinitum.* Just as brain-writing requires brain-writing readers, so the image view requires image-watchers; both views merely postpone true analysis by positing unanalysed man-analogues as functional parts of men.

In fact the last image in the physical process of perception is the image of stimulation on the retina. The process of afferent analysis begins on the surface of the retina and continues up the optic nerve, so that the exact pattern of stimulation on the retina is "lost" and replaced with information about characteristics of this pattern and eventually about characteristics of the environment.[2] The particular physiological facts about this neural analysis are not directly relevant to the philosophical problem of images. The nervous system *might* have transmitted the mosaic of stimulation on the retina deep into the brain and then reconstituted the image there, in the manner of television, but in that case the analysis that must occur as the first step in perception would simply be carried out at a deeper anatomical level. Once perceptual analysis has begun, there will indeed be elements of the process that can be said to be representations, but only in virtue of being interrelated parts of an essentially arbitrary system. The difference between a neural representation of a square and that of a circle will no more be a difference in the shape of the neural things than the difference between the *words* 'ox' and 'butterfly' is that one is heavier and uglier than the other. The upshot of this is that there is no room in the subpersonal explanation of the perceptual process, whatever its details, for images. Let us turn then to the personal level account of mental imagery to see if it is as compelling, after all, as we often think.

Shorter, in 'Imagination',[3] describes imagining as more like depicting—in words—than like painting a picture. We can, and usually do, imagine things without going into great detail. If I imagine a tall man with a wooden leg I need not also have imagined him as having hair of a certain color, dressed in any particular clothes, having or not having a hat. If, on the other hand, I were to draw a picture of this man, I would have to go into details. I can make the picture fuzzy, or in silhouette, but unless something positive is drawn in where the hat should be, obscuring that area, the man in the picture must either have a hat on or not. As Shorter points out, my not going into details about hair color in my imagining does not mean that his hair is colored 'vague' in my imagining; his hair is simply not 'mentioned' in my imagining at all. This is quite unlike drawing a picture that is deliberately ambiguous, as one can readily see by first imagining a tall man with a wooden leg and then imagining a tall man with a wooden leg who maybe does and maybe does not have blond hair, and comparing the results.

If I write down a description of a person, it would be absurd for anyone to say that my description cannot fail to mention whether or not the man is wearing a hat. My description can be as brief and undetailed as I like. Similarly it would be absurd to insist that one's imagining someone must go into the question of his wearing a hat. It is one thing to imagine a man wearing a hat, another to imagine him not wearing a hat, a third to imagine his head so obscured you can't tell, and a fourth to imagine him without going into the matter of headgear at all. Imagining is depictional or descriptional, not pictorial, and is bound only by this one rule borrowed from the rules governing sight: it must be from a point of view—I cannot imagine the inside and outside of a barn at once.[4]

A moment's reflection should convince us that it is not just imagining, however, that is like description in this way; all 'mental imagery', including seeing and hallucinating, is descriptional. Consider the film version of *War and Peace* and Tolstoy's book; the film version goes into immense detail and in one way cannot possibly be *faithful* to Tolstoy's words, since the 'picture painted' by Tolstoy does not go into the detail the film cannot help but go into (such as the colors of the eyes of each filmed soldier). Yet Tolstoy's descriptions are remarkably vivid. The point of this is that the end product of perception, what we are aware of when we perceive something, is more like the written Tolstoy than the film. The writing analogy has its own pitfalls but is still a good antidote to the picture analogy. When we perceive something in the environment, we are not aware of every fleck of color all at once, but rather of the highlights of the scene, an edited commentary on the things of interest.

As soon as images are abandoned even from the personal level account of perception in favor of a descriptional view of awareness, a number of perennial philosophical puzzles dissolve. Consider the Tiger and his Stripes. I can dream, imagine or see a striped tiger, but must the tiger I experience have a particular number of stripes? If seeing or imagining is having a mental image, then the image of the tiger *must*—obeying the rules of images in general—reveal a definite number of stripes showing, and one should be able to pin this down with such questions as 'more than ten?,' 'less than twenty?' If, however, seeing or imagining has a descriptional character, the questions need have no definite answer. Unlike a snapshot of a tiger, a description of a tiger need not go into the number of stripes at all; "numerous stripes" may be all the description says. Of course in the case of actually seeing a tiger, it will often be possible to corner the tiger and count his stripes, but then one is counting real tiger stripes, not stripes on a mental image.[5]

Another familiar puzzle is Wittgenstein's duck-rabbit, the drawing that looks now like a duck, now like a rabbit. What can possibly be the difference between seeing it first one way and then the other? The image (on the paper or the retina) does not change, but there can be more than one description of that image. To be aware₁* of it first as a rabbit and then as a duck can be just a matter of the content of the signals crossing the awareness line, and this in turn could depend on some weighting effect occurring in the course of afferent analysis. One says at the personal level 'First I was aware of it *as* a rabbit, and then *as* a duck', but if the question is asked, 'What is the difference between the two experiences?', one can only answer at this level by repeating one's original remark. To get to other more enlightening answers to the question, one must resort to the sub-personal level, and here the answer will invoke no images beyond the unchanging image on the retina.

Of all the problems that have led philosophers to posit mental imagery, the most tenacious has been the problem of hallucinations, and yet it need hardly be mentioned that there is no problem of hallucinations *unless* one is thinking of awareness imagistically. On the sub-personal level, there can be little doubt that hallucinations are caused by abnormal neuronal discharges. Stimulation by electrode of micro-areas on the visual cortex produces specific and repeatable hallucinations.[6] Having a visual hallucination is then just being aware₁ of the content of a non-veridical visual 'report' caused by such a freak discharge. And where is this report, and what space does it exist in? It is in the brain and exists in the space taken up by whatever event it is that has this non-veridical content, just as my description of hallucinations takes up a certain amount of space on paper. Since spatiality is irrelevant to descriptions, freak descriptions do not require ghostly spaces to exist in.[7]

The one familiar philosophical example that may seem at first to resist the descriptional view of perception and awareness in favour of the imagistic is the distinction, drawn by Descartes, between imagining and conceiving. We can imagine a pentagon or a hexagon, and imagining one of these is introspectively distinguishable from imagining the other, but we cannot imagine a

---

*Two distinct concepts of awareness, indicated by subscripts, are defined in *Content and Consciousness.* Roughly—for present purposes—awareness₁ is the awareness of a (human, language-using) subject who *can say* what the content of his or her consciousness currently is.—D.C.D. 1981

chiliagon (a thousand-sided figure) in a way that is introspectively distinct from imagining a 999-sided figure. We can, however, *conceive* of a chiliagon (without trying to imagine one) and this experience is perfectly distinct from conceiving of a 999-sided figure. From this it might be tempting to argue that whereas conceiving might well be descriptional and not imagistic, imagining must be imagistic, for our inability to imagine a chiliagon is just like our inability to tell a *picture* of a chiliagon from the *picture* of a 999-sided figure. All this shows, however, is that imagining is like *seeing,* not that imagining is like making pictures. In fact, it shows that imagining is *not* like making pictures, for I certainly *can* make a picture of a chiliagon if I have a great deal of patience and very sharp pencils, and when it is done I can tell it from a picture of a 999-sided figure, but this deliberate, constructive activity is unparalleled by anything I can do when I 'frame mental images'. Although I can *put together* elements to make a mental 'image' the result is always bound by a limitation of seeing: I can only imagine what I could see in a glance; differences below the threshold of discrimination of casual observation cannot be represented in imagination. The distinction between imagining and conceiving is real enough; it is like the distinction between seeing and listening to someone. Conceiving depends on the ability to understand words, such as the formula 'regular thousand-sided figure', and what we can describe in words far outstrips what we can see in one gaze.

If seeing is rather like reading a novel at breakneck speed, it is also the case that the novel is written to order at breakneck speed. This allows introspection to lay a trap for us and lead us naturally to the picture theory of seeing. Whenever we examine our own experience of seeing, whenever we set out to discover what we can say about what we are seeing, we find all the details we think of looking for. When we read a novel, questions can come to mind that are not answered in the book, but when we are looking at something, as soon as questions come up they are answered immediately by new information as a result of the inevitable shift in the focus and fixation point of our eyes. The reports of perception are written to order; whatever detail interests us is immediately brought into focus and reported on. When this occurs one is not scanning some stable mental image or sense-datum. One is scanning the outside world—quite literally. One can no more become interested in a part of one's visual experience without bringing the relevant information to the fore than one can run away from one's shadow. For this reason it is tempting to suppose that everything one *can* know about via the eyes is *always* 'present to consciousness' in some stable picture.

To sit and introspect one's visual experience for a while is not to examine normal sight. When one does this, one is tempted to say that it is all very true that there is only a small, central part of the visual field of which one is aware at any moment, and that to describe the whole scene our eyes, our fixation point, and our 'focus of interest' must scan the sensory presentation, but that the parts we are not scanning at any moment persist or remain, as a sort of vague, coloured background. Of this background we are only 'semi-aware'. Here, however, introspection runs into trouble, for as soon as one becomes interested in what is going on outside the beam of the fixation point, one immediately becomes aware (aware$_1$) of the contents of peripheral signals, and this phenomenon is quite different from the ordinary one. While it is true that one can focus on a spot on the wall and yet direct one's attention to the periphery of one's visual field and come up with reports like 'There is something blue and book-sized on the table to my right; it is vague and blurred and I am not sure it is a book,' it cannot be inferred from this that when one is *not* doing this, one is still aware of the blue, booklike shape. We are led to such conclusions by the natural operation of our eyes, which is to make a cursory scanning of the environment whenever it changes and as soon as it changes, and by the operation of short-term memory, which holds the results of this scanning for a short period of time. In familiar surroundings we do not have to see or pay attention to the objects in their usual places. If anything had been moved or removed we *would* have noticed, but that does not mean we notice their presence, or even that we had the experience (in any sense) of their presence. We enter a room and we know what objects are in it, because if it is a familiar room we do not notice that anything is missing and thus it is filled with all the objects we have noticed or put there in the past. If it is an unfamiliar room we automatically scan it, picking out the objects that fill it and catch our attention. I may spend an afternoon in a strange room without ever being aware (in any sense) of the color of the walls, and while it is no doubt true that had the walls been bright red I would have been aware of this, it does not follow that I must have been aware that they were beige, or aware that they were colorless or vaguely colored—whatever that might mean. [8]

It is true, of course, that when we see, we do not simply see *that* there is a table in front of us but a table of a particular color and shape in a particular position and so forth. All this need mean is that the information we receive is vivid and rich in detail. This is not true of the vision of many lower animals. The frog, for example, can see that there is a small moving object before him, but he cannot see that it is a fly or a bit of paper on a string. If the small object is not moving, *he cannot see it at all,* because motion signals are required for the production of the higher-level signals that will initiate a behavioral response. A frog left in a cage with freshly killed (unmoving) flies will starve to death, because it has no equipment for sending the signal: there is a fly (moving or still). Dangle a dead fly on a string and the frog will eat it.[9] The difference in degree of complexity and vividness between frog and human perception does not warrant the assumption that there is a difference in kind—however much we may feel that a picture is worth a thousand words.[10]

Postscript, 1981

My conclusion in 1969 that nothing deserving to be called an image would be discovered in the sub-personal theory of perception and imagination was rash and overstated. A corrective agnosticism is expressed by me in "Two Approaches to Mental Images" (1978), reprinted as Chapter 4 in this volume. I still think the grounds for skepticism presented here are the right sort of grounds, and point out the correct direction for further empirical research and theory-construction.

Notes

1. Optimists who doubt that mental images are still taken seriously in philosophy and even in science are invited to peruse two recent anthologies, R. J. Hirst, ed., *Perception and the External World* (New York, 1965) and J. R. Smythies, ed., *Brain and Mind, Modern Concepts of the Nature of Mind* (London, 1965). The wealth of cross-disciplinary confusions over mental images is displayed in both volumes, both of which include papers by philosophers, psychologists, and neurophysiologists. Neither editor seems to think that much of what he presents is a dead horse, which strengthens my occasionally flagging conviction that I am not beating one. On the other hand, there are scientists who have expressed clear and explicit rejections of imagistic confusions. See, e.g., G. W. Zopf, "Sensory Homeostasis," in Wiener and Schade (1963), esp. p. 118, and D. M. MacKay, "Internal Representation of the External World," unpublished, read at the Avionics Panel Symposium on Natural and Artificial Logic Processors, Athens, July 15–19, 1963.

2. H. B. Barlow, "Possible Principles Underlying the Transformations of Sensory Messages," in *Sensory Communication* (1961), offers a particularly insightful account of the "editorial" function of afferent neural activity and the depletion of information that is the necessary concomitant of such analysis.

3. J. M. Shorter, "Imagination", *Mind,* 61 (1952), 528–542.

4. Counter-examples spring to mind, but are they really counter-examples? All the ones that have so far occurred to me turn out on reflection to be cases of imagining myself seeing—with the aid of large mirrors—the inside and outside of the barn, imagining a (partially) transparent barn, imagining looking in the window and so forth. These are all from a point of view in the sense I mean. A written description, however, is not bound by these limitations; from what point of view is the description: 'the barn is dark red with black rafters and a pine floor'?

5. In the unusual phenomenon of 'eidetic imagery', the subject *can* read off or count off the details of his 'memory image', and this may seem to provide the fatal counter-example to this view. See G. Allport, "Eidetic Imagery", *British Journal of Psychology*, 15 (1924), 99–120. Yet the fact that such 'eidetic memory images' actually appear to be projected or superimposed on the subject's normal visual field (so that if the subject shifts his gaze, the position of the memory image in his visual field remains fixed, and 'moves with the eye') strongly suggests that in these cases the actual image of retinal stimulation is somehow retained at or very near the retina and superimposed on incoming stimulation. In these rare cases, then, the memory mechanism must operate *prior* to afferent analysis, at a time when there still is a physical image.

6. Penfield (1958). Some of Penfield's interpretations of his results have been widely criticized, but the results themselves are remarkable. It would be expected that hallucinations would have to be the exception rather than the rule in the brain for event-types to *acquire* content in the first place, and this is in fact supported by evidence. Amputees usually experience 'phantom limb' sensations that seem to come from the missing limb; an amputee may feel that he not only still has the leg, but that it is itching or hot or bent at the knee. These phenomena, which occur off and on for years following amputation, are nearly universal in amputees, with one interesting exception. In cases where the amputation occurred in infancy, before the child developed the use and coordination of the limb, phantom limb is rarely experienced, and in cases where amputation occurred just after birth, no phantom limb is ever experienced. See M. Simmel, "Phantom Experiences following Amputation in Childhood," *Journal of Neurology, Neurosurgery, and Psychiatry,* 25 (1962), 69–78.

7. Other phenomena less well known to philosophers also favour a descriptional explanation. See, e.g., W. R. Brain's account of the reports of patients who have their sight surgically restored, in "Some Reflections on Mind and Brain," *Brain,* 86 (1963), 381; the controversial accounts of newly sighted adults' efforts to learn to see, in M. von Senden, *Raum- und Gestaltauffassung bei operierten Blindgeborenen vor und nach der Operation* (Leipzig, 1932), trans. with appendices by P. Heath as *Space and Sight: The Perception of Space and Shape in the Congenitally blind before and after Operation* (London, 1960), Vol. 1. Kohler's experiments with inverting spectacles (a good account of these and similar experiments is found in J. G. Taylor, *The Behavioral Basis of Perception,* New Haven, 1962); and the disorder called simultanagnosia, M. Kinsbourne and E. K. Warrington, "A Disorder of Simultaneous Form Perception," *Brain,* 85 (1962), 461–86, and A. R. Luria et al., "Disorders of Ocular Movement in a Case of Simultanagnosia," *Brain,* 86 (1963), 219–228.

8. Cf. Wittgenstein, *Philosophical Investigation,* 'But the existence of this feeling of strangeness does not give us a reason for saying that every object we know well and which does not seem strange to us gives us a feeling of familiarity,' 1953, i. 596. See also i. 597, i. 605.

9. Muntz (1964) and Wooldridge (1963), pp. 46–50.

10. Having found no room for images in the sub-personal account of perception, we can say that 'mental image' and its kin are poor candidates for referring expressions in science. Having found further that nothing with the traits of genuine images is to be found at the personal level either allows us to conclude that 'mental image' is valueless as a referring expression under *any* circumstances.

IMAGISTIC REPRESENTATION

3

Jerry A. Fodor

If I have been unsympathetic about the empirical basis for the existence of stagelike changes in modes of internal representation, it is because I think it would be appalling if the data really did somehow require us to endorse that sort of view. I am, in fact, strongly inclined to doubt the very *intelligibility* of the suggestion that there is a stage at which cognitive processes are carried out in a medium that is fundamentally nondiscursive. I am not, of course, denying the empirical possibility that children may use images more than adults do, or that their concepts may be in some interesting sense more concrete than adult concepts. What I do deny, however, is that the difference could be qualitative in the kind of way that Bruner seems to require. That is, I don't think that there could be a stage at which images are the vehicle of thought in the strong sense that thinking is *identifiable* with imaging at that stage —not, at least, if images are representations that refer by resembling. All this needs considerable sorting out.

Imagine, *per impossible,* that adults think in English—that is, English sentences provide the medium in which adult cognitive processes are carried out. How, on this assumption, would children have to differ from adults if Bruner's ontogenetic doctrines are to hold? That is to say, if we take thinking in English as a clear case of thinking in symbols, what is to count as the corresponding clear case of thinking in icons? Well, one possibility is that the children use a representational system just like the one that the adults use except that the children have *pictures* where the adults have *words*. This suggestion surely *is* coherent; one can, for example, imagine devising a hieroglyphic orthography for English. English sentences would thus be sequences of pictures (rather than sequences of phones) but everything else stays the same. So we have assigned *a* sense to the proposal that children's thought is iconic and adults' thought is symbolic.

But, of course, it isn't the sense that Bruner has in mind. For icons, in Bruner's sense, aren't just *pictures*; they are pictures that resemble what they stand for. That is, it's not just that symbols *look* different from icons; it's also that they are differently related to what they symbolize. The reference of icons is mediated by resemblance. The reference of symbols is mediated by conventions. Or something.[1]

So English in hieroglyphs won't quite do. But we can fix things up. We can imagine a language just like English except that (a) words are replaced by pictures and (b) the only pictures allowed are such as resemble what the corresponding words refer to. Of course, the representational capacity of such a language would be very limited, since we can only use it to refer to what we can picture. Still, it is a coherent suggestion that there could be such a language, and it is a coherent hypothesis that this is the language children think in. The point of the exercise is that one way of understanding the idea that children think in icons is: Children think in a language in which *pictures* (not just hieroglyphs) take the role that words play in natural languages.

I am pretty sure that this is not, however, the sort of account of children's mental processes that Bruner wants to commend either. For one thing, if the difference between children and us were just that we think in something like standard English while they think in (call it) Iconic English, then the difference between us and children might not come to much. For though Iconic English can refer to fewer things than standard English can, they can both express

some of the same semantic relations among the things they do refer to. After all, some such relations are carried by grammatical
features of standard English, and standard English and Iconic
English have the same grammar. Since agency, predication, possession, and the rest are presumably expressible in Iconic English, it
looks as though much of the cognitive incapacity that would be involved in using it would be a relative paucity of *vocabulary*. Bruner makes it pretty clear, however (1966, chap. 2), that he takes
the availability of grammatical structure in representations to be
a proprietary feature of symbolic (that is, noniconic) representational systems.

The preceding remarks are intended as something more than a
commendation of syntax. The point is that we can make sense of
Iconic English as a representational system precisely *because* the
switch to Iconic English leaves the grammar of standard English
unaltered. One way to put the point is this: In Iconic English,
words resemble what they refer to, *but sentences don't resemble
what makes them true.* Thus suppose that, in Iconic English, the
word "John" is replaced by a picture of John and the word
"green" is replaced by a green patch. Then the sentence "John is
green" comes out as (say) a picture of John followed by a green
picture. But *that* doesn't look like John's being green; it doesn't look
much like anything. Iconic English provides a construal of the notion of a representational system in which (what corresponds to)
words are icons, but it provides no construal of the notion of a
representational system in which (what corresponds to) *sentences*
are. Nor do I think that this can usefully be patched up; the notion that sentences could be icons *has* no construal. But if sentences couldn't be icons, thoughts couldn't be either.

The structure of the argument is this: If the role that images
play in a representational system is analogous to the role that
words play in a natural language, then having a thought *cannot* be
simply a matter of entertaining an image, and this is true whether
the image is motoric or iconic and quite independent of any particular empirical hypothesis about the nature of cognitive development. For thoughts are the kinds of things that can be true or

false. They are thus the kinds of things that are expressed by *sentences*, not words. And, while (barring considerations to be reviewed below) it makes a sort of sense to imagine a representational system in which the counterparts of words resemble what they refer to, it makes no sense at all to imagine a representational system in which the counterparts of sentences do.

We have hypothesized a representational system—Iconic English—which differs from standard English in that all the words are pictures but where everything else stays the same. We have remarked that in *that* representational system there is a *noniconic* relation between sentences and what makes them true. Can we do better? What *would* it be like to have a representational system in which sentences are icons of their truth conditions?

For example, what would it be like to have a representational system in which the sentence "John is fat" is replaced by a picture? Suppose that the picture that corresponds to "John is fat" is a picture of John with a bulging tummy. But then, what picture are we going to assign to "John is tall"? The same picture? If so, the representational system does not distinguish the thought that John is tall from the thought that John is fat. A different picture? But John will have to have some shape or other in whatever picture we choose, so what is to tell us that having the picture is having a thought about John's height rather than a thought about his shape? Similarly, a picture of John is a picture of John sitting or standing, or lying down, or it is indeterminate among the three. But then, what is to tell us whether having the picture is having the thought that John is tall, or having the thought that John is sitting, or having the thought that he is standing, or having the thought that he is lying down, or having the thought that one doesn't know whether John is sitting, standing, or lying down?[2]

There are lots of ways of making this sort of point. Suppose that John *is* fat and suppose that John's name is a picture of John. So thinking of John is having a picture which, presumably, shows John fat. And thinking that John is fat is *also* having a picture that shows John fat. But then: What, on this account, is the difference between (just) thinking of John, on the one hand, and thinking that John is fat, on the other?[3]

Let's see where we have got to. The notion that thoughts are images—or that they were images when we were very young—is really viciously ambiguous. On the one hand, the proposal might be that we should identify having an image with thinking *of* something, and, on the other, it might be that we should identify having an image with thinking *that* something. These two proposals don't, by any means, come to the same thing. The former amounts to the suggestion that images might be the vehicle of *reference*, while the latter amounts to the suggestion that images might be the vehicle of *truth*.

So, for example, if Iconic English were the language of thought, then *thinking* of John might consist of entertaining John's image, just as, in the standard use of ordinary English, *mentioning* John (referring to him) might consist just in uttering John's name. It is, in this sense, no more problematic that there should be a language in which reference is defined for images than that there should be a language in which reference is defined for words. I suppose it is just a matter of brute fact that all the natural languages there are happen to be of the latter kind. But I see no way of construing the notion that there might be a language in which *truth* is defined for icons instead of symbols; in which, that is, "formulae" of the system are true of what they resemble. The trouble is *precisely* that icons are insufficiently abstract to be the vehicles of truth.

To a first approximation, the kind of thing that can get a truth value is an assignment of some property to some object. A representational system must therefore provide appropriate vehicles for expressing such assignments. Under what conditions, then, is a representation adequate to express the assignment of a property to an object? Well, one condition which surely must be satisfied is that the representation specify *which* property is being assigned and which object it is being assigned to. The trouble with trying to truth-value icons is that they provide no way of doing the former. Any picture of a thing will, of necessity, display that thing as having indefinitely many properties; hence pictures correspond (and fail to correspond) in indefinitely many ways to the things they resemble. Which of these correspondences is the one that makes the picture true?

But if pictures correspond to the same world in too many

different ways, they also correspond in the same way to too many different worlds. A picture of John with a bulging tummy corresponds to John's being fat. But it corresponds equally to John's being pregnant since, if that is the way that John *does* look when he is fat, it is also, I suppose, the way that he *would* look if he were pregnant. So, if the fact that John is fat is a reason to call a picture of John with a bulging tummy true, then the fact that John isn't pregnant is as good a reason to call a picture of John with a bulging tummy false. A picture which corresponds to a man walking up a hill forward corresponds equally, and in the same way, to a man sliding down the hill backward (Wittgenstein, 1953, p. 139). For every reason that we might have for calling a picture true, there will be a corresponding reason for calling it false. That is, there is no reason for calling it either. Pictures aren't the kind of things that can have truth-values.

Notice that symbols (as opposed to icons) are exempt from these worries; that's one of the respects in which symbols really *are* abstract. A picture of fat John is also a picture of tall John. But the sentence "John is fat" abstracts from all of John's properties but one: It is true if he's fat and only if he is. Similarly, a picture of a fat man corresponds in the same way (that is, by resemblance) to a world where men are fat and a world where men are pregnant. But "John is fat" abstracts from the fact that fat men *do* look the way that pregnant men *would* look; it is true in a world where John is fat and false in any other world.

Taken together, these sorts of considerations strongly suggest that there isn't much sense to be made of the notion that there might be an internal representational system in which icons are the vehicles of truth—that is, in which entertaining an image is identical to thinking *that* such and such is the case. But we've seen that a certain kind of sense *can* be made of the suggestion that there is an internal representational system in which icons are the vehicles of reference—that is, in which thinking *of* such and such is identical with entertaining an image. It should now be remarked that even this concession needs to be hedged about.

In Iconic English, John's name is a picture of John. So if the language of thought were Iconic English, thinking of John might consist of entertaining an image of John, in just the sense that, in real English, referring to John might be identical with uttering "John." But what sense is that?

Clearly not every utterance of "John" *does* constitute a reference to John. For example, I just sat back from my typewriter and said "John." But I referred to no one; a fortiori, I did not refer to John. One might put it as follows: In the case of natural languages, utterances of (potentially) referring expressions succeed in making references only when they are produced with the right intentions. I cannot, as it were, refer by mistake; no utterance of "John" counts as a reference to John unless it was at least produced with the intention of *making* a reference.

In natural languages, to put it succinctly, the vehicles of reference are utterances that are taken under (that is, intended to satisfy) descriptions. In paradigm cases of referring to John, I utter "John" intending, thereby, to produce a form of words, and moreover to produce a form of words standardly used to refer to John, and moreover to refer to John by producing a form of words standardly used to refer to John. But on other occasions when I make the sound "John," none of these things is true, and in those cases (though not only in those cases) my utterances of "John" don't count as references to John.

So sometimes uttering "John" constitutes making a reference to John, but only when the speaker intends his behavior to satisfy certain descriptions; only when he intends his utterance in a certain way. I think the same kinds of remarks apply, *mutatis mutandis*, to the use of images as vehicles of reference in systems like Iconic English: If Iconic English were the language of thought, there might be cases in which entertaining an image of a thing constituted thinking of it; but only when the image is taken to satisfy certain descriptions; only when it is entertained in the right way. Iconic English is, by hypothesis, a language where the referring expressions are images. But even in Iconic English resemblance wouldn't be a sufficient condition for reference since, even in Iconic English, what refers aren't images but images-under-descriptions. Iconic English doesn't succeed in being *very* nondiscursive after all.

Figure 1 is a picture of a pinwheel sort of thing. Close your eyes and form an image of it. If thinking is forming an image of a thing, and if images refer to whatever they resemble, then you must just have been thinking of a cube viewed from one of its corners. For the image you just entertained does, in fact, resemble a cube viewed from one of its corners, just as (and in just the same way that) Figure 2 resembles a cube viewed from one of its edges. But, surely, many readers will have formed the image and *not* have thought of the cube. Having the image will have constitued thinking of a cube only for those readers who both formed the image and took it in a certain way: i.e., took the point in the center to be a corner of the cube, took the lines radiating from the point to be edges of the cube, etc.

The moral is: Yes, we can make a certain sort of sense of children having icons where we have symbols, viz., they have pictures where we have words (*n.b.* words, not sentences).[4] But no, we cannot make much sense of the notion that the relation between thoughts and their objects is basically different for children and for us. To make sense of that, we would need to suppose that images refer by resembling while symbols refer by convention. (Or, as we remarked above, something.) And that they patently do not do. (Images usually don't *refer* at all. But when they do— as, e.g., in Iconic English—they do so in basically the same way that words and phrases do: viz., by satisfying, and by being taken to satisfy, certain descriptions.)

This is not, of course, to deny that pictures look like the things they are pictures of. It is rather to deny that *looking like a thing* could be a sufficient condition for *referring* to that thing, even in a language like Iconic English, where pictures are the referring expressions. There is, in fact, a perfectly good way of using a picture to make a reference, viz., by embedding it in a description. So one might say "I am looking for a man who looks like this . . ." and show a picture of a man. It's true that in such a case the form of words wouldn't usually succeed in communicating a reference

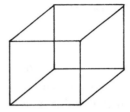

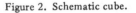

Figure 1. A pinwheel sort of thing.   Figure 2. Schematic cube.

unless the picture of the man looks like the man one is seeking.
But, equally, the picture is no use without the description which
tells you how it is intended to be taken. Compare the ways in
which the picture would be used in 'I am looking for a man who
(looks like/dresses like/is taller than) this . . . (picture of a short
man wearing a toga)'. What carries the reference here is the picture
together with the 'symbols' that interpret it.

I can, in short, see no way of construing the proposal that there
might be a representational system in which resembling is a *sufficient* condition for referring, still less that there might be a representational system in which resembling and referring come to the
same thing. To put it briefly, even if Bruner is right and the *vehicles*
of reference are different for adults and children, the *mechanisms*
of reference—whatever they are—must be pretty much the same
for both.

I have been trying to undermine two notions about images that
have played a long and dubious role in cognitive psychology: that
thinking might *consist* of imaging, and that the means by which
images refer to what they are images of might be fundamentally
different from the means by which symbols refer to what they
denote. But, of course, nothing I have said denies that images exist or that images may play an important role in many cognitive

processes. Indeed, such empirical evidence as is available tends to support both claims. This is interesting from the point of view of the major preoccupations of this book. The fact that the data come out the way they do throws light on the nature of the representational resources that people have available. And the fact that the data come out *at all* supports the view that the nature of such resources is a bona fide empirical question.

The relevant studies have recently been extensively reviewed (see, in particular, Paivio, 1971; Richardson, 1969). Suffice it here to sketch one or two of the findings which seem to argue forcibly for the psychological reality of images.

1. If there are images, and if, as introspection suggests, imaging is very like visual perception, one might plausibly expect that experimental tasks which elicit images should produce mode-specific interference with other cognitive processes in which vision is implicated. Tasks which require visual imagery, e.g., should induce decrements in the performance of simultaneous tasks which require visually guided responses. An elegant series of experiments by Brooks (1968) suggests that they do so. In one condition, *Ss* are asked to form a memory image of a figure like Figure 3. They are then asked to trace around the memory image following the arrows and indicating, for each corner, whether it occurs on a top edge of the figure. (The appropriate responses for Figure 3 are thus: 'no, yes, no, no, no, yes, yes, no, no, no.') Depending on the experimental group to which the subject is assigned, responses are indicated either by pointing to written yeses and noes or by some form of nonvisually guided gesture (like tapping or saying 'yes' or 'no'). The relevant result is that performance is significantly better for subjects in the latter (nonvisually guided) groups. Visual images interfere with visually guided tasks.

Moreover, they interfere selectively. Brooks had another condition in which *S's* task was to produce sequences of yeses and noes depending on the form class of the words in a previously memorized sentence. A subject might be given a sentence like 'Now is the time for all good men to come to the aid of the party' and told to indicate 'yes' for each word that is a noun or verb and 'no' for each

Figure 3. Stimulus diagram of the kind used by Brooks (1968).

word that is neither. In this condition, the effect of response mode upon performance reversed the relation found in the visual image case: Performance was best for subjects who point or tap, worst for subjects who gave their responses verbally. Visually guided responses don't, apparently, much interfere with auditory images.

2. If there are images, and if, as introspection suggests, images are very much like pictures, then there ought to be demonstrable similarities between the processes of comparing an object with an image of that object and comparing two objects that look alike. There are, in fact, a number of experiments in the literature which suggest that this is so. (See, e.g., Cooper and Shepard, 1973). The paradigmatic study is owing to Posner, Boies, Eichelman and Taylor (1969).

To begin with, it is possible to show that there is a reliable difference in the speed with which subjects can make judgments of type identity in the case where the tokens are physically *similar*, on the one hand, and in the case where the tokens are physically *different*, on the other. Thus, e.g., Ss are presented with tachistascopic displays consisting of two letters and asked to respond 'yes' if the letters are the same and 'no' if they are different. In this situation, Ss are faster when the members of the positive pairs (i.e., the pairs for which the correct response is 'yes') are of the *same case* (like *PP* or *pp*) than when they are of *different case* (like *Pp* or *pP*).

Now suppose the paradigm is changed. Instead of presenting S with two letters in the visual mode, we present him first with an auditory case-and-letter designation, then with a *single visual* letter to match to the auditory description. So the subject might hear 'capital *P*' and then see *P* (to which his response would be 'yes') or *p* or *Q* or *q* (to all of which the right response would be 'no'). It turns out that *S*s performance in this situation depends critically on the length of the interval between the auditory and the visual stimulus. Subjects for whom the visual stimulus comes on immediately after the auditory stimulus give response latencies comparable to those for visually presented letter pairs whose members *differ* in case. If, however, the interstimulus interval is increased to about 0.7 second, the response latencies *decrease* and approximate those for visually presented letter pairs whose members are *identical* in case. It is not mandatory, but it is extremely natural, to assume that what happens during the 0.7 second of interstimulus interval is that the subject constructs a letter image to fit the auditory description, and that it is that image which gets matched to the visual display. If this is true, and if, as we have supposed, matching images to things is fundamentally similar to matching things that look alike, we have some sort of explanation of the behavioral convergence between *S*s who judge the relation between pairs of letters both of which they *see,* and *S*s who judge the relation between pairs of letters one of which they only hear described.

The studies just reviewed are by no means the only possibilities for the empirical investigation of the psychological reality of mental images.[5] Consider just one further line of argument.

Discursive symbols, as Bruner remarked, are deployed in time. Or, rather, *some* discursive symbols are (viz., spoken sentences). Pictures (and written sentences), on the other hand, are deployed in space. There may be conventions for determining the order in which information is retrieved from a picture (as in certain kinds of didactic paintings which 'tell a story' and are meant to be scanned in a certain order) but, in general, there needn't be. In principle, all the information is available simultaneously and can be read off in whatever order the observer chooses.[6]

Suppose, then, that subjects *can* employ mental images to display the information pertinent to performing an experimental task, and suppose that mental images are relevantly similar to real pictures. One should then predict that Ss who can use images ought to enjoy considerable freedom in the order in which they can report the information that their images present, while Ss who use discursive forms of representation (e.g., sentences) ought to be relatively restricted in the order in which their information can be accessed. To take an extreme case, imagine an experiment in which the subject is shown a red triangle and then asked about what he has seen. Ss who stored an *image* ought to be about equally quick in answering 'Was it red?' and 'Was it triangular?' Ss who stored the sentence 'It was a red triangle' ought to be faster in answering the first question than in answering the second.[7]

As things stand this is, alas, largely a *gedanken* experiment; I mention it primarily as a further illustration of techniques that might be used to subject hypotheses about the nature of internal representations to experimental test. It is worth mentioning, however, that precisely this interpretation *has* been suggested by Paivio (1971) to account for differences in order-of-report effects exhibited by subjects in an experiment by Haber (1966). Paivio remarks that "while the implications of the present analysis have not been independently tested using the appropriate perceptual tasks, evidence from several sources is consistent with the hypothesis" (p. 130).

The preceding should suggest that the existence and functioning of mental images can be handled as an experimental issue and that techniques more subtle than brute appeals to introspection can be employed in the experiments. This may strike the philosophical reader as surprising, since it has recently been fashionable to treat the nonexistence of images as demonstrable a priori. Before we round off this discussion, it is worth digressing to see what can be said for so implausible a view.

Dennett (1969) has put succinctly what appears to be the paramount philosophical worry about images.

Consider the Tiger and his Stripes. I can dream, imagine or see a striped tiger, but must the tiger I experience have a particular number of stripes? If seeing or imaging is having a mental image, then the image of the tiger *must*—obeying the rules of images in general—reveal a definite number of stripes showing, and one should be able to pin this down with such questions as 'more than ten?', 'less than twenty?'. If, however, seeing or imagining has a descriptional character, the questions need have no definite answer. Unlike a snapshot of a tiger, a description of a tiger need not go into the number of stripes at all; 'numerous stripes' may be all the description says. Of course in the case of actually seeing a tiger, it will often be possible to corner the tiger and count his stripes, but then one is counting real tiger stripes, not stripes on a mental image. [pp. 136–137]

A number of philosophers appear to hold that this sort of argument provides something like a *demonstration* that there aren't mental images. If they are right it is an embarrassment since, as we have seen, there is some persuasive empirical evidence in the field, and it suggests that what goes on in imaging is very like picturing and very unlike describing. Moreover, the introspective plausibility of the image theory is enormous, so if the striped tigers do show what they are alleged to show we are without an explanation of either the introspections or the experimental data. Any theory is better than none; clearly, we should undermine the striped tiger argument if we can.

There are, I think, at least three ways that one might attempt to do so. I don't suppose that any of these counterarguments is conclusive, but I do think that, between them, they suggest that striped tigers don't clinch the case against images. Given the persuasiveness of the a posteriori arguments for imagery, that should be good enough.

To begin with, one might try simply denying what the striped tiger argument primarily assumes. That is, one might argue that there *is* some definite answer to 'How many stripes does the image-tiger have?' but that, because our images are labile, we usually can't hold on to them for long enough to count. It's to be said in favor of this view (a) that it seems introspectively plausible to many people who claim to have images (if you don't believe it, ask a few);[8] (b) it makes everyday mental images qualitatively like idetic images, from which even Dennett admits "the subject *can* read off or count off the details" (p. 137); (c) this view is anyhow less hard to swallow than the alternative suggestion: that what goes on when I think that I am picturing a thing is that I am, in fact, describing it to myself.[9]

This is, I think, the kind of suggestion that sophisticated philosophers take to be naive; perhaps because they are impressed by the following sort of argument. 'Having images is supposed to be part of the perceptual process. But now, if images themselves have to be perceived (scanned, etc.) to recover the information they contain, then surely we have taken the first step in a regress which will eventually require the postulation of images without number and endless perceivers to look at them.' This is, however, a bad argument. It assumes, quite without justification, that if recovering information from the external environment requires having an image, recovering information from an image must require having an image too. But why should we assume that? Moreover (and more to the present point), even if this were a *good* argument, it would be no good here. For the most it could show is that images don't play a certain role in perception (i.e., that perceiving a thing couldn't always and everywhere require forming an image of that thing). It shows nothing about whether having and scanning an image might play a role in *other* mental processes (such as comparing, remembering, or imagining things).

The second point that one might want to make about striped tigers is this: It simply isn't true that a picture of a striped tiger must be determinate under such descriptions as 'has n stripes.'[10] Of course the *tiger* has to have precisely n stripes for some n or other (barring problems about the individuation of stripes), but there are all kinds of cases in which a picture of an n-striped tiger may not show any definite number of image stripes. Blurring is the main (but not the only) problem.[11]

What *is* true, what does follow from what Dennett calls "the rules of images in general," is that if what you've got is an image, then necessarily there will have to be *some* visual description under which it is determinate. For a picture in a newspaper, e.g., the pertinent description is one which specifies a 'gray-matrix'—an assignment of a value of black or white to each of the finitely many points that comprise the image. So far as I can see, this is the *only* kind of visual description under which newspaper pictures are *always* determinate. Whether a given such picture happens also to be determinate under some *other* visual description (as, e.g., has *n* stripes) will depend on such matters as what it's a picture of, the angle from which the picture was taken, how good the resolution is, etc.

If this is right, it means that the striped tiger argument is a good deal weaker than it started out to seem. What that argument shows *at most* is that there are *some* visual descriptions under which mental images *aren't* fully determinate. But what would need to be shown to prove that mental images fail to satisfy 'the rules of images in general', i.e., to prove that they aren't images—is that there are *no* visual descriptions under which they *are* fully determinate. Surely nothing that strong follows from the sort of observations Dennett makes.[12]

The third point to make against the striped tiger is that it is more dogmatic about the distinction between images and descriptions than there is any need to be. A paradigmatic image (say a photograph) is *nondiscursive* (the information it conveys is displayed rather than described) and *pictorial* (it resembles its subject). The present point, however, is that there is an indefinite range of cases in between photographs and paragraphs. These intermediate cases are, in effect, images under descriptions; they convey *some* information discursively and *some* information pictorially, and they resemble their subjects only in respect of those properties that happen to be pictured. In particular, they are determinate under the same visual descriptions as their subjects only for such properties.[13]

An example may help to make this clear. Dennett says: "Consider the film version of *War and Peace* and Tolstoy's book; the film version goes into immense detail and in one way cannot possibly be *faithful* to Tolstoy's words since the 'picture painted' by Tolstoy does not go into the details the film cannot help but go into (such as the colors of the eyes of each filmed soldier" (1969, p. 136)). There are, however, other kinds of images than photographs. Consider, for example, *maps*. Maps are pictorial in respect of some of the information they convey; geographical relations are pictured when the map is oriented right. But they are, or may be, nonpictorial in respect of other information. Population densities or elevations above sea level may be given by coloring or shading, and then we need to use the legend to determine what the image means.

To put it briefly, since images under descriptions are images, they are typically pictorial vis-à-vis some set of visual properties, and, of course, they will be determinate vis-à-vis any set of properties they picture. But since it is in part the description that determines what such an image is an image *of*, the properties for which the image has to be determinate can have arbitrarily little in common with the visual properties of whatever the image images. Images under descriptions share their nondiscursiveness with images *tout court*. What they share with descriptions is that they needn't look much like what they represent.

We can now say what all this has to do with the tiger's stripes. Suppose that what one visualizes in imaging a tiger might be anything from a full-scale tiger portrait (in the case of the ideticist) to a sort of transient stick figure (in the case of poor imagers like me). What makes my stick figure an image of a tiger is not that it looks much like one (my drawings of tigers don't look much like tigers either) but rather that it's *my* image, so I'm the one who gets to say what it's an image of. My images (and my drawings) connect with my intentions in a certain way; I *take* them as tiger-pictures for purposes of whatever task I happen to have in hand. Since my mental image *is* an image, there will be some visual descriptions under which it is determinate; hence there will be some questions whose answers I can 'read off' the display,[14] and the more pictorial the display is, the more such questions there will be. But, in the case of any given image, there might be arbitrarily many visual properties which would not be pictured but, as it were, carried by the description under which the image is intended. The image will, ipso facto, not be determinate relative to these properties. We thus return, by a different route, to the conclusion mooted above: To show that mental images violate 'the rules of images in general,' one would have to show not just that they are indeterminate under some visual description or other, but rather that they are determinate under no visual descriptions at all. There *may* be a way of showing this, but I doubt it and the striped tiger argument doesn't do it.

All this points toward some plausible speculations about how images may integrate with discursive modes of internal representation. If one recalls the Posner et al. experiment discussed above, one notices that there are two psychological processes postulated by the proposed explanation of the results. In the first phase, an image is constructed in accordance with a description. In the second phase, the image is matched against a stimulus for purposes of perceptual identification. The explanation thus implies (what common sense also suggests) that we have psychological faculties which can construct images which display the information that corresponding descriptions convey discursively; i.e., faculties which permit us to construct images *from* descriptions. The experiment demonstrates that having the information displayed *as* an image facilitates performance in certain kinds of tasks. (In effect, using the image rather than the description permits the subject to do the job of perceptual categorization in parallel rather than in series; he can check letter case and letter type *at the same time*.)

These remarks about the Posner experiment fit very well with the view that images under description are often the vehicles of internal representation. For insofar as mental images are constructed *from descriptions*, the descriptions can function to determine what the images are images of, and how their properties are to be interpreted. Here, then, is the general outline of the picture I have been trying to develop:

1. Some behaviors are facilitated when task-relevant information is nondiscursively displayed (e.g., when it is displayed
   as an image).
2. One of our psychological faculties functions to construct
   images which accord with descriptions. That is, we have
   access to a computational system which takes a description as input and gives, as output, an image of something
   that satisfies the description. The exploitation of this system is presumably sensitive to our estimates of the demand
   characteristics of the task at hand.
3. The image that gets produced may be quite schematic since
   how the image is *taken*—what role it plays in cognitive processing—is determined not only by its figural properties but
   also by the character of the description it is paired with. We
   have seen that this point is important for evaluating the
   striped tiger argument. It may now be added that it goes
   some way toward meeting one of the empirical arguments
   that is frequently urged against taking mental images very
   seriously.

Psychologists who don't think that images could play any very
important role in internal representation often insist upon the idiosyncratic character of the images that subjects report (see, e.g.,
Brown, 1958). Clearly the content of images does vary quite a lot
from person to person, and it might well be that a given image can
function to effect different representations in different computational tasks (what counts as the image of a duck for one purpose
might count as the image of a rabbit for another). The present
point is that if mental images are images under descriptions, then
their idiosyncrasies might have very little effect on the role they
play in cognitive processes. Suppose your image of a triangle is
scaline and mine is isosceles. This needn't matter to how we use
the images to reason about triangles so long as we agree on how
the images are to be taken; e.g., so long as we agree that they are
to represent *any* closed three-sided figure whose sides are straight
lines.

This is, in fact, quite a traditional sort of point to make. The empiricists were on to it, though the significance of their views has frequently been overlooked. Thus Hume acknowledged Berkeley's insight that images can't resemble the referents of abstract ideas, but held that there is a sense in which entertaining an abstract idea might be identical with having an image all the same. Hume says: 'the image in the mind is only that of a particular object, tho' the application of it in our reasoning be the same as if it were universal' (1960 ed., p. 28). Viewed one way, this is tantamount to the abandonment of the image theory of thought, since the vehicles of internal representation are taken to be (not images *tout court* but) images under one or another interpretation; what we have been calling images under descriptions. What has been abandoned, in particular, is the doctrine that mental images refer to what they resemble and resemble what they refer to. But, viewed the other way, Hume's point is that the abandonment of the resemblance theory of reference is compatible with preserving the insight that (some) internal representations are, or may be, nondiscursive. The importance of distinguishing between these two claims—and the failure of lots of latter-day psychologists and philosophers to do so—has, of course, been one of the main themes of our discussion.

What we have so far is not more than a sketch of a theory: The questions it leaves open are more interesting than the ones that it proposes answers to. For example, granted that there is such a thing as mental imagery, is there any reason to suppose that it plays more than a marginal role in internal representation? What kinds of tasks are facilitated by the availability of nondiscursive displays? What is it about nondiscursive displays that makes them useful in such tasks? How much freedom do we have in opting for nondiscursive representation in given cases? What are the mechanisms by which images are constructed from descriptions?[15] Above all, it would be interesting to know whether *all* mental images are generated from descriptions, or whether some psychological processes are, as it were, nondiscursive from beginning to end.[16] If, for example, I use images to recall the look or smell of a thing, do I invariably recruit information which was discursively represented at some stage in its history? Was what Proust had stored a *description* of how madeleines taste soaked in tea? Or are there psychological mechanisms by which nondiscursive engrams are established and deployed? Certainly the enormous amounts of information which get handled in some tasks where images are implicated make it implausible that the information displayed went through a stage of digital encoding. The discussion has, in any event, returned to an area of straightforwardly empirical psychological research, and I propose to leave it there. Interested readers are referred to Pribram (1971) and Penfield and Roberts (1959).

Notes

1. Bruner stresses the *conventionality* of noniconic representational systems (like English), but, surely, it isn't their conventionality which makes them noniconic; English would be a discursive (i.e., a symbolic; i.e., a noniconic) representational system even if it were innate (i.e., nonconventional). It is, in fact, a major problem in the philosophy of language to give a plausible account of the relation between symbols and what they symbolize. What Burner's theory comes to is that icons refer by resembling and symbols refer in some other—as yet unspecified—way. The latter claim is certainly true.

2. This form of argument is owing to Wittgenstein (1953). It is, I think, entirely convincing.

3. The obvious way out of this won't do. Suppose thinking of fat John *doesn't* involve having a picture that shows John fat. Still, the picture one has will have to show John *somehow*; i.e., as having some properties or other. And then what will be the difference between just thinking of John and thinking that John has those properties?

4. I want to emphasize that I am not *endorsing* the view that the thinking of children is iconic in *any* sense. I am simply trying to make clear what a coherent version of that view might come to. As will be apparent by now, I find that proposal a good deal less transparent than some of the psychologists who have sponsored it seem to do.

5. The most impressive finding is perhaps that steroptic depth perception can be produced by imposing an idetic memory image upon a visual stimulus. (See the very remarkable findings reported by Stromeyer and Psotka, 1970. For a general discussion of ideticism, see Haber, 1966.) It seems hard to deny that imaging is like perceiving when it is possible to produce typical perceptual illusions whose objects are images rather than percepts. It's worth remarking, in this respect, that it has been known for some time that there are circumstances in which subjects can be induced to confuse (*non*idetic) images with percepts (Perky, 1910; Segal and Gordon, 1968).

6. This point is related to one that Kant makes in the *Critique of Pure Reason*. Kant distinguishes between 'subjective' and 'objective' temporal sequences, where the latter, but not the former, are independent of the scanning strategies of perceiver. Thus we may choose to examine the façade of a building from portal to pediment. But since all of the bits of the building are, in fact, contemporaneous, we could equally have chosen to go the other way around. Events which constitute an objective sequence, on the other hand, can be scanned in one order only. The same kind of point applies, *mutatis mutandis,* to the contrast between recovering information from pictures and from spoken sentences.

7. *Ss* who stored, as it might be, the sentence 'It was a triangle and it was red' ought, of course, to show the reverse asymmetry. The point is that *some order of report effect or other* should be associated with any form of discursive representation, while imagists ought to be relatively free from such effects. If *Ss* who claim that they are imaging turn out to be the ones who exhibit relatively weak order of report effects, that would be a reason for taking the hypothesis that they *are* using images seriously.

8. I *will not* get involved in the question whether introspection is infallible; but it seems to be perverse to hold that the deliverances of introspection are *eo ipso* always wrong. The subject's views about what he's doing appear to have as good a right to be considered as yours or mine or the experimenter's.

9. What's still harder to believe is that what goes on in typical cases of *perceiving* a thing is significantly like what goes on in typical cases of describing it. This is pertinent because the natural view of imaging is that to image a thing is to be in a psychological state qualitatively similar to the state that one would be in if one were perceiving the thing. If, therefore, imaging is like describing, perceiving must be too.

10. By stipulation, a picture is *determinate under a description* iff the statement that the picture satisfies the description has a determinate truth value.

11. Think of an out-of-focus photograph of a page of type. There is a definite answer to 'How many letters on the page?' Need there be a definite answer to 'How many image letters on the photograph?'

12. My discussion begs the question of what is to count as a 'visual' description. However, the striped tiger argument does too since, presumably, it is only for visual descriptions that it follows from 'the rules of images in general' that images must be determinate.

13. It isn't even the case that images under descriptions are necessarily pictorial in respect of all the information in respect of which they are nondiscursive. Taking 'nondiscursive' and 'pictorial' as coextensive is one of the root sources of confusion in thinking about images. Thus the line on the globe that shows where the equator is presumably conveys information nondiscursively. But it doesn't look like the equator. Such cases suggest how rough-and-ready the unanalyzed contrast between images and descriptions really is. For present purposes, I am using the materials at hand, but serious work in this area would require sharpening (and perhaps ultimately abandoning) the framework of distinctions that I have been assuming.

14. It is, presumably, because images do allow some information to be 'read off' that people bother with constructing images in memory tasks. A standard psychological anecdote concerns the man who can't tell you how many windows his house has unless he constructs an image of the house and then counts.

15. Some hints might be garnered from an examination of 'digital to analog' computer routines. It argues for the possibility of psychologically real devices which map descriptions onto images that machines can already be built to realize such functions. See Sutherland (1970).

16. I assume, for the kinds of reasons just discussed, that insofar as internal representations are images, they must be images-underdescriptions. What I regard as an open empirical question is the mechanisms by which descriptions and images are related. One way to relate them—the one sketched above—would be to generate the images *from* the descriptions. The present question is whether there are other ways and, if so, what they are.

It may be worth remarking, by the way, that there are similarities between what I have been saying about how images might be deployed in recognition tasks and the so-called 'analysis by synthesis' theories of perceptual categorization. The point of such theories is precisely that representation—in effect, templates—are generated from descriptions and then matched to the input that needs to be categorized. The description from which the template is generated then provides the perceptual analysis of the input. It is an attractive feature of such models that they provide for an infinite stock of templates so long as the formation rules for the descriptions are iterative. (For discussion, see Halle and Stevens, 1964; Nesser, 1967.) I very much doubt that analysis by synthesis could yield anything like a general theory of perception, but it is quite plausible that such mechanisms are involved in perception *inter alia*.

TWO APPROACHES
TO MENTAL IMAGES

4

Daniel C. Dennett

> *"You don't believe in me," observed the Ghost.*
>
> *"I don't," said Scrooge.*
>
> *"What evidence would you have of my reality, beyond that of your senses?"*
>
> *"I don't know," said Scrooge.*
>
> *"Why do you doubt your senses?"*
>
> *"Because," said Scrooge, "a little thing affects them. A slight disorder of the stomach makes them cheats. You may be an undigested bit of beef, a blot of mustard, a crumb of cheese, a fragment of an underdone potato. There's more of gravy than of grave about you, whatever you are!"*
>
> *Scrooge was not much in the habit of cracking jokes, nor did he feel, in his heart, by any means waggish then. The truth is, that he tried to be smart, as a means of distracting his own attention, and keeping down his terror; for the spectre's voice disturbed the very marrow in his bones.*
>
> —Dickens, A Christmas Carol

Of all the controversies currently raging in philosophy and psychology, none is being conducted with more vigor—if not rigor—than the debate over the nature of, and even the very existence of, mental images. Although the issues are various and complex, and although the arguments exhibit at least some of the variety and complexity the issues demand, one can describe the situation with negligible sociological distortion by saying that there is a *single* war being fought on many fronts (or at least there seems to be in the minds of the participants), a war between the believers and the skeptics, the lovers of mental images—let us call them *iconophiles* —and those who decry or deny them—the *iconophobes*. Both sides have apparently decided to pretend to know what *mental representations* are, and the issue is whether there are mental representations with properties peculiar to images.[1] Whatever *mental* representations are, they must be understood by analogy to *non*-mental representations, such as words, sentences, maps, graphs, pictures, charts, statues, telegrams, etc. The question is whether any of one's mental representations are more like *pictures* or *maps* than like *sentences,* to take the favored alternative.

A curious feature of the debate is the passion it evokes, which is unlike the normal passion of scientific controversy in being as accessible to the layman and spectator as to the proprietors of the various theories. People often take a lively interest in a controversy in physics or biology or astronomy without feeling the need to take sides, and indeed without deeming themselves equipped to have an opinion worth promoting, but everyone, it seems, has a fiercely confident opinion about the nature and existence of mental images. This manifests itself in remarkable ways: in unhesitating predictions of the results of novel psychological experiments, in flat disbelief in the integrity of recalcitrant experiments, in gleeful citation of "supporting" experimental evidence, coupled with bland imperviousness to contrary evidence. Since this relatively uninformed or pretheoretical partisanship comes in both varieties —iconophile and iconophobe—one breathtakingly simple explanation of the phenomenon, and one that is often proposed, is that in fact some people do have mental images and others don't. Each side naively extrapolates from its own experience. There are a variety of data that independently support this hypothesis. It is very likely that there are quite radical differences in people's "imagistic" powers. That cannot, however, be the whole explanation of this confident partisanship. I wish to show that a subtle misconception of the issue underlies this curious phenomenon, a misconception that is as apt to beguile the theorist as the innocent bystander.

I will try to bring out the misconception by first setting out a picture of the issue from the point of view of the iconophile. This picture is familiar, but *out of focus, untuned.* I will then show how the issue is transformed by attention to a few distinctions. Here, then, is the *untuned* version of the iconophile's case.

The iconophile asserts that *there are* mental images, and moreover is prepared to back up this ontological claim by saying just *where* in the scheme of things the mental images are. First, they are the typical *effects* of certain sorts of causes. Mental images are, let us say, the typical effects of veridical visual perception, the ingestion of hallucinogens, the desire to solve geometry problems in one's head, and so forth. There are all manner of mental images, but let us take a particular case for discussion. On being asked whether it is possible to touch one's right elbow to one's left knee while touching one's left elbow to one's right knee, Lucy refrains from contortions and instead *forms a mental image* of herself attempting this feat. Call the image itself, the target item in this debate, α. Here we have a certain train of events including, *inter alia,* Lucy's (A) hearing the question, (B) coming to understand it, (C) coming to desire to answer it, (D) deciding not to contort herself, and finally (E) attempting to frame an image. These are all plausibly held to be events in the causal ancestry of α. No one of them itself is, or contains, or need be held to be or contain, a mental image, but as a sequence they form a particular natural prelude to a particular mental image, namely α.

Moreover, says our iconophile, mental images are the typical *causes* of certain sorts of effects. That is to say, the occurrence of a mental image such as α *makes a difference:* had it not occurred, later things that happened would not have happened, or would have happened differently. In making this claim, our iconophile rejects epiphenomenalism, wisely, since no version of that bizarre doctrine merits attention.* Of all the effects typically produced

---

*I find there are different senses of the term "epiphenomenal" in currency today. The epiphenomenalism I have just rudely dismissed is the view that there are epiphenomena that are more or less accompanying shadows of

by the occurrence of a mental image, one is singled out by its immediacy and the consequent dependence of other effects on it; let us call it the *apprehension* of the mental image, being as neutral as possible about what apprehension might be. Perhaps there could be unapprehended mental images. If so, the people visited by them *do not believe* they are visited by them, do not *make use* of them (e.g., to solve problems, to answer questions, simply to perceive), do not remember them. That is what we shall mean by apprehension. A mental image that fails to be apprehended is like a stimulus that fails to stimulate; one can rule either out by definition if one wishes. Note that we have left it open whether one can *mis*-apprehend a mental image or *unconsciously* apprehend a mental image. As I said, we are being as neutral as possible about what apprehension might be.

But whether or not there might be unconsciously apprehended mental images, there certainly are mental images that are consciously apprehended, supposing for the moment that all we mean by "consciously apprehended" is "believed by the subject to have occurred in virtue of having been apprehended at occurrence." Thus one of the effects of α is Lucy's subsequent belief that α has occurred. Now we could say that this belief (partially) *constituted* Lucy's apprehension of α,

$$A \rightarrow B \rightarrow C \rightarrow D \rightarrow E \rightarrow \alpha \rightarrow \text{Apprehension of } \alpha \ (= \text{belief that } \alpha \text{ occurred } \& \ldots),$$

or we could say that this belief was *caused by* an interveining apprehension of α.

events in the brain, but that these epiphenomena *have no physical effects at all.* One might say this is one half of Cartesian interactionism: bodily events cause (or occasion) mental events (epiphenomena), but these are themselves causally inert. Some people, notably psychologists, often use "epiphenomenal" to mean, roughly, "nonfunctional." Thus if I engrave curlicues and filagrees on the connecting rods of an engine they are merely epiphenomenal in this sense—they don't contribute to or detract from the normal functioning of the engine, but of course they do have effects in the world by which their presence may be determined: they reflect and absorb light, for instance. That there are nonfunctional physical properties of brain events (or nonfunctional brain events) we already know; we will need an impressive argument to show there are nonfunctional (but physically efficacious) nonphysical events or properties.

A→ B→ C→ D→ E→ α→ Apprehension of α→ belief that α occurred.

In either case, we will acknowledge that such a belief is at least a typical consequence of the occurrence of a mental image such as α. It is a familiar fact that beliefs spawn beliefs with great fecundity, and no sooner would Lucy believe that α had occurred than she would also believe a host of other things about α. Let us both arbitrarily and vaguely distinguish the manifold of beliefs *quite* immediately produced by and "focussed on" or "about" α, and call this assemblage of beliefs β.

A→B→C→D→E→α→β (= a manifold of beliefs about α).

Up to now, "α" has been the proper name of a particular mental image of Lucy's, and "β" the proper name of one of its effects. Now generalize this bit of nomenclature. Let α be any mental image and β be its relatively direct effect in the realm of belief. There can be debate and disagreement among iconophiles over the scope and population of particular β-manifolds, but surely the conscious apprehension of an α will produce *some* beliefs about α. Put the uncontroversial beliefs in that α's β-manifold and ignore the rest, since nothing will hinge on them. The outer boundary of a β-manifold will not be important to us, but the joint between an α and its β-manifold will.

To some theorists, beliefs are themselves images or at least *like* images. Armstrong, for instance, likens beliefs to maps[2] and contrasts them to sentences. Since I want the β-manifolds to be agreed by all to be purely *non*-imagistic (whatever that means) believers in the imagistic nature of belief, if there are any, are asked to direct their attention to a slightly different item among the causal descendants of any α, namely to the causally-first entirely non-imagistic typical psychological effect of that α, and call *it* the β-manifold of that α. It might, for instance, be a manifold of *dispositions to say and do various things* in virtue of one's (imagistic) beliefs about α.

This concept of a β-manifold is unavoidably lax, but perhaps its flavor can be conveyed by another example. Suppose I am inspired by my current mental image of a unicorn to draw a picture of a unicorn, indeed to *render* my current mental image on the page. There are then *two* images: my mental image, and its good or bad copy, the drawn image. Something intervenes between them. Of all that intervenes there are myriad descriptions possible, no doubt, most of them quite unknown to us. A plausible sketch of one such description would include in roughly this sequence: first, the mental image of the unicorn; then apprehension of that image, followed by (or constituting) belief that one is having just such an image; then delight in it; a subsequent desire to produce it for others; then an intention to draw, leading to an intention to grasp the pencil *just so*—and so forth. Of all of this, I want to focus on the earliest and most immediate non-imagistic products of (or constituents of) apprehension, the manifold of beliefs about the mental image that one might suppose would remain relatively constant over changes in artistic desire, delight, boredom, and incidental knowledge, provided only that the image remained constant (supposing that notion to make sense—remember, this is the iconophile's story). One cannot get entirely precise about this. For instance, the *desire to draw* arrives hand in hand with the *belief* that the image is, shall we say, artworthy, and does *this* belief belong in the β-manifold or not? I don't think it makes any difference to my case one way or another.

Now I have tried to define β-manifolds in such a way that any iconophile will be happy to acknowledge the existence of β-manifolds as the first cognitive but non-imagistic difference the having of a mental image typically makes in us. By characterizing the β-manifold as itself non-imagistic, I mean to obtain a similar acquiescence from the iconophobe, for iconophobes do not for a moment wish to deny the existence of those manifolds of belief called by the iconophile β-manifolds. To deny that would be to deny the one truly obvious fact about mental imagery: people generally do think they have mental images and are disposed to say so. Iconophobes differ from iconophiles in denying that the normal or typical proximate causes of those manifolds are things or events having the earmarks of, hence deserving to be called, *images*. The debate is entirely over the nature of the occupants of the α role, *the nature of the normal causes of* β-manifolds.

So far neither category is all that well characterized—not by me, and not by the participants in the psychological and philosophical debates, so it is not surprising that disagreement between iconophile and iconophobe should persist, should lack agreed-upon methods of resolution, should look like a *philosophical* dispute. It is not. It is merely *embryonic-scientific*. What is remarkable is that so many people find it so difficult to let this issue be what it ought to be: a scientific, empirical question, amenable to experimental probing. Why should anyone feel differently? Most of us laymen are quite content to be not only ignorant but opinionless about the normal causes of dandruff, inflation, earthquake, and schizophrenia. We will let science tell us if only it will. But, one is mightily tempted to say, the normal cause of my β-manifold to the effect that I am having a mental image of sort *x* is (of course!) a mental image of sort *x,* and I already know more about that mental image of mine, simply in virtue of having it, than science could ever tell me. This temptation is at the heart of the misconception I hope to uncover and dispel. I hope to dispel it by pointing out and clarifying two approaches to mental images that are very different, but not at war. The *first* approach has just, in fact, been sketched, if fuzzily. It can be called, without intending thereby to do it special honor or dishonor, the *scientific approach*. It proceeds by defining mental images as the *normal causes* of β-manifolds. (The existence of β-manifolds is uncontroversial, however murky and ill-defined the concept is.) This approach treats the hints, avowals, and protestations of image-havers as issuing in the normal way from their β-manifolds. Having various beliefs about what is going on in them, people come to say various things, and these utterances are useful *data* about the nature of mental images. The subjects have no more special authority about the nature of their own mental images, on this approach, than about the nature of their genes or germs. This approach calmly ignores the claim of the image-haver to be *authoritative* about the nature of his or her mental images.

By defining mental images as the normal causes of β-manifolds, the scientific approach virtually guarantees the *existence* of mental images—since it is highly probably that β-manifolds have some normal pattern of causation—and conducts an investigation to see whether mental images are well named. Are mental images *images* of any sort? Similarly, atoms came to be defined as the smallest units of a chemical element, and then it remained a question whether atoms were well named. They weren't, as it turned out, and the scientific approach to mental images is just as prepared to discover non-imagistic mental images as physicists were to discover splittable atoms.

The stance of the scientific approach to the avowals of image-havers will benefit from further characterization. The scientist confronted by an organism that "talks" is free to treat the vocal emissions of the specimen as mere sounds, the causes of which are to be investigated. This is the way we treat human snores, for instance. If one makes this choice, one is not then confronted with questions concerning the semantic interpretation of the sounds, their meaning, truth or falsity. For snores this proves to be no hardship, but all attempts to treat those sounds we call human utterances in this non-semantic way have failed to produce credible accounts of their etiology, to put it mildly. Once one makes the decision to treat these sounds as utterances with a semantic interpretation, on the other hand, one is committed to an intentionalistic interpretation of their etiology, for one has decided to view the sounds as the products of communicative intentions, as the expressions of beliefs, or as lies, as requests, questions, commands, and so forth. Under the scientific approach to mental images, the image-haver is *not* subjected to the indignity of having her avowals and commentaries treated as mere noise: they are granted the status of expressions of belief, assertations made with both reason and sincerity. The scientific approach simply refrains from granting at the outset that the beliefs being expressed are *true* or even well grounded. In this the scientific approach deviates slightly from the normal mode of interpersonal communciation. If in the course of conversation I assert that p and you set to wondering out loud what might *cause* me to believe that p, you bid fair to insult me, for your wondering leaves open the gaping possibility that my belief that *p* might lack the proper epistemic credentials, might be *merely* caused (might be caused in some way other than that mysteriously *right* sort of causal way alluded to in the various causal theories of perception, reference, memory, inference, etc.). It is this possibility that the scientific approach to mental images leaves explicitly open, just in order to investigate it. What normally causes people to believe that the sun is shining is the sun's shining, but what normally causes people to believe that everything they are now experiencing they have experienced once before is not their having experienced it all once before. The scientific approach to mental images leaves open the possibility that mental image beliefs, β-manifolds, might have an explanation more akin to the explanation of *déjà vu* than to that of normal visual perception.

The *other* approach to mental images, which I will name in due course, is initially more congenial in *not challenging* or questioning the epistemic credentials of image-havers' beliefs. Indeed, the β-manifold of a person can be endowed with a certain authority: the authority to *create a world,* the world that is the logical construct of the manifold of beliefs. Any set of beliefs determines a world; if the beliefs are all true, the world thus determined coincides with a portion of the real world. If any are false, the set determines a world that is at least partly fictional (e.g., the world of Dickens' London). If the set of beliefs is inconsistent, the world determined will contain objects with contradictory properties, but that is all right, since the objects are not real objects but merely *intentional objects.*[3]

The second approach to mental images defines them not as the *normal causes* of β-manifolds, but as the *intentional objects* of β-manifolds:

$$\text{intentional object}$$
$$\vdots \;(\text{the path of logical construction})$$
$$A \rightarrow B \rightarrow C \rightarrow D \rightarrow E \longrightarrow \alpha \longrightarrow \beta \cdots$$

By defining mental images as the intentional objects of β-manifolds, the second approach guarantees the *existence* of mental images *as logical constructs.* That is, it guarantees them the odd but surprisingly robust existence of intentional objects generally, what Brentano called "intentional inexistence." On this approach, mental images are at least as real as Santa Claus. Just as one might set out to learn all there is to be learned about Santa Claus, the intentional object, so one might set out to learn all there is to be learned about those intentional objects, people's mental images.

Note that there are truths and falsehoods about Santa Claus. It is true that Santa Claus has a white beard and drives a flying sleigh, false that he is tall and thin. Focusing on intentional objects like this does not require a presumption of fiction or falsehood. Consider the difference between setting out to learn all there is to know about Queen Elizabeth II, and setting out to learn all there is to know about Queen Elizabeth II, the intentional object constructable from the beliefs of British school children under the age of ten. The latter investigation might prove both more interesting and more useful than the former.

But to return to our second approach to mental images, why would one be interested in the logical construction route in this instance? The scientific approach was seen to be blandly *uncommitted* to the truth of β-manifolds; *its* mental images, the normal causes, exist with the features they do whether or not people's beliefs about them are true. This second approach seems blithely *unconcerned* with the truth of β-manifolds; *its* mental images, the logical constructs, or intentional objects, exist (as logical constructs) with precisely the features they are believed to have— whether or not the beliefs are true (true *of* anything real). Could one claim that this second approach would be a serious pursuit?

An extended analogy may convince us that it could be, by exhibiting in more detail the program of such a study. Suppose anthropologists were to discover a tribe that believed in a hitherto unheard-of god of the forest, called *Feenoman.* Upon learning of Feenoman, the anthropologists are faced with a fundamental choice (not a deliberate, intentional choice, but a choice-point, an opportunity): they may convert to the native religion and believe wholeheartedly in the real existence and good works of Feenoman, or they can *study the cult* with an agnostic attitude. Consider the agnostic path. While not believing in Feenoman, the anthropologists nevertheless decide to study and systematize as best they can the religion of these people. They set down descriptions of Feenoman given by native informants; they look for agreement, seek to explain and eliminate disagreements (some say Feenoman is blue-eyed, others say he—or she—is brown-eyed). Gradually a logical construction emerges: Feenoman, the forest god, complete with a list of traits and habits, and a biography. These infidel scientists, or Feenomanologists as they call themselves, have described, ordered, catalogued, inventoried the relevant belief-manifolds of the natives, and arrived at the *definitive* description of Feenoman. Note that the beliefs of the natives are authoritative (he's *their* god, after all), but only because Feenoman is being treated as *merely* an intentional object, a mere fiction as we disbelievers insist, hence entirely a *creature* of the beliefs of the natives, a logical construct. Since those beliefs may contradict one another, Feenoman as logical construct may have contradictory properties attributed to him. The Feenomanologists try to present the best logical construct they can, but they have no overriding obligation to resolve all contradictions—they are prepared to discover unresolved and undismissible disagreements among the devout.

The believers, of course, don't see it that way—by definition, for they are the believers, to whom Feenoman is no *mere* intentional object but someone as real as you or I. Their attitude toward their own authority about the traits of Feenoman is—or ought to be—a bit more complicated. On the one hand, they do believe they *know* all about Feenoman—they are Feenomanists, after all, and who should know better than they? Yet unless they hold themselves severally to have some sort of papal infallibility, they allow as how they could *in principle* be wrong in some details. They could just possibly be instructed about the true nature of Feenoman. For instance, Feenoman himself might set them straight about a few details. Thus a native Feenomanist who fell in with the visiting Feenomanologists and adopted their stance would have

to adopt an attitude of distance or neutrality toward his own convictions (or shouldn't we have to say his own *prior* convictions?),
and would in the process suffer some sort of crisis of faith, and
pass from the ranks of the truly devout. (Cf. the old joke about
Santayana's curious brand of Roman Catholicism: Santayana's
creed, it was said, is that there is no God and Mary is His Mother.)

We can imagine another group of anthropologists who study the
Feenomanists and their religion, who are also disbelievers or ag-
nostics, like the Feenomanologists, but who set out to plot the
normal causes of Feenomanist belief-manifolds. Their first step
would be to learn what the Feenomanologists had charted out of
those belief manifolds. This might provide valuable clues about the
normal causes of the manifolds. This would be especially true if
Feenomanism turns out to be true religion; we leave it open, that
is, for the scientific cause-seekers to discover Feenoman and con-
firm the native religion. The whole investigation might, however,
prove fruitless; perhaps there are no normal or projectible or sali-
ent patterns in the events that lead Feenomanists to their creed.
(Cf. the conditioning of "superstitious" behavior in pigeons via
random reinforcement schedules by Herrnstein et al.). What
if these cause-seekers ask the Feenomanists, the believers, about
the normal causes of their beliefs? The Feenomanists will insist,
naturally, that the normal causes of their Feenomanist belief manifolds are the words and deeds of Feenoman. The anthropologists
might discover otherwise. They might discover that the normal
cause of the bulk of Feenomanist belief manifolds was the trickery
of Sam the Shaman. This would be a particularly interesting case
for us, for no matter how directly and reliably Sam the Shaman's
activities determined the content of Feenomanist beliefs about
Feenoman, we would not on that account alone be entitled or inclined to *identify* Feenoman as Sam the Shaman. Identification
depends on the truth of the beliefs caused. If an impressive number of the most important traits of Feenoman are traits of Sam the
Shaman, we will be tempted to identify the two. So, for that matter, will the Feenomanists themselves—a telling test. But probably
two overridingly important traits of Feenoman are his immortality

and his supernatural power, and no doubt the lack of these in Sam the Shaman would count decisively, both in our eyes and the Feenomanists', against identifying the intentional object of their creed with its normal cause. It seems, however, to be a matter almost of taste: we will learn which traits of Feenoman are *essential,* and for whom, when we see which Feenomanists (if any) accept the proposed identity.

It is time to start drawing morals from this extended analogy. I expect the morals I wish to draw are obvious, but since there are so many of them, and since I mean to draw them all, I must try your patience by making them all explicit. The second approach to mental images I shall *call* the *phenomenological approach,* but with the following warning: I mean to be *prescribing* an approach rather than *describing* an existing discipline. When I speak of the phenomenological approach I shall mean the approach I am here outlining *whether or not* any people who call themselves phenomenologists would accept it as an accurate description of their enterprise. My position, to put it bluntly, is that if what I call the phenomenological approach does not describe the program of Husserl, Sartre, and their followers, so much the worse for their program. I intend to *defend* the phenomenological program as I describe it, and I call it the phenomenological program because it seems to me—no Husserl scholar, but an amateur of long standing—to do justice to what is best in Husserl.[4] I am even less of a Sartre scholar, but my reading of Sartre also encourages me to use this name for the approach described.[5] I would be happy to learn that my description finds favor among self-styled phenomenologists; if it does not, I shall change the name of the approach, not its description.

The phenomenological approach, then, sets out to rationalize the β-manifolds of people by describing the intentional objects that are their logical constructs. It proceeds independently of any search for the causes of those β-manifolds, and can *afford* to ignore experimental data about reaction times, interference effects and the like (I don't recommend that it turn its back on these data, but it may).[6] Its master, like the master of the New Critics, is the *text,* in this case the protocols, the introspective declarations, avowals, revisions, confessions of *subjects* or image-havers.[7] It treats these declarations, once care has been taken to allow for editorial revision, as authoritative, as *constituting* the features of the intentional objects being studied. In so viewing these declarations, the phenomenologists adopt an attitude fundamentally if subtly different from the attitude of the subjects themselves, for the phenomenologists must view the mental images that are the focus of *their* investigation as possibly only *mere* intentional objects, while by the subjects the mental images are *believed to be real*—"by definition," provided the subjects are sincere. Phenomenologists will be interested to discover inconsistencies between the accounts of different subjects, and even within the accounts of a single subject on a single occasion, and will make more or less standard efforts to remove these by queries and challenges designed to provoke thoughtful expression, retraction of misspoken claims, and so forth. But if inconsistencies remain after such purification of the text has gone as far as it can go, then the phenomenologists will be under no obligation to force consistency onto the β-manifolds they are cataloguing. Of course, the probing and challenging may well *effect a revision* in their subjects' β-manifolds, just as the anthropologists' sophisticated questions might well provoke doctrinal revision, invention, or clarification in the Feenomanists' creed. Under such probing some subjects might even come, rightly or wrongly, so to alter their β-manifolds that they no longer could be said to believe in mental images—and so *in the sense of the phenomenological approach* they would *cease to have* mental images. (Under intense anthropological scrutiny from Feenomanologists, Feenoman might cease to exist. That seems to have happened to Satan, for instance.)

Like the Feenomanists, subjects ought to have a complicated attitude toward their own authority about their mental images. On the one hand, believing as they do, they take their introspective descriptions to be truths, but if so, they ought to grant that the real objects they are attempting to describe might turn out to have properties unrecognized by them, might turn out to be not

as they believe them to be, *might* even turn out not to exist.[8]
There is thus a tension between their attitude as subjects and the
attitude of the phenomenologists studying them, and just as the
Feenomanist turned Feenomanologist could not both cling un-
problematically to his faith and study it, the *auto*phenomenologist
studying his own mental images must find a built-in frustration in
his efforts at "bracketing" or *epoché,* in divorcing himself from
the implications of those of his beliefs he is studying at the very
moment he is drawing out those implications. If he succeeds in
suspending belief in them, to that extent he succeeds in altering
the β-manifold he is attempting to study. Autophenomenology is
so difficult that even experts typically fail, and end up studying
some artifact of their own enterprise.*

The tension between the attitude that takes mental images to
be constituted "authoritatively" by β-manifolds and the attitude
that takes mental images to be the real, normal causes of those
β-manifolds helps to create a spurious *third* approach to mental
images, an approach that tries to treat mental images as both
incorrigibly known and causally efficacious. Such marvelous
entities would have to inhabit a medium more transparent to
cognition than ordinary physical space, yet more actual and concrete than the mere logical space in which logical constructs,
possible worlds, and the like reside. Call it, as many have, *phenomenal space.* It is as if our Feenomanist turned Feenomanologist
were to grasp in his confusion at the desperate stratagem of in-
venting a god-space, or heaven, for his beloved Feenoman to reside in, a space *real* enough to satisfy the believer in him, but

---

*For example, imagine the plight of the autophenomenologist who set out
to study the intentional objects that accompanied his engagement in wildly
abandoned sex; he would end up studying the intentional objects of someone
engaged in sex while simultaneously performing *epoché*—hardly the same experience at all. According to Schacht, "Phenomenology proper is characterized by Husserl as 'the critique of transcendental experience' (*I[deas]* 29);
'transcendental experience' is said to be 'a new kind of experience' (I, 27),
distinct from ordinary experience; and the 'phenomenological reduction' is
held to be the operation through the performance of which this 'new kind
of experience' becomes accessible to us." (Schacht, 1972, p. 298).

remote and mysterious enough to hide Feenoman from the skeptic in him. Phenomenal space is Mental Image Heaven, but if mental images turn out to be *real,* they can reside quite comfortably in the physical space in our brains, and if they turn out not to be real, they can reside, with Santa Claus, in the logical space of fiction.*

This point is so central to my purpose, and people are often so resistant to it, that I wish to take a bit of time to explore its implications. I have been speaking as if β-manifolds were uniform from subject to subject, but of course they are not. Not only do people differ in the kinds of imagery they report, but they hold all manner of different *theories* about what they call their mental images, and, hence, their β-manifolds vary widely in content. Some people think their mental images are epiphenomena; some people think their mental images are something-or-others that happen in their brains; some may think their mental images are *merely* intentional objects, fictitious things they are mightily tempted to believe in, hence, when they let their guard down, do believe in. (Cf. Scrooge.) Now, if anyone believes his mental images are information-carrying structures in his brain that deserve to be called images because they have certain structural and functional properties, and if science eventually confirms that the normal causes of that person's β-manifolds are just such structures, then he can happily *identify* intentional object with cause. It will turn out for him that imaging is, and has been, like normal veridical perception: just as pigs cause one to see pigs and cows cause one to see cows, images have caused him to believe he is having images. That is the scientific iconophile's prediction. If, on the

---

*Nothing I have said here *requires* materialism to be true. If the followers of the scientific approach wish to be dualists, they can set out to study dualistic causation of α, of β by α, and of behavior, etc., by β. My objections to dualism are of the familiar sort, and are recounted in other writings, but no appeal is being made to them here. Even for the dualist, I am insisting, there is no way to *merge* the two approaches. The dualist must either be investigating, or talking about, the occupants of the α-role, or intentional objects. A non-physical cause would have to bear the same relation to an intentional object as a physical cause.

other hand, that person's beliefs turn out to be false, if they turn out to be caused by things in the brain lacking the peculiar features of images, then the scientific iconophobe will turn out to be right, and we will have to say that that person's β-manifolds are composed of (largely) false beliefs, what one might call systematically illusory beliefs. We ought to be able, in such a case, to convince the person of this. Success in this attempt would eliminate those beliefs, but not necessarily the temptation or disposition to lapse back into them. (Some illusions are "stronger" than others.) Complete success would "cure" the delusions, and, from the phenomenological point of view, eradicate the mental images.

What if someone holds that his mental images are not physical events or structures in his brain at all, but rather either epiphenomena or items in phenomenal space, having automatically cognizable features, obeying a different logic from that of images in physical space, etc.? It is *not,* I am saying, an empirical question whether *he* is right: he is wrong, and it doesn't take science to prove it; it takes philosophy to prove it. Philosophy's job in this entire issue is to clear away hopeless doctrines like these, and leave the issue between scientific iconophile and scientific iconophobe as the only issue with *ontological* significance. *In principle* there could be a parallel question to dispute within the purely phenomenological approach. The debate between iconophile and iconophobe phenomenologists could only concern the correct or best extrapolation of intentional objects from β-manifolds. Such questions can be discussed with serious intent and rigor, but if scientific iconophobia turned out to be the truth, they would be of rather rarefied and diminished significance. They would be parallel to such questions as "Does Santa Claus have eight or nine reindeer? (Is Rudolph *established?*)" and "Was Apollo a murderer?" If scientific iconophilia turns out to be true, there could be a rich and interesting interaction between the scientists and the phenomenologists. It would not follow from the truth of scientific iconophilia that the images of phenomenology could be identified with the newly discovered or confirmed images in the α-position, for the latter might be, while undeniably *images,* very unlike the intentional objects they produced. Of course for any particular mental image creed that turns out to be *true religion,* the scientific approach will answer all the questions the phenomenological approach leaves indeterminate. There is always more to learn about *real* things about which we have (some) true beliefs.

A third approach of sorts to mental images can be obtained by noting the possibility of an equivocation in the notion of a *logical construct.* Suppose someone says, as I guess many philosophers are tempted to say: "*Whatever* science discovers, it can't discover that I don't have mental images when I think I do, and not merely as intentional objects of my beliefs." This is a powerful intuition, I grant, but one best combatted. If one wants, however, one can grant the point by a simple logical maneuver: define mental images as logical constructs out of β-manifolds in a different sense of logical construct: make having the β-manifold *criterial* for having a mental image; make it tantamount to having a mental image. One could then say, "What it *means* to say I am having a mental image is that I am having a certain β-manifold." This view might be called logical internal behaviorism. It is an approach of sorts, but an approach that has already reached its goal. It leaves nothing more (of interest) to be said about mental images. It is like the phenomenological approach in not being at war with the scientific approach, though people who hold such doctrines often cast their claims in terms that strongly suggest otherwise. (Cf. Malcolm, 1959). Note, too, that on this view we already know what mental images are, and one thing is clear: they are *not* images of any sort, or anything *like* images. They are no more like images than home runs are like baseballs or fences.

Is my position, then, best described as iconophile or iconophobe? With regard to the legitimate scientific disagreement about the nature of mental representations, this paper is so far entirely neutral. It has so far merely attempted to clarify that issue by distinguishing it sharply from spurious—if traditional—debates about entirely mythical species of mental images: the various non-physical, phenomenal or epiphenomenal, self-intimating, transparent to cognition, unmisapprehensible, pseudo-extended, quasi-imagistic phantasms that have often been presented as mental images in the past. About these I am a devout iconophobe. What do I put in their place? What is left to be going on in one once these pretenders have been dismissed? In their place there are only the α's—the causes, and the β-manifolds—the effects, and about these I have been neutral, for the question whether either of these is properly imagistic is not a pure philosophical question, but a question of psychological theory or meta-theory. At the outset I required a definition of β-manifolds that had them non-imagistic, but now we can see that that was a temporary bit of scaffolding; at the time there seemed to be just *one* question about mental images, and that proviso was needed to isolate that one question. Now we can see that in fact there are two—indeed many more than two—roles in cognitive theories that *might* be filled by information-bearing structures that deserved to be called images. Armstrong, you recall, likens beliefs themselves to maps, and perhaps he is right: perhaps when psychological theory develops— if it ever does—to the point where there are well behaved and well attested theoretical entities playing roughly the α and β roles, it might prove appropriate to conceive of the β items as images of some sort. That is, of course, an issue that is far removed from any introspector's authority to settle. The considerations that count concern the power and versatility of different kinds of information-bearing structures, or data-structures as they are called in computer science. There is much that can already be said by iconophiles and iconophobes in support of their positions, but this is not the time to review that debate.* The goal of this essay has just been to clear the decks so that debate can proceed unhindered by misconceptions about what we might call the metaphysical status of mental images.

---

*In *Content and Consciousness* (Dennett, 1969), in spite of my efforts to distinguish what I distinguish here in terms of the two approaches (there I spoke of the personal and sub-personal levels of explanation), I mixed metaphysical iconophobia, the view I have just espoused, and scientific iconophobia, a view I still favor, though cautiously. That is, many of the iconophobic arguments and claims of *Content and Consciousness* are properly viewed as contributions (good or bad) to psychology, not philosophy. [See Chapter 2 of this volume.—Ed.]

Notes

1. The psychological literature on mental images is growing so fast that a citation of current work will be out of date before the ink is dry. There is even a new journal, the *Journal of Mental Imagery*. A few classic papers are R. N. Shepard and J. Metzler, "Mental Rotation of Three-Dimensional Objects," *Science*, (1971), 701–703; L. A. Cooper and R. N. Shepard, "Chronometric Studies of the Rotation of Mental Images," in W. G. Chase, ed., *Visual Information Processing* (1973): 75–115; Allan Paivio, *Imagery and Verbal Processes* (New York: Holt Rinehart and Winston, 1971); Zenon Pylyshyn, "What the Mind's Eye Tells the Mind's Brain: A Critique of Mental Imagery," *Psychological Bulletin* (1972), and "Imagery and Artificial Intelligence," in C. Wade Savage, ed., *Minnesota Studies in the Philosophy of Science*, Vol. 9; and M. Kosslyn, "Information Representation in Visual Images," *Cognitive Psychology*, 7 (1975), 341–370.

2. D. M. Armstrong, *Belief, Truth and Knowledge* (Cambridge University Press, 1971).

3. Cf. my "Geach and Intentional Identity," *Journal of Philosophy* 65 (1968), 335–341.

4. I find support for my reading of Husserl in Richard Schacht's excellently lucid article, "Husserlian and Heideggerian Phenomenology," *Philosophical Studies*, 23 (1972), 293–314. Schacht proposed there to distingush what he calls *phenomenography* from *phenomenology*. In the terms of this chapter, phenomenography would be the mere gathering and cataloguing of protocols (one's own, not others') without attempting the further extrapolation of intentional objects from them—which is phenomenology.

5. I find support especially in Alastair Hannay's "Sartre's Illusion of Transcendence," chapter 5 of *Mental Images—A Defence* (London, 1971). "The term 'image' itself should be used to refer to the way the object appears, or rather, to the way in which an imaging-consciousness 'gives itself an object'" (p. 99).

6. Husserl speaks of the *hyle* or hyletic phase, and I am tempted to claim that the occupants of the α-role are Husserl's *hyle*, but perhaps the hyle are only some constituents of or raw material for the α. See "The Hyletic and Noetic Phases as Real, the Noematic as Non-real Phases of Experience," Section 97 of Husserl's *Ideas*, trans. W. R. Bryce Gibson (London, 1931). Bo Dahlbom has both clarified and complicated my thinking on this issue.

7. Cf. my *Content and Consciousness*, and for an account of the relation between such utterances and the "propositional episodes" that evince them, see my "On the Absence of Phenomenology," in B. L. Tapscott and D.

Gustafson, eds., *Body, Mind and Method: Essays in Honor of Virgil Aldrich* (Dordrecht, Reidel, 1979).

8. Cf. Strawson's insightful discussions of the dangers and prospects of conceiving of (without believing in) "phenomenal figures," in "Physical and Phenomenal Geometry," in *The Bounds of Sense* (London, 1966), pp. 281–292: "The problem is whether the nature of phenomenal geometry can be described without a dangerous reliance on the possibly dubious concept of the phenomenal figure—a concept which, though dubious, is satisfying to one's simple-minded wish for a set of *objects* to be the peculiar matter of the study" (p. 288).

IMAGERY—

There's More to It Than Meets the Eye

5

Robert Schwartz

The public image of private imagery is showing signs of a come-back. Not only does it again seem legitimate to talk about "hav-ing" images, there has been a tremendous revival of interest in the role of imagery in all aspects of cognition. But while the experi-mental work on imagery has been progressing nicely, there is little agreement over how best to interpret the empirical results. The newly gathered data not only have not convinced everyone of the importance of imagery, it has spawned a whole new generation of critics who are sure that imagist explanations of cognition are without merit. These critics generally do not deny that people experience images; rather they deny the significance of these phe-nomena for psychological theory. Some go so far as to maintain that the very notion of an imagist explanation is in principle mis-guided. And so the debate goes on, fueled by the fact that there is no consensus on either side on such crucial matters as what counts as imagery, what it means for an activity to be explained imagisti-cally or what evidence is to be taken as for or against imagist theories.[1]

Now much of the recent psychological literature on imagery is concerned with the nature of the neural or mental "representations" thought responsible for the storage and generation of images, i.e., on how the image itself is represented. I, on the other hand, have pointed this study in the opposite direction, focusing on the question of how images may serve to represent. For I believe that a better understanding of this relationship—between an image and what it purports to be an image of—is a necessary precondition for unravelling many of the conceptual perplexities that plague current discussion. In fact, as will be developed in the final section of this paper, debates over the nature of the underlying representation of images often turn on the same points that come up in analyzing representation via images.

But first, two caveats. Perhaps the most bothersome problem in talking about imagery phenomena is that it is hard to say just what is being talked about. Images cannot be readily located in physical space and cannot, in the ordinary sense of the words, be touched, heard, smelled, or seen. Yet our usual ways of describing imagery are in seemingly physical and perceptual terms, and this raises difficulties about the ontological status of images. Indeed, the bulk of the philosophical literature on imagery has centered on ontological matters. The main topic has been whether we must accord existential status to images or whether we can account for the relevant phenomena without being ontologically committed to an independent realm of such mental entities. I think avoiding reification of images has its advantages and would go a long way toward resolving various psychological controversies over whether people actually "manipulate," "rotate," or "scan" images in "mental space." Nevertheless, as an expository convenience, I will talk cavalierly in substantive terms of images and the relations images may bear to other things.

My second caveat has to do with the scope and classification of imagery episodes. While visual imagery tends to hold center stage in image research, it is usually admitted that the phenomena are not limited to just this modality. We may have auditory, gustatory, and kinesthetic images as well. Deciding which category a given image event falls into poses some delicate questions, but as a start, I propose that we allow that "sound-like" experiences count as auditory, "smell-like" as olfactory, etc. On this account, image type is a function of the phenomenal quality of the image experience. All this talk is admittedly vague, and the opaque notions, "sound-like" or "smell-like," are sure signs of trouble—some of which will press in on us quite soon. In any case, I intend to make use of examples from the auditory realm, so it is important to bear in mind that I construe imagery as encompassing more than just the visual.

1. The Symbolic Use of Images

In focusing on the way images serve to represent, I am proposing to treat imagery as a kind of symbolization. All I mean by the claim that images have symbolic functions is that they may bear semantic-type relations to things; they can play a role in describing, depicting, or representing objects, relationships, or "states of affairs." This is not the only function of imagery, but it is a prominent one. Consider, for example, reports that people depend on "mental pictures" to help them answer such questions as: "How many windows are there in your living room?" or "What's the shape of a German shepherd's ear?" On analogy with ordinary pictures, these picture-images can help provide the right answers if they accurately represent the *actual* number of windows or the *real* shape of the ears. I stress the words 'actual' and 'real' in order to emphasize the fact that for the tasks at hand, the question is not how accurately the images represent the subject's possible past visual perceptions of the room or dogs. What is relevant for solving these problems is that the images represent the physical situations correctly. Representing or otherwise symbolizing an object is not the same as representing a percept of the object. And while images may serve to do either, a correct account of the symbolic function and accuracy of the image will depend on which representative relationship is being considered.

Keeping track of distinctions among different possible symbolic functions is important for understanding other forms of imagery as well. For example, in a typical auditory imagery experiment a subject may be asked to say if the sixth note of the Star Spangled Banner (S.S.B.) is higher or lower than the fifth. The person claims that the song ran-through-her-head and that it was on the basis of this experience that she answered "yes." Correctness of her answer will depend on how accurately the mental sound pattern represents for her the pitch structure of the S.S.B., i.e., the musical piece. It is a totally independent matter whether the image accurately replicates a previously experienced performance of the S.S.B. The subject may have never heard the S.S.B. played. Or she might accurately represent the tune in auditory imagery, although it was misplayed in the one performance she did attend. Of course, the subject might have been tested on her ability to recall the notes played at that performance or asked to recall what it was like to experience that performance. These, however, would be different tasks and the symbolic function of the imagery would have to alter accordingly.[2]

2. Mode vs. Medium

Suppose we accept at face value the subject's claim that imagined sounds ran-through-her-head, and that this experience played a role in her attempt to answer the initial question about the pitch structure of the S.S.B. This would seem like a paradigm case of someone having an auditory image of the S.S.B. It is classified as auditory, since it is sound-like; the image does purport to describe the S.S.B., and it does so reasonably well. Also it should make little difference to its status as an S.S.B.-image if it is "heard" as a full orchestral rendering, or as a solo piano version, or as a vocal without accompaniment. The fact that the last experience contains word-like sounds does not preclude it from informing us about the sound sequence of the S.S.B. But now suppose what runs-through-her-mind's-ear is not the sound of music but the sound of music note names. She "hears" a voice, perhaps her own, saying in monotone, "G, E, C, E, G, C." The experience is akin to that of subvocal talking-to-oneself, or "hearing" verbalizations of some thought or idea. The difference is that in place of full-blown English words she hears letter sounds that denote pitches.

Should this last case too be considered an instance of having an auditory image of the S.S.B.? Settling on a definitive "yes" or "no" answer, I think, is less important than establishing the basis for either decision. For my purposes, it is enough to notice that this case shares important features with our paradigm cases of auditory S.S.B. images. The image is phenomenally sound-like, and it purports to and reasonably well does characterize the S.S.B. Where it differs from the more standard musical image is in the mode of symbolization, in *how* the image relates to what it purports to characterize. The obvious point is that alternative modes of symbolization may function within the very same medium, the auditory realm.

Making the mode-medium distinction is especially important when analyzing visual imagery. Here there is a tendency to identify the visual with the pictorial, and either exclude other forms of symbolization from consideration or mistakenly analyze them as if they fell entirely within the pictorial mode. This issue surfaces nicely in the experiments on reasoning reported by Huttenlocher (1968). Subjects are given three-term series problems such as: "J. is taller than M.," "S. is shorter than M.," "Who is tallest?" Many subjects claim they solve these problems by visually imaging a line, entering height information along the line (e.g., $\left|\begin{smallmatrix} J \\ M \\ S \end{smallmatrix}\right.$), and "reading" off the answer. Are such phenomena then examples of visual imagery? "Yes" in the sense that the image has "visual-like" qualities rather than "sound-like" or "odor-like" ones. Is the mode of symbolization "pictorial"? That depends on which symbolic relationship is being analyzed. For although the image may be understood to picture a possible graph, this is not the only symbolic function it serves. The image also represents or symbolizes the comparative heights of J., M., and S. And it is this latter symbolic relationship—between image and height—that is important for solving the three-term series problem. Unless the image is interpreted in terms of what it says "graphically" about heights, it will not help with the reasoning task, no matter how well it "pictures" an actual or hypothetical graph.

While the three-term series example may not sever sharply the connection between the visual medium and the pictorial mode (some may wish to construe the graphic representation of height as itself being in the pictorial mode), my next case is invented to do just that. Three roommates are asked the familiar imagery question, "How many windows are there in your living room?" The first reports imaging a vague picture of each wall and counts represented windows. The second reports no visual aid but subvocally hears "There are two windows on the far wall, one on the right wall" and calculates the answer. The third person is the more unusual. She reports visualized input, but instead of imaging a sketchy picture of the room, as does the first, she images a "spatial" counterpart of the sentence auditorily rehearsed by the second. She "sees" in her mind's eye the sentence "There are two windows on the far wall, one on the right wall" and uses the display to work out the answer.

How are we to analyze the symbolic function of this last person's imagery episode? By hypothesis her images have the phenomenal earmarks of the visual medium and on that score, at least, are instances of visual imagery. Along with the images of the other roommates, these sentential visual images bear a symbolic relationship to the living room. Do they characterize the room by picturing it? Surely not. They do not depict the living room, they describe it. But do not the visualized sentences picture or pictorially represent English sentences? Here, as in the previous graph case, we must be careful not to run together different symbolic roles. If all this last picturing claim amounts to is that the image itself may be characterized as "looking" sentence-like and not room-like, there is no difficulty. However, this is not to say that in this context the sentential image serves merely to represent a particular sentence pictorially. In order to answer the windows problem, it must be interpreted as a description of the living room. If it is to be efficacious, it must function symbolically to characterize windows, not just words.

Of course, visual images of this very same sort may have other uses and different symbolic functions in other contexts. For example, the subject's task might have been to recall sentence shapes. A person is shown a sentence on a blackboard; the sentence is erased. Five days later she is asked to select from a set of alternatives the sentence that matches the original in handwriting. In this context, the qualitatively same sentence image as before would serve to characterize mark shapes, not rooms (the person may not even understand the sentence), and an analysis of its representative functions solely along pictorial lines would be more appropriate. Or, for another example, a sentential visual image with the exact same phenomenal shape qualities might be brought in to aid in answering the spoken question, "How many O's are there in the sentence: "There are two windows on the far wall"? In this example, exact shape representation is not at stake but letter denotation is.[3]

3. Symbolization and Interpretation

The examples just discussed were chosen to highlight what I am calling the mode-medium distinction. Of necessity they also exhibit another important aspect of the symbolic use of imagery in cognition—the need for interpretation. Whether a state or item is functioning as a symbol, what it symbolizes, and the mode of symbolization it exhibits are all dependent on and relative to what if any system of interpretation is employed. The recently canvassed variety of functions of the phenomenally same sentence image already demonstrated this. Perhaps a few additional examples can help spell out matters more explicitly.

In front of you is a series of three ink marks: S O N; (or close your eyes and visualize the marks). Is it a symbol? In and of itself no more than the random inkblot: ●. S O N functions as a word only relative to a linguistic system of interpretation, and it is the system that determines its semantic status. Its denotation in English is one thing and in French another. S O N might equally well, however, be a picture. It may be my sketched depiction of the pattern of cracks found in the sidewalk; I may be totally unaware that the shape is a character in a language.

Similar remarks hold for other spatial displays and modes of symbolization. ⌂ may be a sketch of a mountain range, a letter or word in a foreign language, a graph of car sales or a diagram of electrical circuitry. Even a "realistic" photograph (or image) of the Empire State Building may have only non-pictorial symbolic functions, as in a system where it and like shaped displays are used to signify products made in New York City, while Eiffel Tower shapes indicate Paris-made items. Determining if a given spatial display is functioning pictorially or not is thus a matter of how it is being interpreted. When an Empire State Building shaped display is representing pictorially, it is depicting features of the building; when used to label product origins, it functions more like words. In both cases, though, we are employing a mode of interpretation. What a shape display tells us, what information it provides, is relative to the type of reading we give it.

4. Counting Modes

Distinguishing mode from medium of imagery allows for the possibility that within a particular sensory medium alternative modes of symbolization may be employed. How many, say, in the visual medium? Debates in the imagery literature seem to assume the answer must be either two (the pro-imagist's view) or really only one (the anti-imagist's position). I believe there is no unique answer to this question, nor good reason to assume the maximum number is two. Counting modes of symbolization depends on how they are individuated. In turn, individuation of modes depends on which properties of symbolization are found significant and which differences in function are taken as sufficient to determine distinctive modes. If my arguments so far are correct, however, mode difference will be importantly a matter of differences among the systems of interpretation associated with given displays. So individuating modes will require a set of principles for classifying systems of interpretation.

To my mind, the most carefully worked out analysis of this aspect of symbolic functioning can be found in Goodman (1968). In that work, Goodman develops a set of three syntactic and three semantic properties, as well as additional related concepts. He then shows how symbol systems can be differentiated according to

which of these independent properties they have or lack. Now
there is nothing absolute or sacrosanct in Goodman's principles of
individuation. For different purposes some of his categories might
be collapsed or entirely new properties for classifying symbol systems developed. Relative to such deletions or additions, the count
of modes will differ. In any event, I find the popular dichotomous
classification of systems into pictorial and linguistic (or propositional) both obscure in application and too broad to be very helpful in understanding differences in cognitive function.

Recall the three-term series example, $\begin{vmatrix} J \\ M \\ S \end{vmatrix}$. Is this graphic representation of heights to be allied with pictures or with language? I
am not sure how to tell. And a moment's consideration of the
numerous and varied symbol systems we constantly encounter—
maps according to various projection schemes, music notation,
diagrams, bar graphs, continuous line graphs, assorted kinds of
models and samples, gestures, gauges, traffic signals, as well as
mathematical systems, artificial and natural languages, and pictures ranging from caricatures or stylized stick-man drawings to
color photographs—should warn us of the complexities involved
in individuating modes. While the point cannot be argued here (although related issues will come up immediately), it seems to me
that no simple dichotomy of pictorial vs. linguistic is likely to reflect the richness of the phenomena at hand, nor is it obvious
where or why many of the symbol systems just listed would fall
in such a dual classificatory scheme. The virtue of Goodman's
analysis is that it does provide a principled set of distinctions that
more readily handles this variety, and the syntactic and semantic
properties he elaborates seem to reflect significant distinctions in
symbolic function. But if we count modes Goodman's way, the
number of types of symbol systems involved in cognitive activity
is very much more than two.

5. Analog—Digital

Much ink has been spilled arguing whether imagery phenomena
show that cognition involves analog processing or that minds are

analog as well as digital mechanisms. Pro-imagists tend to argue that imagery phenomena demonstrate the importance of analog activity. Anti-imagists generally maintain that imagery experiences do not indicate that cognition is at all analog. A serious problem with a lot of this debate, though, is that it is often unclear just what the analog-digital distinction is and what is being claimed when something is said to be either 'digital' or 'analog'. Uses of the term 'analog' can be found that range from identifying the concept with pictorial representation to others that would require that the physical processes underlying neural firings be continuous, to others that would require that the ultimate materials of the universe be wavelike and not particulate.[4] Given the ambiguity in construals of the notion 'analog', there can be no unambiguous answer to the question whether cognitive activity in general or imagery phenomena in particular are analog.

In keeping with my concern with the symbolic function of imagery, I suggest that one fruitful way to proceed is to ask if imagery processes make use of analog systems of symbolization. This then turns on specifying a set of criteria for distinguishing analog symbol systems from others. I find the classificatory scheme Goodman (1968) proposes perspicuous. Details of Goodman's analysis are complex and cannot be gone into here. Roughly, Goodman defines separate notions of syntactic and semantic density and contrasts these with the syntactic and semantic properties of finite differentiation. "A scheme is syntactically dense if it provides for infinitely many characters so ordered that between each two there is a third" (p. 136). A system is semantically dense if it "provides for an infinite number of compliance-classes so ordered that between each two there is a third" (p. 153). A symbol system that is both syntactically and semantically dense is said to be analog, whereas a system that is syntactically and semantically differentiated throughout is said to be digital. To use some of Goodman's own examples: A circular-faced pressure gauge with rotating pointer will count as analog if (a) every difference in absolute pointer position is taken to constitute a different character (syntactic density) and (b) the field of reference of these characters is densely ordered (semantic density). The gauge will be part of an analog system even if its face has numbers marking divisions, as long as these marks serve only as aids in approximating absolute pointer position. In contrast, a gauge with the same face, but used to register the number of dimes in a toy bank will typically be interpreted in a non-analog manner. Each point around the circumference is not taken as a different character, and the ordering of dimes provided for is not dense.

While I believe Goodman's explication of the analog-digital distinction is a useful one and more precise than most, I do not want to argue for the merits of his specific formulations. What is important for our concerns is that his approach provides a framework for linking together the symbolic function of imagery with considerations of analog systems. And it is from this perspective that I want to make several points about some claimed relationships between imagery and analog processing. I can do little more than list these points and suggest Kolers and Smythe (1979) for more detail on several of them: (1) Whether a symbol is functioning digitally or in an analog fashion cannot be determined by the physical properties (or in the case of imaged representations, the phenomenal properties) of the symbol display. It is the syntactic and semantic properties of the system that determine this. The same dial face and pointer may be interpreted in an analog manner, as with the pressure gauge, or digitally, as with the dime counter. Facts about the physical makeup of the dial or that it moves continuously in space are irrelevant to these distinctions. (2) Analog systems need be no less conventional or arbitrary than comparable digital systems. (3) There is nothing especially visual or spatial about analog systems. A system that correlates intensity of tone with pressure may be analog, although its employment makes use of the auditory modality. A system that correlates absolute intensity of light with pressure will be analog and operate in the visual medium, but it will not depend on spatial properties of the symbol. And, as all of these examples show, there is no need for the field of reference of the symbols to be spatial. (4) The idea of a system's symbols having or lacking one-to-one correspondence or isomorphism with their referents does not match up readily with the analog-digital distinction. The gauge points correlate one to one with pressure and function as part of an analog scheme. The Arabic numerals correlate one to one with their respective numbers but presumably form a digital system. Notice, too, when talking about structural correlations, it is important to distinguish between structural features of the symbol *scheme* and those of individual symbols. In cases of pictorial representation, it may make sense to talk about certain shape or structure properties of the given symbol (e.g., a picture) and compare these to those of its referent. But in those analog systems where the individual symbol is a particular light or sound intensity or pointer position, there will be no relevant structure of the single symbol to correlate with its referent. (5) While various aspects of pictorial representation require analog modes of interpretation, analog is not identical with pictorial. This is so even in those systems where distinctions among the characters depend on spatial dimensions. (6) Cases frequently thought to be analog are not obviously so. The initially described S.S.B.-image understood as a notation for picking out discrete notes will not be analog. And the oft-cited chess diagram

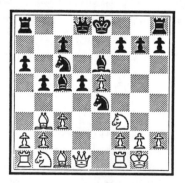

read as a notation for characterizing chess-significant board positions is not being interpreted as part of a syntactically or semantically dense system. (7) If it is admitted that within the visual medium we may imagistically employ different modes, it follows that there is no unique way by which visual imagery phenomena symbolize. Some of the systems used will be analog, some digital, some neither, and others mixtures. If, however, we restrict the concept of visual imagery, including only cases of "pictorial" representation or only those aspects of the symbolic functions that serve to depict, then it will turn out that analog modes of symbolization will be prominent.

6. Pictures and Percepts

I have just noted again that there is a tendency to limit the term "visual-imagery" to cases of visual "picturing." Given the prevalence of this construal, it is evident why arguments for and against imagery often debate whether image processes show enough similarity to pictures and picturing to sustain the analogy. But the issue cuts both ways. The extent of analogy found will depend not only on features of imagery, it will depend equally on how we conceive the mode of pictorial representation to operate. Now this is no place to undertake an analysis of the nature of pictorial representation. There are, however, several claims about the picturing relation that pervade accounts of imagery, and a brief examination of why these claims are problematic should be helpful.[5]

To start, it is just not clear how to delimit the domain of the pictorial. Maps, graphs, diagrams, and various models all differ in important ways from linguistic descriptions, but are they to be included in the pictorial? What of cubist portraits, Japanese line drawings, caricatures, geometrical renderings in reverse perspective, or stick-man drawings? If a person's image is "qualitatively" of one of these sorts, should it count as visualizing or picturing the object? If not, why not?

One prominent line of argument attempts to draw the distinction among forms of symbolization in terms of some notion of resemblance. Pictorial symbols are said to resemble (look like, be similar to, share properties with, be isomorphic with, bear structural correspondence to) what they represent.[6] In turn, a process or experience will count as imagistic, in this narrower sense, only if it too resembles what it purports to represent.[7] The difficulty with this sort of approach to imagery is that it relies on a flawed account of picturing.

The initial stumbling block is that the notion of resemblance is too vague to underpin an insightful analysis of pictorial representation. It is a commonplace that every two things resemble each other along some dimensions and any two things share the same number of properties as any other pair. So the unqualified claim that a picture (or picture image) resembles its referent is vacuous. Furthermore, relativizing the notion of resemblance to shape or spatial properties does not get very far either. Shared spatial properties are not necessary for pictorial representation. Depending on context, perspective, and style of rendering: (a) $\vert$, (b) ⬭ , (c) ⌒ , (d) ( ) may all represent a circle although none of the first three are of circular shape, and (a), (c), and (d) are not even topologically equivalent to a circle. Alternatively, ● may serve to represent a dot, a line (seen end on), or the last horse in the file (in a picture of horses parading off into the sunset). The situation with color properties is much the same. The green leaf, part in and part out of the shade, will be represented by two different colors, although the leaf itself is of uniform color. And neither of the colors in the picture may match the actual color of the leaf. Given such variety in the ways a particular shape or color may be represented and the wide range of objects that can be represented by the same pictorial shape or color, attempts to analyze pictorial representation on the basis of one-to-one correspondences or isomorphisms between picture and objective referent do not seem very promising.

One way taken to avoid these last difficulties is to claim that the resemblance required is not between the picture (image) and the object but between the picture (image) and a percept of the object. ⬭ does not resemble a circle; it resembles how the circle looks or would look if perceived from a certain angle. And the two colors do not resemble the color of the leaf itself, but that of a look of the leaf. Unfortunately, this approach too has its shortcomings. For even if a notion of image-percept resemblance could be spelled out clearly, it would still leave us a long way from an adequate account of the symbolic function of images. That such resemblance is not sufficient for representation should be obvious from earlier considerations. No matter how much a person's Empire State Building image resembles a possible percept of the building, in a given context the image may be serving solely to denote New York City products—it may not be being interpreted pictorially. Nor is image-percept resemblance sufficient to account for representation when restricted to those contexts in which the image is read pictorially. Such resemblance might be more to the point if the image were construed as representing the perceptual state it was most like. But, in general, images represent persons, places, and things and not percepts; my initial discussion of the symbolic use of living room and S.S.B. images was meant to highlight this. Thus, likeness of image to percept cannot by itself provide an account of the link to the objective referent.

At this stage there is a temptation to try to bridge this remaining gap by assuming that the percept must be structurally similar to or bear a one-to-one correspondence to its object. However, the claim that percepts resemble their objects is no better off than the original claim of image-object correspondence. If we interpret resemblance loosely, the claim is contentless; if we read it as demanding equivalence or sharing of shape, color, etc., it is false. A particular green circular surface may give rise to percept displays having an infinite range of shapes and an unbounded variety of colors throughout or in part. So granting some sort of resemblance between image and percept does not amount to accepting a pure resemblance account of the cognitive content of either.[8]

Several other related issues found in discussions of pictures, percepts, and image representation deserve at least some mention here: (1) We often imagine non-existent objects or situations. In such cases there will be no readily available referent for the percept or image to correspond to. Also, images may not "resemble" the object or a percept of the object they represent because they are mistaken. While attempting to answer a question about Benjamin

Franklin, I may call to mind an image that better depicts Alexander Hamilton. The referent of the image is still Franklin, although the image may more accurately characterize or "look like" Hamilton. (2) It is sometimes said that since percepts are always of particulars, pictures and hence picture images can only represent particulars. This argument seems incorrect. Pictures or images can be used to tell us about a general class of objects and not represent any one member of the class. The picture that accompanies the entry "tiger" in an encyclopedia is used to depict characteristics of the species. It may not "correspond" to an individual tiger; it may display a "prototypical" average that best informs us about the species as a whole. To construe the picture or image as describing a given tiger or as claiming that all tigers have all the displayed properties is to misread it. (3) It is claimed that pictures, unlike propositions, cannot provide limited bits of information. The sentence may merely say that John is tall; the picture, of necessity, must characterize his physical features more completely. Anti-imagists sometimes cite this supposed difference in arguing against the cognitive significance of pictorial imaging. Roughly, their claim is that since imagery experiences provide selective information, they must really be discursive and not pictorial forms of symbolization. But the grounds for these arguments fall apart once it is recognized that no depiction or description can approach completeness. Of necessity, pictures are highly selective. They can only depict some features, leaving others unspecified, and within a set of features specified, they may range in the amount of detail conveyed. A picture may suggest that Tom the tiger is striped but not indicate how many stripes he has, or as with encyclopedia pictures, display a definite number of stripes but make no specific number claims. A skillfully executed drawing may, with a single line, represent a basketball player in motion, yet specify little else about his physical makeup. It is not even necessary that pictures indicate spatial relations among the objects depicted or that all the spatial properties of a display have representational significance. If when asked to imagine J. and M., I succeed in picturing them, I will not suppose that J.'s being to the right of M. has any more relevance than display orientation has in a page completely filled with portraits of the senior class. And while it may be true that J.'s being next to M. cannot be specified in a pictorial system without also showing whether J. is to the right or left, this is not unique to picturing. Many digital and non-pictorial systems, like music notation or discrete graphs, cannot indicate nextness relations without giving more directional information as well.

7. Propositions and Pictures

Although the focus of much of the current imagery literature has been on the nature of the so-called "internal representation" of the image, I have been more concerned with the relationship between the image and what it purports to represent. Yet I have put heavy emphasis on the relativity of symbolic function to interpretation, and such talk of underlying systems of interpretation would seem to bring these two concerns closer together. In this concluding section, I wish to indicate where my position enjoins some of the debate over internal codes—in particular the argument over images vs. propositions.

Very early debates over imagery often made it sound as if the issue was whether there was a cognitive mode of information processing that required no interpretation at all. It was this feature that images were thought to share with pictures and in turn was one of the features that was supposed to set pictorial modes of representation apart from linguistic modes. Now notice that this construal requires identifying visual imagery with pictorial imagery, and this restriction is itself of questionable warrant. But even if we limit attention to pictorial imagery, the distinction rests on an untenable premise. Pictures too require interpretation when they are serving to represent. Furthermore, I have argued in the previous section that it is unlikely that a satisfactory account of pictorial understanding can be based on unqualified notions of resemblance, similarity, or one-to-one correspondence between an image and what it represents.

In one way or another, I believe that anti-imagist theorists have been picking up on this need for interpretation when they express qualms over the idea that we can have *purely* iconic or pictorial thoughts. And I have sympathies with their concerns. Nevertheless, image opponents often go on to assume (or argue) that once we realize that pictures and other modes of representation require interpretation, the differences between the various modes must only be surface differences. In addition, it is often claimed that since all modes require interpretation, if they are to function symbolically, the underlying understanding of pictures and other modes must be itself propositional. The reasons usually offered for these latter anti-imagist claims, however, seem to me to be unconvincing.

To begin, the claim that a symbol has content only relative to a system of interpretation does not entail that understanding or using a symbol requires first translating or encoding it into a *different* internal symbol system. Whether there is such a thing as "mentalese" or a "language of thought" or "lingua mentalis" is a complex problem the ramifications of which cannot be explored. All I want to maintain here is that talk of readings, construals, or interpretations can be understood in ways that do not require postulating an additional symbol system in which the content of the original resides. Indeed, some such account must be possible, for the requirement of a distinct encoding language for every understood symbol system leads to a regress. But, for argument's sake, let us suppose that some version of an encoding model of interpretation is correct. It still would not follow that comprehension of different symbol systems requires decoding them all into one and the same underlying code. The fact that one can go from information presented in one type of system to a representation in another or produce comparable information in each of several systems just does not show that there must be a third independent system into which all of the originals are reduced. And the long history of frustrated attempts to spell out theories of comprehension and translation of natural languages in terms of neutral propositions or meanings should make us wary that the arguments needed to support such claims will be easy to sustain.[9]

The fact, furthermore, that we can, to an extent, translate from pictures into words or vice versa does not mean that pictures are really a propositional mode of representation. Nor do I see why it is reasonable to suppose that our understanding or the "internal representation" of our understanding of pictorial and other non-linguistic systems must be propositional in nature. Of course, all this talk of propositional vs. pictorial codes (either external or internal) depends on how we construe the differences between these two categories of symbolization. And although I have considered primarily image-external object relations, the points raised throughout carry over to talk of underlying codes as well. Just as the mode classification of the spatial display S O N depends on how it is read, categorizing neural or internal codes will depend on the syntactic and semantic properties of their systems of interpretation. Discussions in previous sections of this paper should make it apparent why I am skeptical of drawing a propositional/non-propositional distinction in terms of the lack of presence of such features as generality, selectivity, spatiality, digitalness, and resemblance. What's more, many of the properties typically mentioned as being distinctive of propositional systems do not seem to me to provide promising bases for individuating systems in the manner intended.

The properties cited in Anderson (1978) are representative. He claims that what is distinctive of propositional systems is that (a) they are abstract, (b) they have an explicit set of rules or a syntax determining well-formedness, and (c) their symbols have truth values. Unpacking the significance of these supposed distinctive features, however, is not an easy task. As far as I can tell, there is no uniform construal in the literature of the label "abstract." It is used in a variety of ways, many of which apply to all systems or no system (e.g., need or do not need interpretation), some of which apply equally to various pictorial and analog graphic systems (e.g., can convey information about the general and non-observable), and others of which, if applicable, would make it impossible for the symbols of the system to be realized physically in psychological states of the relevant sort (e.g., the symbols are

Platonistically abstract objects). Difficulties too arise with the syntax requirement. If all that is meant by 'rules of formation' is that there are some systematic principles of use, the feature will not make fine enough cuts. On the other hand, the sorts of constraints on systems like music notation—presumably a propositional system —are far removed from the syntactical restrictions and semantically relevant syntactic structures that characterize natural languages and standard logical systems. And a further attenuated notion of syntax would be needed to encompass such digital, non-pictorial systems as traffic lights, discrete scattergram graphs, and unordered lists of names specifying membership in political parties.

The third and perhaps most important feature Anderson claims for propositions is that they have truth values; propositions are either true or false. But this criterion says more about our use of the words 'true' and 'false' than it does about any principled distinction among symbolic modes. For while we may restrict the use of the terms 'true' or 'false' to language-like systems, comparable terms of evaluation may be employed across the board. The map of New Jersey provides accurate or inaccurate information about the shoreline, the analog pressure gauge correctly or incorrectly reflects the state of the container, and the composite police sketch of the suspect rightly or wrongly indicates the snubness of his nose. So once it is admitted that pictures and other non-language-like systems can be evaluated for aptness and fit, the point of identifying propositionality with having truth values becomes otiose. Moreover, allowing that these systems can be evaluated for rightness does not mean that they must or insightfully can be subject to the kinds of combinatorial recursive semantic analysis usually applied to formal and natural languages. Nor does it entail that understanding such symbols and deciding on their correctness requires that they be translated into modes of symbolization that do contain more linguistic-like features. The important notions of discrete and disjoint alphabets and vocabulary, predicate argument structure, logical connectives, quantifiers, and demarcated complete statements would seem to have no counterparts in many of these systems.

Finally, even if it were the case that at some highly abstracted level of analysis, there were a "language of thought" that is "ultimately" employed in processing symbols of all types and is "propositional" on some construal, I am not convinced how important that would be. Surely, it would not show that psychologically significant processes and principles cannot be isolated at other levels. Alternate systems of the propositional calculus are about as close as we come to systems that are mere notational variants of one another; they have the logically same expressive power. Yet one would expect to find differences in ease of learning, memory, processing times, and task simplicity, depending on which system a person is employing. Thus, differences of merely a notational sort may affect the nature of cognitive activity. All the more reason to believe that pictures, words, graphs, maps, gauges, and diagrams offer genuine alternative modes for incorporating, storing, and conveying information.

Notes

1. See, for example, Anderson (1978) and subsequent discussion of his paper in *Psychological Review* 86 (1979), 379 ff.

2. It should be mentioned too that images are often used creatively, to think up new tunes or imagine unrealized situations. In such cases symbolic accuracy will not be at stake, and questions about the storage of information or the memory of past experiences will not be relevant.

3. Notice, however, that in all three cases there may be "visual" processing, left-right "scanning," and longer reaction times were the sentence longer.

4. Kolers and Smythe (1979, pp. 161–162), for example, claim to isolate three different usages in just the work of Shepard and his colleagues.

5. My remarks here draw heavily on Gombrich (1960), Goodman (1968), and Black (1972) and also reflect points developed in Schwartz (1975).

6. I use the word 'resemblance' as short-hand for all of these various terms. Although there are differences among the concepts, the problems I consider pretty much cut across them all.

7. This is often the view of anti-imagists as well as pro-imagists. Dennett 1969, pp. 132 ff.), for example, argues that pictures are our paradigm case of images, and they represent by resemblance. So he says the question about mental images is "are there elements . . . that represent in virtue of resembling what they represent?" (p. 133). Along with other anti-imagists, he then goes on to argue against mental imagery on the grounds that purported cases are not instances of pictorial representation by resemblance.

8. In Schwartz (1975) I do attempt to sketch out a role for picture-percept resemblance as part of an account of pictorial realism. Some of those moves may be applicable to image representation as well.

9. Exploring these issues fully would require an extended discussion of meaning, comprehension, and translation. Suffice it to say that the very idea of a complete meaning preserving translation between systems of the structurally same kind is a suspect notion. When one extends the claim for the reducibility of cognitive content to include symbol systems in general (i.e., systems having vastly different syntactic and semantic properties), the hypothesis of a single decoding language becomes less plausible still.

ON THE DEMYSTIFICATION
OF MENTAL IMAGERY

6

Stephen M. Kosslyn, Steven Pinker,
George E. Smith, and Steven P. Shwartz

A history of mental imagery would almost require a complete
history of the idea of mental representation, so intimate is the relationship between the two concepts. The objections to mental
imagery have traditionally been of two forms. First, it has been
argued that imagery cannot serve the functions that have been
attributed to it. Most notably, it has been pointed out (at least
by Berkeley's time) that an image cannot represent an object or
scene uniquely without some interpretive function that picks out
certain characteristics of the image as being important and others
as being incidental. That is, an image of John sitting could represent John, John's head, bent knees, and so forth, depending on
what one pays attention to in the image. And the "stage direc-
tions" indicating what is important in an image cannot *themselves*
be images—if they were, the problem would only be pushed back
a step. This class of objections is to the point: images cannot be
the *sole* form of internal representation that exists in human
memory. But this does not mean that images cannot be one form
of representation in memory.

The second class of objections historically leveled against the use
of mental imagery as an explanatory construct in psychology has
two thrusts: first, it has been claimed that there are incoherencies

and inconsistencies inherent in the concept. Pylyshyn (1973) has recently summarized and developed these claims, and Kosslyn and Pomerantz (1977) have provided counterarguments. Not surprisingly, neither the arguments nor the counterarguments have been definitive, and neither seems to have had enough force to sway most people from whatever position they found most congenial in the first place. In the present paper we will not attempt to argue from purely rational grounds that mental imagery is a suitable topic for scientific study and a suitable explanatory construct in psychology. Rather, our argument will consist of a demonstration that progress can in fact be made in studying imagery scientifically. The second thrust of these objections against the use of imagery as an explanatory construct focuses on the claim that imagery is not a well-formed domain in its own right, but is merely one special aspect of a more general processing system (see Pylyshyn, 1973). Again, if this were the case, one would not expect to see much progress in attempts to develop a special theory of imagery. However, if a coherent theory that treats imagery as a distinct "mental organ," a theory having explanatory power and predictive utility, *can* be developed, this alone should make us hesitate to abandon the construct. In the course of describing the theory and its development, we will raise questions about how imagery—or any other mental structure or process—ought to be studied and how theories of mental phenomena ought to be evaluated.

The present research program has had two phases. In "Phase I" we attempted to delimit the class of acceptable models empirically; this work will be described in this chapter. In "Phase II" we formulated the core theory, as will be described in the following chapter. We began with a simple conception of how the imagery representation system might operate. This conception hinges on the notion that visual images might be like displays produced on a cathode ray tube (CRT) by a computer program operating on stored data. That is, we hypothesized that images are temporary spatial displays in active memory that are generated from more abstract representations in long-term memory. Interpretative mechanisms (a "mind's eye") work over ("look at") these internal displays and classify them in terms of semantic categories (as would be involved in realizing that a particular spatial configuration corresponds to a dog's ear, for example).* This metaphor seemed capable of providing accounts for most of the available data on imagery (see Paivio, 1971); on this view images not only have some pictorial properties, but they are of limited capacity and actively composed. This simple "protomodel" was used as a heuristic to help construct a "decision tree," where the nodes represented issues and the branches stood for alternative positions on the issues. Sets of experiments were conducted to eliminate (as far as possible) branches, allowing us to descend to the next issue.

The CRT protomodel directed our attention to the following four key issues: First, it suggested that the quasi-pictorial image people report experiencing is not an epiphenomenal concomitant of more abstract, non-pictorial processing; second, it led us to ask whether such images are simply retrieved or whether the representation system is built such that images can be generated; third, if images can be generated, we may then ask whether generation is simply a piecemeal retrieval of stored information, or whether it can involve retrieving and actively amalgamating units that are stored separately; lastly, we were faced with the question whether images are composed solely by retrieving encodings of how something appeared (the products of "seeing as"), or whether "descriptive" information (such as the products of "seeing that") can also be used. At the end of Phase I, then, we had a set of constraints on the viable structures and processes of a theory of imagery.

Thus there were three key aspects to the initial research program:

1. It was guided by a conception of the imagery system, the CRT metaphor. This metaphor was computational and it specified possible components of the system and their interactions. The metaphor was used to raise issues.

---

*In this paper the term "image" is used to refer to representations in active memory, not to an experience. The experience of "having an image" is taken as an indication that an image representation is present in active memory; the question whether one can have an image representation without the experience is left open.

2. The issues raised by the metaphor are issues about capacities, about things the representational system can do. Thus, for example, we do not ask whether images *are* always, or even typically, generated—we ask whether the system is constructed such that images *can* be generated. If so, any theory of imagery will have to account for this capacity.

3. Issues are raised in order to generate opposing hypotheses. One class of hypotheses is eliminated, as best as any hypotheses in isolation can be "eliminated," by a method of converging evidence. Numerous different experiments are conducted with an eye toward rendering one class of accounts more plausible than the other.

1.1 Issue 1: Are Images Epiphenomenal?

The cathode ray tube metaphor posits that quasi-pictorial images are produced and then processed by other mechanisms. This image is not strictly pictorial because it does not share all the properties of pictures (e.g., it cannot be hung on a wall). Rather, it is quasi-pictorial in that it *depicts* information, as opposed to *describing* information in a discursive way. Presumably, information implicit in long-term memory becomes explicit in an image (e.g., if asked which is higher off the ground, a horse's knees or the tip of its tail, people claim that this information becomes apparent only when they form an image of the beast). Alternatively, the experience of quasi-pictorial images could be a nonfunctional, epiphenomenal by-product of nonconscious processing of descriptive representations. On this view, images could simply be like the flashing lights on the outside of a computer; although they vary systematically with the functioning of an information-processing mechanism, they take no part in the processing (see Kosslyn and Pomerantz, 1977). None of the models of imagery based on Artificial Intelligence research treats the quasi-pictorial properties of images that people report when introspecting as functional properties of the representation (see Baylor, 1971; Farley, 1974; Moran, 1973; Pylyshyn, 1973; Simon, 1972). Thus there must be some resolution of this issue before we can even begin to theorize about imagery. Chapter 3 of Kosslyn (1980) presents a detailed review of our research on this issue, which is summarized below.

Four classes of experiments were performed to address the image-as-epiphenomenon view. These experiments were motivated primarily by the claim that quasi-pictorial images "depict" information in a spatial medium (in relation to the interpretive processes that operate on the image). If a representation depicts an object, than (a) every portion of the representation corresponds to a portion of the represented object such that, (b) the inter-point distances among portions of the representation preserve the distances among the corresponding portions of the object (cf. Shepard, 1975). It follows from this that any arbitrary part of a depictive representation is a representation of the corresponding part of the object. For example, the rear portion of my *image* of a car is a representation of the rear portion of the *car*. This property is not true of non-depictive representations. For example, "my" is part of "my car," but "my" is not part of the car itself. In addition to this formal property, because a quasi-pictorial image depicts, it has the following property: size, location, and orientation of an object must be represented whenever a shape is represented. The foregoing dimensions are inextricably linked in the quasi-pictorial format (see Kosslyn, 1980, chapter 3 for a formal treatment of the properties of depictive representation). Thus if images are in fact depictive, then factors like spatial extent—which is inherent in the way visual images depict information—should affect information processing when images are used. In contrast, if images are not depictive representations, then the spatial properties of images revealed by introspection (which do not characterize list-like linguistically based representations) would not be expected to affect information processing.

Scanning visual images. If images depict spatial extent, then they should be capable of preserving relative metric distances between portions of objects. If so, then we might expect that more time should be required to scan longer distances across images. Kosslyn (1973) in fact found that the farther a property was from an initial focus point on an imaged object, the longer it took to see it in the image. Unfortunately, there was a major flaw in this experiment: more properties of the imaged object were scanned over when subjects scanned longer distances (see Lea, 1975). Thus the apparent effects of distance can be explained without referring to depictive images, but rather by arguing that the underlying representations are networks of propositions (simple language-like descriptions; see Anderson and Bower, 1973; Pylyshyn, 1973). When subjects are told to focus on a location of an image, what they do, the argument goes, is activate a region of a network. When a to-be-located property is presented, the relevant variable is the number of links in the network that must be traversed before reaching the representation of the property. Because representations of properties located further apart on the object are separated from the activated location by more intervening links, more time is required to traverse the network before locating the sought representations. Kosslyn, Ball and Reiser (1978) report a number of experiments that eliminated the confounding between distance and number of items scanned. In one, subjects scanned 3 different distances and scanned over 0, 1, or 2 letters. The number of letters scanned over and distance scanned were varied orthogonally. Time to classify the case of the "destination letter" increased linearly with distance and—independently—with numbers of letters scanned over. In another experiment, people first learned to draw a map with a mythical island that contained seven objects (e.g., a hut, tree, rock). These objects were located so that each of the 21 interobject distances was at least ½ cm. longer than the next shortest. After learning to draw the map, subjects were asked to image it and to focus mentally on a given location (each location was used as a focus point equally often). Following this, a probe word was presented; half the time this word named an object on the map, and half the time it did not. On hearing the word, the subjects were to look for the object on their images. If it was present, they were to scan to it and push a button upon arriving at it. If it was not found on the imaged map, they were to push another button. As before, the longer the distance, the more scanning time was needed. The map and results are illustrated in Figure 1.

Figure 1. The map scanned, and the time to scan different distances across an image of it.

A control was included in the map-scanning experiment to rule out explanations that some sort of (unspecified) underlying non-depictive representation was actually being processed. These subjects participated in the same task as the experimental group, but with one change: after imaging the map and focusing on a location, they were simply to decide—without necessarily referring to the image—whether or not the probe word named an object on the map. Thus if the distance effects observed before were due to processing non-depictive representation merely associated with experience of imagery, we should find the same pattern of results here. In fact, distance had absolutely no effect on judgment time in this situation.

Finally, another experiment reported in Kosslyn, Ball and Reiser (1978) allows us to rule out one more counterexplanation for the scanning results: on this view, (1) the closer two objects or parts are, the more likely they are to be encoded into the same "chunk," and (2) encodings in the same chunk are accessed more quickly than those in different chunks. In this experiment, subjects imaged three schematic faces, with eyes three different distances above the mouth. Immediately after the picture was removed, the subjects were asked to image the face at one of three "subjective sizes" (i.e., such that they seemed to subtend different visual angles). Interestingly, time to scan from the mouth to the eyes (and classify their color) increased not only with the amount of separation between the eyes and mouth, but also as subjective size (and overall distance) increased. Thus the effects of distance on scanning time cannot be attributed to encoding into "chunks," given that subjective size was not manipulated until after the picture was removed.

On any straightforward account, these results are most perspicuously explained if image representations depict metric distance, and this property affects real-time processing of images.

Imaging to the point of overflow. The notion that images have spatial extent suggests that they also have spatial boundaries (after all, they don't extend on indefinitely). If images occur in a structure specialized for representing visual spatial information (e.g., within an array, as suggested by the CRT protomodel), then the maximum extent of an image should be constrained by the extent of the structure. This idea was tested in the following way: Subjects first were asked to image an object as if it were being seen from very far away, and then were to imagine that they were walking toward the object. All subjects claimed that the object seemed to loom larger as they imagined approaching it. At some point, it was suggested, the image might loom so large as to "overflow." At this point, the subjects were to stop their "mental walk" and to estimate the apparent distance of the object. Estimates were made either verbally (in feet and inches) or nonverbally (by moving a tripod apparatus the appropriate distance from a blank wall). The distance estimates and the length of the longest axis (which accounted for the most variance in distance estimates in a regression analysis) of each imaged object were then used to calculate a visual angle subtended by the image at the point of overflow. This basic experiment was performed in a variety of ways, which differed in terms of how distance was estimated and in terms of whether subjects mentally imaged pictures that were visually presented or animals that were described.

If images occur in a spatially constrained medium, then larger objects should appear further away at the point of overflow. In addition, objects should seem to subtend a constant visual angle at the point of overflow. And in fact, both of these predictions were borne out when subjects imaged pictures (of rectangles, animals) and estimated distance nonverbally (by positioning a tripod away from a wall). The distance at the apparent point of overflow increased linearly with the size of the object, and the angle subtended at the point of overflow was the same for different-sized objects. The results of a typical experiment, in which subjects imaged different-sized line drawings of animals, are illustrated in Figure 2. The size of the angle obtained varied somewhat with the stimuli being used (e.g., smaller angles were obtained for imaged rectangles than for images of animals that were simply named; see Kosslyn, 1978a, for details).

In addition, to the distance-estimation technique, similar results

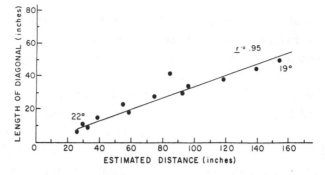

Figure 2. Judged distance at the point of overflow for different-sized images.

were obtained using two other kinds of tasks. In one task subjects imaged and scanned lines subtending various amounts of visual arc, and the time to scan each degree was computed. This measure of scan rate then allowed us to estimate the length of a line subjects imaged "to be as long as possible without overflowing" and then scanned. The angle obtained here was virtually identical to one obtained using the first technique with a separate group of subjects. In the other task the subjects were simply asked to indicate the apparent size at which an image overflowed by gesturing, and the spread between the hands and the distance from the eyes was measured. This estimate converged nicely with those obtained from the other two tasks. These results, then, support the claim that the representations underlying the images we experience are spatial entities and that their spatial characteristics have real consequences for some forms of information processing (see Kosslyn, (1978a).

Subjectively smaller images are more difficult to examine. The CRT proto-model suggests that images are classified by the same sorts of procedures used in classifying perceptual representations. If so, some of the same constraints that affect ease of classifying percepts also should affect the ease of classifying parts of mental images. One obvious example is apparent size: parts of objects subtending smaller visual angles are harder to see in perception, and hence we might expect that they are also harder to see in a mental image. Kosslyn (1975) tested this idea in a variety of experiments requiring subjects to image animals at different subjective sizes. In all of these "imagery detection experiments" the subject was told that we were interested in how long it took to see a property on the image or to see that it was not there. Only after the property was either clearly in view or clearly not to be seen was the subject to respond by pushing the appropriate button. As expected, more time was required to see properties on subjectively smaller images. Subjects often reported having to "zoom in" on an initially small image to see a property, which presumably required time. The larger images, being better resolved, presumably did not require such zooming in.

As before, these findings might be able to be explained by a model in which all information is stored in networks of abstract propositions (e.g., see Bower, 1978). Perhaps the representation of information about an object consists of a list of properties, and subjects merely activate more properties when asked to form a larger image. That is, people realize that they would be able to see more things on closer objects, and hence interpret the instructions to require activating more information about the object when it is to be "imaged larger." If so, then there would be a greater probability that a given probed property was already activated prior to query when subjects were asked to form large images. And verification time is faster if the queried property is already activated than if it is inactivated and one must search long-term memory— as would be more likely to occur when subjects were asked to form small images, and hence presumably activated fewer properties (cf. Anderson, 1978).

If subjectively smaller images are inspected more slowly than larger ones because of the probability that a property representation is activated on a list, then subjects should be faster in verifying properties stored near the "top" of the list (because these properties would be more likely to be activated at the time of query). The fact that more highly associated properties are verified more quickly in standard semantic memory tasks, in which imagery is presumably not used (see Smith, Shoben and Rips, 1974), has been taken to indicate that the association strength between an object and its properties reflects the ordering of the properties on a list. If lists are so ordered, then the association strength of a property, and not its size, should dictate the time subjects require when asked to see a property on an imaged object.

This idea was tested by having subjects evaluate items such as "cat claws" and "cat head," with the smaller property being more associated with the object (as determined by ratings obtained from other subjects). Interestingly, people saw these larger properties more quickly when asked to find them on an image of the object. But when no imagery instructions were given, people verified the smaller, more closely associated properties more quickly. These results are illustrated in Figure 3. The same results were obtained in a regression analysis of times to evaluate items not selected for the size-association strength tradeoff (see Kosslyn, 1976). These results, then, clearly distinguish between processing of depictive representations and non-depictive, list-like representations.

Effects of subjective size of an image on later recall. If smaller images are less resolved than larger ones, then it should be more difficult to remember the identity of an object if one encoded a small image of it instead of a larger one. And in fact, we have demonstrated that smaller images are remembered less well in an incidental memory task. This result was found in four experiments, which controlled for the amount of effort required to form the image at different sizes and the relationship between two objects in an image (one of which may have been imaged at a tiny size; see Kosslyn and Alper, 1977).

The total weight of the evidence, then, supports the view that images are not simply epiphenomenal concomitants of more abstract underlying processing. The results are much more simply explained by positing functional, quasi-pictorial images than by formulating "Rube Goldberg" non-imagery models (which not only are ad hoc, but have failed to have the heuristic value for predicting new results that is evident in the imagery models). Thus, all told, we decided to descend the branch that rejects the claim that the depictive properties of images are epiphenomenal and proceed to the next issue.

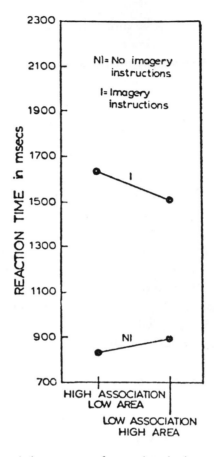

Figure 3. The time to judge two sorts of properties using imagery or not using imagery.

1.2 Issue II: Are Images Stored Intact in Long-Term Memory and Later Retrieved in Toto?

The second node of our decision tree is at the bottom of the branch representing the hypothesis that images depict information. This new node represents the issue of the way in which the active memory representation is produced from long-term memory. Two branches extend from this node: One one hand, images could be stored in long-term memory as single units that later are retrieved;

on the other, there may be more flexibility in how image representations are stored and activated. All of the existing experiments in the literature bearing on image formation (e.g., Paivio, 1975; Weber and Harnish, 1974) required subjects to image scenes containing multiple objects. These results do not tell us whether images of individual objects are simply stored holistically and later retrieved. Chapter 4 of Kosslyn (1980) presents a detailed review of our research that bears on this and the following two issues; only the highlights of the relevant findings are mentioned here.

We claimed earlier that people can find properties of larger images more quickly because more information is apparent (to the "mind's eye" interpretive procedures) on them. If so, then subjectively larger images may require more time to form if images are in fact constructed by elaboration (adding more parts or detail). Kosslyn (1975) found that people do generally require more time to form subjectively larger images, independent of the actual size of the imaged object (within a relatively narrow range). This result could reflect a "criterion effect," however, and not the effects of adding more parts. That is, since more material is concentrated into a smaller area, perhaps subjectively smaller images are retrieved holistically but they reach some level of brightness sooner than do corresponding subjectively larger images. If subjects consider an image complete when it has reached a given level of vividness, then smaller images will seem to be formed more quickly—even if images are retrieved all of a piece, with no construction.

If this counter-interpretation were correct, subjects should require less time to report that images of pictures with more detail have been formed. If the construction idea is correct, people should require more time to image more detailed pictures. These contrasting predictions were tested in an experiment in which subjects imaged more or less detailed versions of pictures of animals. Subjects studied a picture, imaged it (pushing a button when the image was completed, which allowed us to measure the time required to form the image), answered a question about the image, and then chose which picture (from a set of two) they had just imaged. The data of primary interest here were the image formation times, with the other manipulations being included primarily to mask the purpose of the experiment and to encourage the subjects to form accurate images. The results were straightforward: people do, in fact, require more time to image more detailed pictures.

A control group was not asked to use imagery in this task, but was asked to remember descriptions of the pictures. Instead of pushing the button when they had an image, these subjects pushed it when they had "quickly reviewed the properties of the drawing" in their minds. This review process required the same amount of time for detailed and undetailed pictures. Thus, forming images was distinguished from retrieving non-imaginal information, and the view that images are not necessarily retrieved in toto was supported.

But consider the following counter-interpretation of the results: more detailed pictures required more time to image not because they were constructed, but because there were more things to check after the image was retrieved. That is, people may indeed store images as simple units that are later retrieved, and in fact require the same amount of time to form images of detailed and undetailed objects. But after the image is present, the subjects may first check it over before deciding that the image is in fact fully retrieved (even retrieval of a single unit need not be instantaneous). And because they scan to more parts on more detailed images, more time is consumed before they decide to respond that the image is present. This idea was examined in a number of experiments (see chapter 4 of Kosslyn, 1980). In one, subjects were asked to image sets of objects at different distances from each other. Image formation time increased with the number of objects, but not with the distance—although time to scan between pairs after the image was formed did increase with distance (replicating the earlier results). If the effects of number of objects were due to scanning, distance should have affected times here, but did not. Further, in another experiment more detailed drawings required more time to image, but now there were no effects of size on image formation time. The stimuli used here were simple line drawings, the parts of which were equally easy to see (and hence presumably equally easily inserted into the image during construction) at the two sizes. In this case, if scanning were at the root of the complexity effect, we again would have expected less time to scan over and examine the smaller images. Further, if subjects scanned images after retrieving them, the effects of complexity should have been amplified for the larger images because more distance had to be scanned on the average—which also was not found.

1.3 Issue III: Are Images Retrieved Piecemeal or Can They Be Retrieved in Units?

Given that images are not merely turned on like slides in a projector, are they simply retrieved piecemeal, not in any organized fashion, or can they be composed by amalgamating information stored as distinct, separate units? This issue essentially separates the structure and process assumptions that underlie the previous issue. Now we consider the possibility that the imagery representation system can only store image representations as single units, but these units can be activated a portion at a time. Alternatively, the system may be built such that coherent units can be retrieved and composed in the act of construction. This question was addressed in an experiment in which people imaged drawings of geometrical forms. In this experiment we used "top down" conceptual processes to vary how many units were in an encoding while keeping the number of lines, area subtended and so on, constant. The subjects in one group were unaware of the existence of the other, and the number of units in a figure was varied between the two groups. Subjects were shown a set of geometric figures, each of which could be described in two different ways: as sets of relatively few overlapping forms or as sets of relatively many smaller adjacent forms. For example, one figure could be described either as "two overlapping rectangles" or "a central square with four squares attached." One group of subjects received the set of descriptions using overlapping forms and one received the set using adjacent forms. Time to form images of the figures later was indeed dictated by the number of units in the description. In fact, image formation time increased linearly with the number of units in the description, even though different subjects contributed to the different data points.

One interpretation of these results would be that the image is stored integrally but that at the time of retrieval it is segregated into units. That is, perhaps the image and description of it are stored separately and the description is used to retrieve the long-term memory representation a part at a time. We find this implausible, but it is possible and—if true—does not implicate a system that can store separate encodings and integrate them together into a single image. To consider this possibility, another experiment was performed. In this experiment units were defined by presenting parts of a stimulus separately over time. Thus even though the final product occupied the same area and had the same numbers of lines, the number of units was varied by varying how the stimulus was broken up into parts initially. In this experiment, then, people learned to image a set of drawings prior to the experiment proper. A given drawing was presented in one of three ways (but counterbalancing resulted in each stimulus occurring equally often in each presentation condition), defined by whether (1) an animal was drawn completely on one page, (2) parts were separated and presented on two separate pages (in correct relative locations), or (3) parts were separated and presented on five pages (again with the parts being in the correct relative locations on the pages). When parts were presented on more than one page, the subjects were told to study each page as long as they needed, and to mentally "glue" the parts together so that they formed an image of the whole animal. This procedure forced subjects to encode separate units and to integrate them in memory. If images were later constructed by composing these units, we would expect subjects to require more time to construct images of drawings distributed over more pages. And this is just what we found. In fact, image formation time increased *linearly* with the number of pages used to present a stimulus. Interestingly, however, no more time was required to "see" parts of imaged drawings once the images were formed; thus, it was not simply that subjects were more confused about the appearance of drawings that were presented on multiple pages.

Given the results of the foregoing experiments, then, we have good reason to posit that the imagery system has the capacity to retrieve and integrate "chunks" stored separately in long-term memory. Thus, we are justified in positing that a theory of imagery must explain how images are constructed from organized units stored in long-term memory.

1.4 Issue IV: Are Images Generated Only from "Depictive" Information or Can "Descriptive" Information Also Be Used?

Images could be generated by simply composing information in depictive encodings, or image construction could at least sometimes involve an interplay between depictive and descriptive memories. A number of experiments were conducted to investigate this issue. In one (see Kosslyn, 1978b) subjects first viewed a 3 × 6 array of letters. After the array was removed, these people either were told it would be referred to as "6 columns of 3" or were told it would be referred to as "3 rows of 6." When the matrix was described the first way, with more units predicated initially (and in terms of columns rather than rows), more time was later required to image it. Given that the same matrix was imaged in both cases and the labels were given after the matrix was removed, these results indicate that descriptive information can be used in image construction. Kosslyn (1980, see chapter 4) reports an additional experiment that also makes this point. Here, subjects were able to use verbal descriptions to form images of scenes with objects at different distances from each other. Not only did image formation time increase with the number of items in the scene, but time to scan between items later was determined by the distance between them. Beech and Allport (1978) present further evidence that conceptual information can be used in the formation of mental images. In addition, Weber, Kelley, and Little (1972) present some data indicating that actual verbal (not simply abstract discursive) information is sometimes used in imaging sequences of letters of the alphabet (see Kosslyn, 1980, for a detailed review of this literature).

It may help the reader to gain a better picture of the overall research strategy if we summarize the four points established during Phase I somewhat more abstractly. The first point established that there are data that are promisingly construed in terms of the central feature of the CRT protomodel, the "quasi-pictorial display." Because this issue is at the heart of the protomodel, data that make it plausible lend credence to the protomodel itself as a conceptualization of the imagery system. The systematicity in the data initially collected was especially important because in the absence of a reasonably defined range of diverse yet well-behaved data, the task of theory construction is hopeless. At the close of research on the first issue, then, we had data that fit together and complemented one another in an appropriate way, if they are construed in terms of the CRT protomodel. Thus we felt comfortable in letting the protomodel lead us to ask additional questions. The second point followed from an investigation of a question left open by the CRT protomodel, namely, how the information underlying the images we experience is represented in, and later retrieved from, long-term memory. Given the data, it seemed reasonable to conclude that images are not stored holistically in long-term memory, and simply "activated" when one experiences a surface image. Hence the study of image processing will have to answer questions about the nature of the underlying representation and the way it is mapped into a surface image. The third point established was that the image system is built to allow one to construct images from organized units stored in long-term memory. Hence, one thing a process model will have to include is provision for combining units to form a surface image. The final point established during Phase I was that image construction can exploit non-pictorial as well as pictorial information from long-term memory, which also must be explained by a theory of the mental image processing system.

Thus at the end of Phase I there are a number of constraints on the form of a model and a body of data in need of explanation. The model will include a CRT-like display medium, techniques for forming an image on this display, and techniques for interpreting ("seeing") and transforming information in such a display. What requires explanation, then, is how the image is formed from information in long-term memory and how, once formed, the image is used in various cognitive tasks. It was at this point, then, that it made sense to begin to formulate a theory and a model.

THE IMAGERY DEBATE
Analog Media versus Tacit Knowledge

7

Zenon Pylyshyn

The study of mental imagery continues to be a major concern in cognitive psychology. Since regaining acceptance about 15 years ago, the study of processes underlying the sort of reasoning that is accompanied by perceptionlike experiences has become one of the focal points of the new mentalistic psychology. The purpose of this article is to comment on some of the recent theoretical work in this area in the light of the debate over the nature of mental imagery that has been recurring in the literature over the past 6 or 7 years. The various positions in this debate have been summarized in a number of places, including most recently in Shepard (1975, 1978), Kosslyn and Pomerantz (1977), Kosslyn, Pinker, Smith, and Shwartz (1979), Paivio (1977), Anderson (1978), and Pylyshyn (1973, 1978, 1979a, 1979b). What I shall do in this article is pick out what I consider to be the most substantive strand in this disagreement and discuss it in relation to some of the most persuasive recent empirical findings and the most widely accepted theoretical accounts of these findings. For this purpose I shall make extensive reference to the overview article by Kosslyn et al. (1979), since it represents the most explicit formulation of the "imagistic" (or "pictorial" or "analogical") position to date. In doing this I shall be highly selective in the questions I shall address. There is much in the imagery literature that can be (and has been) debated, not all of which is equally significant from a theoretical standpoint. Thus one could argue over whether images are continuous or discrete, concrete or abstract, holistic or articulated, pictorial or discursive (whether they depict, like pictures, or refer, like descriptions), and whether they constitute a fundamentally different form of cognition or are merely a species of a single form used in all cognitive processing (and at what level they are considered to be the same or different). There have even been arguments over whether images are epiphenomenal or whether they are functional in cognition; but questions such as the latter cannot even be addressed until one takes a theoretical stand concerning the properties of images. One cannot say of something that it is or is not epiphenomenal until one has a clear statement of what that something is. For example, to the extent that *image* refers to what I experience when I imagine a scene, then surely *that* exists in the same sense that any other sensation or conscious content does (e.g., pains, tickles, etc.). If, on the other hand, *image* refers to a certain theoretical construct that is claimed to have certain properties (e.g., to be spatially extended) and to play a specified role in certain cognitive processes, then the appropriate question to ask is not whether the construct is epiphenomenal but whether the theoretical claims are warranted, and indeed whether they are true.

In my view, however, the central theoretical question in this controversy is whether the explanation of certain imagery phenomena requires that we postulate special types of processes or mechanisms, such as ones commonly referred to by the term *analog.* I shall discuss one plausible interpretation of this notion—one that does indeed represent a fundamental difference in approach from the one I have been advocating. In addition to this issue, several of the other distinctions mentioned above can also be touched upon if we focus as sharply as possible on one particular claim often made in the imagery literature, namely, the alleged spatiality of images, and on a set of prototypical experimental findings that have been taken as establishing this particular property of images, namely, those that demonstrate "mental rotation" and "mental scanning" of images. In this regard I shall argue that the only real issue that divides the proponents of what has unfortunately become known as the "images versus propositions" debate is the question of whether certain aspects of cognition, generally (though not exclusively) associated with imagery, ought to be viewed as governed by tacit knowledge—that is, whether they should be explained in terms of processes which operate upon symbolic encodings of rules and other representations (such as beliefs and goals) or whether they should be viewed as intrinsic properties of certain representational media or of certain mechanisms that are not alterable in nomologically arbitrary ways by tacit knowledge. I have elsewhere referred to such mechanisms as constituting the "functional architecture" of the mind (Pylyshyn, 1980a, 1980b). In this article I will present arguments and evidence in support of the view that most of the empirical phenomena involving transformations of images (such as the image scanning results of Kosslyn et al., 1979) are better explained according to the tacit knowledge theory.

The Appeal to Properties of an Analog Medium

In discussing the question of whether images are epiphenomenal, Kosslyn et al. (1979) assert that "none of the models of imagery based on Artificial Intelligence research treat the images that people report experiencing as functional representations" (p. 536). This strange yet widely held view is based in part on a misconception concerning what in fact is reported in imagery. As Hebb (1968) has pointed out, what people report is properties not of their image but of the objects that they are imaging. Such properties as color, shape, size, and so on are clearly properties of the objects that are being imagined. This distinction is crucial. The seemingly innocent scope slip that takes *image of object X with property P* to mean *(image of object X) with property P* instead of the correct *image of (object X with property P)* is probably the most ubiquitous and damaging conceptual confusion in the whole imagery literature.

To see that this slip is not a mere way of speaking but carries considerable weight in explanations of imagery phenomena, consider the case of the generally accepted "spatial" character of images. Take, for example, the elegant experiments by Kosslyn (1973, 1975) and by Kosslyn, Ball, and Reiser (1978) involving "mental scanning" of images, which show that the further away an item is from the place on an image that is currently being focused on, the longer it takes to see or focus on and report that item in the image. I shall take up the question of the interpretation of these results in the Tacit Knowledge and Mental Scanning section below. For the present I simply wish to point out that the story that goes with Kosslyn's interpretation inherits its plausibility and compellingness from a systematic equivocation over which particular entity has the property *length* in precisely the manner suggested in the previous paragraph.

For example there can be no disputing the Kosslyn et al. (1979) claim that "these results seem to indicate that images do represent metrical distance" (p. 537). But in the very next sentence this format-neutral claim becomes transformed into the substantive assertion that "images have spatial extent"—that is, that the image itself has rather than represents length or size. This transformation, moreover, is essential to the particular account of the scanning experiments that Kosslyn et al. wish to promote. That is because the naturalness of the scanning notion comes from the lawfulness of

$$T = \frac{D}{S}. \tag{1}$$

In this equation, of course, T, D, and S are to be interpreted as real time, real physical distance, and real mean speed, respectively. If Equation 1 were literally applicable to the image, then this account of the scanning results would be a principled one, since the equation represents a universal principle or basic fact of nature. If, on the other hand, we were to keep with the first way Kosslyn et al. put their claim (viz., that images represent, rather than have distance), we would, instead, have to appeal to a different sort of regularity, one that might for instance be expressed roughly by

$$T = F(D', S'), \tag{2}$$

where $D' = R_1(D)$ is some representation of distance using encoding R_1, $S' = R_2(S)$ is some representation of mean speed using encoding R_2, and F is a function that maps pairs of representations D' and S' onto real time such that for all distances, d, and speeds, s, it will be the case that $F[R_1(d), R_2(s)] = d \div s$.

Now, Equation 2 is clearly not a law of nature. There can be no general universal law governing the amount of time that it takes to transform representations, since obviously that depends upon both the form of the representations and the available operations for transforming them. The equation $T = R_1(D) \div R_2(S)$ is far from expressing a nomological law. In fact, if F is to be realized computationally, we must view Equation 2 as asserting that there is some process, P, which, given the representations D' and S' as inputs (together with other specifications such as a beginning and ending state) takes T sec to complete, where T in this case has to equal $D \div S$. Obviously, unless the various representations and the process P are especially selected, Equation 2 will be false. For example, it is a nontrivial exercise to design an algorithm that always terminates after $D \div S$ sec when given two expressions representing the numerals for D and S (except for the degenerate case in which the algorithm calculates $D \div S$ and then simply waits idly for that amount of time to go by). Now by systematically leaving out the words *representation of* or by using ambiguous descriptions, such as saying that images "preserve relative metrical distances" (which can be interpreted as meaning either that they have or that they represent distances), it is possible to create the illusion of having the explanatory power provided by Equation 1 while at the same time avoiding the ontological claim that goes with it (viz., that images are actually laid out in space somewhere in the brain).

Another way to put the point about the relative explanatory power of the literal account based on Equation 1, compared with the representation account based on Equation 2, is in terms of the degrees of freedom in these two explanatory principles. If we assume that it is literally the case that physical space is involved, then the form of the relation among distance, speed, and time would be fixed as in Equation 1. If, on the other hand, only a representation of space is involved, and thus the regularity is expressed by Equation 2, the form of the function F is actually a free empirical parameter that is obtained by observing instances of the very phenomena that require explaining. This means that an explanation based on Equation 2 has more degrees of freedom and, hence, less explanatory power than an explanation based on Equation 1. Even more seriously, however, if we take Equation 2 as the appropriate formulation, then we need a theoretical account of why the relation holds and by what mechanisms it is realized. Even if we maintain that the cognitive system has evolved that way for one reason or another we still want to know what cognitive mechanisms are responsible for that behavior. There have traditionally been two approaches to providing such an account.

1. The first is to say that a subject makes Equation 2 come out (perhaps voluntarily, though often unconsciously) because he or she has tacit knowledge of Equation 1. In other words, regardless of the form of his or her representation, the subject knows that Equation 1 holds in the world and therefore makes it be the case (using some form of symbolic analysis, the exact nature of which need not concern us here) that the amount of time spent imagining the scanning will conform to this relation. We shall discuss this possibility in greater detail in the Tacit Knowledge and Mental Scanning section below.

2. The second way is to say that Equation 2 is the case because of properties of the representational medium. This is just to say that the observed function has that form as a consequence of the intrinsic lawful relations that hold among the particular physical properties that in fact represent distance and mean speed in the brain. For example, if distance were represented by the electrical potential between two points separated by a certain electrical capacitance, and mean speed were represented by current flow, then (within limits) the time taken would have the form given by Equation 2. This corresponds to what I would call the *analog* view.

It should be appreciated that Alternatives 1 and 2 represent two fundamentally different ways of explaining the underlying process responsible for the observed behavioral regularities. Alternative 1 appeals to symbolically encoded facts about the world and to rules for transforming representations and drawing inferences. It is a "cognitivist" approach such as advocated by Fodor (1975, 1980), Chomsky (1980), Newell and Simon (1976), and others. On the other hand, Alternative 2 represents what I would call the analog approach to mental representation and mental processing. The term *analog* has been used to refer to a wide range of characteristics of models and representations covering everything from the mathematical continuity of representations to the simple requirement that the representation go through intermediate states representing the intermediate states that the actual system being represented would go through (e.g., Shepard,1975). All of these capture something of what we intuitively mean by analogue. In my view, however, the only aspect of analogs that is relevant to the imagery debate (i.e., that differentiates among the major competing views) is the one raised by the distinction between Alternatives 1 and 2,—that is, an analog process (represented by Alternative 2) is one whose behavior must be characterized in terms of intrinsic lawful relations among properties of a particular physical instantiation of a process, rather than in terms of rules and representations (or algorithms). Whenever people appeal to an "analog representational medium" (e.g., Attneave, 1974) or to a "surface display" (e.g., Kosslyn, et al., 1979), they take it for granted that this medium incorporates a whole system of lawfully connected properties or intrinsic constraints (some of which have mathematical properties isomorphic to Equation 1 above) and that it is precisely this set of properties and relations that determines how objects represented in that medium will behave. Such people specifically contrast these accounts with ones like our Alternative 1, which claims that how the representation will behave is a function of what the person knows about the actual behavior of the things represented, rather than of properties of the medium in which it is represented.

Although there are various conceptions of what analog processing is (as I suggested above), I suspect that the other senses are actually derivative from the sense I am adopting. Thus, for instance, any process can be made to go through an appropriate sequence of intermediate states, and even to do so in very small (quasi-continuous) steps—even a purely verbal process. Yet we would not want to count such a model as analogue if the mechanism were not naturally constrained to go through such a sequence. Thus we would count the process as analogue if its going through particular intermediate states were a necessary consequence of intrinsic properties of the mechanism or medium, rather than simply being a stipulated restriction that we arbitrarily imposed on a mechanism that could carry out the task in a quite different way. Palmer (1978) has taken a similar position with regard to the distinction between analogical and nonanalogical processes. From this, however, Palmer draws the unwarranted conclusion that only biological evidence will distinguish between the two forms of processing. But, as I have argued at some length (Pylyshyn, 1979b, 1980b), if we contrast analog mechanisms with ones that operate on representations or tacit knowledge, the distinction can be seen to be a functional one that can be empirically decided by behavioral criteria. An example of one such criterion is discussed below. Other criteria are discussed in Pylyshyn (1979b, 1980b).

The Appeal to Tacit Knowledge

The distinction between analog processes and rule-governed or cognitive processes (also referred to as computational or informational processes) is one that, in its most general form, needs to be drawn with some care, since after all, both are physically realized in the brain, although in quite different ways. The issue reduces to the question of when different forms of explanation of the behavior are appropriate. I have attempted to develop the general argument at length elsewhere (Pylyshyn, 1980a, 1980b). For the present purposes, however, a brief sketch of that discussion will do, since the only cases relevant to the imagery debate are unproblematic.

The operation of some processes can be explained perfectly well by giving an account of how various of their physical properties are causally connected, so that, for instance, altering some physical parameter here (e.g., by turning a knob) leads to specifiable changes in another parameter there because of some law connecting these two properties. Such a physical causal account will not do, however, to explain connections that are independent of the particular physical form the input takes yet that follow a single general principle that depends only on the semantic content of what might be called the input *message.* Thus, for example, if being told over the telephone that there is a fire in the building, seeing the word *fire* flash on a screen, hearing what you take to be a fire alarm, smelling smoke in the ventilator duct, seeing flames in the hallway, and so on without limit, all lead to the same building-evacuation behavior, the relevant generalization cannot be captured by a purely causal input-output story, since each such stimulus would involve a distinct causal chain and the set of such chains need have no physical laws in common. In that case, the generalization can only be stated by postulating internal belief and goal states (e.g., the belief that the building is on fire and knowledge about what one ought to do in such circumstances, as well as other tacit knowledge and the capacity to make inferences). Such processes are explainable only in terms of the mediation of rules and representations (since it is clear, for example, that neither a behavioral principle such as "Make sure you don't get too close to a fire" nor a logical principle such as modus ponens expresses a physical law and that they hold regardless of what kind of physical substance they are instantiated in).

A corollary of this explainability claim is that if a certain behavior pattern (or input-output function) can be altered in a way that is rationally connected with the meaning of certain inputs (i.e., what they refer to, as opposed to their physical properties alone), then the explanation of that function must appeal to operations upon symbolic representations such as beliefs and goals: It must, in other words, contain rule-governed cognitive or computational processes. A function that is alterable in this particular way is said to be *cognitively penetrable.* The criterion of cognitive penetrability (among other considerations) will be used in later discussions as a way of deciding whether particular empirically observed functions ought to be explained by Alternative 1 or by Alternative 2 above. Specifically, I shall maintain that if the form of certain image transformation functions reported in the literature can be altered in a particular sort of rationally explicable manner by changing what the subject believes the stimulus to be or by changing the subject's interpretation of the task (keeping all other conditions the same), then the explanation of the function must involve such constructs as beliefs, goals, or tacit knowledge, rather than the intrinsic properties of some medium—that is, some part of the explanation must take the form of Alternative 1.

The essence of the penetrability condition is this: Suppose subjects exhibit some behavior characterized by a function, f_1 (say, some relation between reaction time and distance or angle or perceived size of an imagined object), when they believe one thing, and some different function, f_2, when they believe another. Suppose further that which particular f they exhibit bears some logical or rational relation to the content of their belief: For example, they might believe that what they are imagining is very heavy and cannot accelerate rapidly under some particular applied force, and the observed f might then reflect slow movement of that object on their image. Such a logically coherent relation between the form of f and their belief (which we refer to as the "cognitive penetrability of f") must be explained somehow. Our claim is that to account for this sort of penetrability of the process, the explanation of f itself will have to contain processes that are rule governed or computational, such as processes of logical inference, and that make reference to semantically interpreted entities (i.e., symbols). The explanation cannot simply say that there are some causal (biological) laws which result in the observed function f (i.e., it cannot cite an analog process), for exactly the same reason that an explanation of this kind would not be satisfactory in the building-evacuation example above: because the regularity in question depends on the semantic content (in this case of beliefs) and on logical relations that hold among these contents. Although in each particular case some physical process does cause the behavior, the general explanatory principle goes beyond the set of all observed cases (i.e., there may be token reduction but no type reduction of such principles to physical principles (see Fodor, 1975). A process that is sensitive to the logical content of beliefs must itself contain at least some inferential (or other content-dependent) rule-governed process. It should be emphasized that cognitive penetrability refers not merely to any influence of cognitive factors on behavior but to a specific kind of semantically explicable (e.g., rational or logically coherent) relationship. The examples we shall encounter in connection with discussions of imagery will be clear cases of this sort of influence (for more on this particular point, see Pylyshyn, 1980a). It should also be noted that being cognitively penetrable does not prevent a process from having analogue components: It simply says that it should not be explained *solely* in terms of analogues with no reference to tacit knowledge, inference, or computational processes.

The concept of tacit knowledge—as a generalization and extension of the everyday notion of knowledge (much as the physicists' concept of energy is an extension of the everyday notion)—is one of the most powerful ideas to emerge from contemporary cognitive science (cf. Fodor, 1968), although much remains to be worked out regarding the details of its form and function. It is already clear, however, that tacit knowledge cannot be freely accessed or updated by every cognitive process within the organism, nor can it enter freely into any logically valid inference. For example, much of it is not introspectable or verbally articulable (relevant examples of the latter would include our tacit knowledge of grammatical or logical rules, or even of most social conventions). A great deal needs to be learned about the control structures of the cognitive system that constrains our access to tacit knowledge in various elaborate ways. The existence of such constraints is no doubt what makes it possible for people to hold contradictory beliefs or to have beliefs that are only effective within certain relatively narrow classes of tasks. For example, it might well be that many people only have access to their tacit knowledge of physics when they are acting upon the world (e.g., playing baseball) or perhaps when they are engaged in something we call *visualizing* some physical process, but not when they have to reason verbally or answer certain kinds of questions in the abstract. Nonetheless, in all of these cases it would clearly be inappropriate to view such visualizing as being controlled by a medium or "surface display" that caused the laws of physics to hold in the image. A better way to view the cause of the regularities in the movement of objects in the visualized scene is in terms of subjects' tacit knowledge about the physical world and in terms of the inferences that they make from this knowledge. I shall consider other such examples in the next section when I argue that the appearance of autonomous un-folding of imagery sequences may be very misleading.

Incidentally, when one constructs a computer model using some-thing called a matrix data structure rather than something called an analogue representational medium, one is not thereby relieved of the need to make a distinction between Alternatives 1 and 2. Because the existence of a computer model often carries the im-plication that there can no longer be any ambiguity or terminolog-ical confusions, it is worth examining one such model briefly.

In describing the Kosslyn and Shwartz (1977) computer model, Kosslyn et al. (1979) appear ready to admit that much of the model's explanatory and predictive capacity derives from what they refer to as the "cathode ray tube proto-model." In this proto-model there is no problem in seeing how a principled account of the scanning results can be derived. The CRT is a real physical de-vice to which properties such as distance apply literally, and thus our earlier explanation of the observed scanning function applies in virtue of the applicability of Equation 1. But as we have already noted, such an explanation is a principled one only when it refers to a physical system whose intrinsic lawful behavior is described by Equation 1. Thus the explanatory power of the CRT proto-model only transfers to the human cognition case if there is some-thing in the brain to which Equation 1 also applies. On the other hand, the version of the model that uses the matrix data structure, in which there is no actual physical CRT, lends itself equally to either one of the following two interpretations. In the first interpretation, the part of the model that contains the two-dimensional image (i.e., the 2-D matrix and its relevant access operations) is considered as merely a simulation of the physical screen, in which case the model really does assume the existence of a spatially laid out pattern in the brain. In the second interpretation, the matrix and the set of relevant accessing operations is viewed as a specific proposal for how the function F required by Equation 2 might be realized. In the latter case, however, when we give a theoretical interpretation of the claims associated with that part of the model, we still have a choice of the two basic views I have been calling Alternatives 1 and 2, exactly as we did when we were examining the informal account of the scanning results (e.g., does the adjacency relation in the matrix represent subjects' knowledge that the elements referred to are next to one another, or is it an intrinsic constraint of that particular format?).

Appealing to a matrix in explaining certain imagery results is only useful if matrices constrain the representations or operations on representations in specified ways. If they do constrain the form of representations, then they function essentially as a simulation of an underyling analog representational medium. (It might be noted in passing that if we were to take the matrix structure seriously, we would be stuck with the unavoidable conclusion that mentally represented space is necessarily nonisotropic. This is a formal consequence of the fact that a matrix is a tesselation of cells of some fixed shape and hence has certain essential nonisotropic properties. For example, if the cells are assumed to be square, then regardless of how fine we make them, scanning diagonally will be faster by a factor of the square root of two than scanning vertically or horizontally. Such an entailment cannot easily be glossed over, except by viewing the matrix as merely a metaphor for some unspecified spatial characteristics.)

The distinction between analogue and what I have sometimes referred to as propositional, but is perhaps better thought of as simply symbolic, is fundamental to a wide range of issues in the foundations of cognitive science (see Pylyshyn, 1980b). In the specific case of models of mental scanning, the distinction is important because Alternative 1 allows for the possibility that the results of mental scanning experiments may represent a discovery about what subjects believe and what they take the goal of the experiments to be, rather than a discovery about what the underlying mechanisms of image processing are. A consequence of the former alternative is that if subjects perceived the task differently or had different tacit beliefs about how the objects in question would move or about properties of space, then the experimental results could be quite different. On the other hand, if Alternative 2 were correct, then manipulation of such things as the form of the task and the instructions should not have a corresponding, rationally explainable effect (provided, of course, that imagery was still being used). Otherwise we would have to say that the medium changes its properties to correspond to what subjects believe about the world, in which case appealing to the existence of an analog medium would serve no function.

Before turning to a discussion of some specific theoretical proposals, let me summarize the picture I have presented. Figure 1 illustrates the structure of alternatives available in explaining a variety of imagery findings. We can, first, choose a literal spatially extended brain-projection model. Although there is no a priori reason for excluding this alternative, it does raise some special problems if we try to explain the full range of imagery phenomena this way, and as far as I can tell, no one since Wertheimer has taken it seriously (though some, for instance Arbib, 1972, have come close). In any case the literal approach can be viewed as a special case of the analog approach I shall be discussing in detail later. Continuing down our tree of alternatives, if we take the functional, as opposed to the literal or structural, approach, our task becomes to explain how this function could be realized by some possible mechanism (e.g., how Equation 2 could be realized in the case of mental scanning). Here we come to what I take to be the fundamental bifurcation between the two camps in the imagery debate, between those who advocate the analogue (or intrinsic property of a medium) view and those who advocate the symbolic or tacit knowledge view. Much confusion arises in this debate because there is considerable equivocation regarding exactly what the referents of ambiguous phrases such as *spatial representation* or *preserves metric spatial information* are intended to be from the point of view of this tree of alternatives. However, once the problem has been formulated so as to factor away the misleading implications associated with the use of a physical vocabulary, or a vocabulary that is appropriate for describing the represented domain as opposed to the psychological processes or mechanisms (see the next section), we are left with a basic empirical question: Which aspects of an organism's function are attributable to intrinsic (analog) processes, and which are attributable to transactions on a knowledge base? It is to this empirical question that I now turn.

The Autonomy of the Imagery Process

It seems to me that the single most intriguing property of imagery, and the property that appears, at least on first impression, to distinguish it from other forms of deliberate rational thought, is that it has a certain intrinsic autonomy—both in terms of requiring that certain properties of stimuli (e.g., shape, size) must always be represented in an image and with respect to the way in which dynamic imagery unfolds over time. Consider the second of these. The literature contains many anecdotes suggesting that in order to imagine a certain property, we first have to imagine something else (e.g., to imagine the color of someone's hair, we must first imagine the person's head or face; to imagine a certain room, we must first imagine entering it from a certain door; to imagine a figure in a certain orientation, we must first imagine it in a standard orientation and then imagine it rotating; to have a clear image of a tiny object, we must first imagine "zooming in" on it, and so on). Sometimes imagery even seems to resist our voluntary control. For example, in conducting a study of mental rotation of images, I instructed subjects to imagine moving around a figure, pictured as painted on the floor of a room. A number of subjects reported considerable difficulty in one of the conditions because

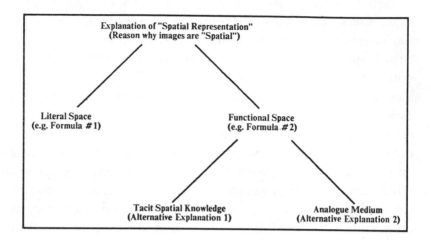

Figure 1. Theoretical positions on the nature of spatial representations.

the path of the imaginal movement was impeded by a wall visible in the photograph. They reported that they could not make themselves imagine moving around the figure because they kept bumping into the wall! Such responsiveness of the imagination to involuntary processes and unconscious control is one of the main reasons why imagery is associated with the creative process: It appears to have access to tacit knowledge and beliefs through other than deliberate intellectual routes.

Other examples involving imaginal movement may be even more compelling in this respect. Imagine dropping an object and watching it fall to the ground or throwing a ball and watching it bounce off a wall. Does it not naturally obey physical laws? Imagine rotating the letter C counterclockwise through 90°. Does it not suddenly appear to have the shape of a U without your having to deduce this? Imagine a square with a dot inside it. Now imagine the width of the square elongating until it becomes a wide rectangle. Is the dot not still inside the figure? Imagine the letters A through E written on a piece of paper in front of you. Can you not simply see by inspection that the letter D is to the right of the letter *B*? In none of these examples is there any awareness of what Haugeland (1978) calls "reasoning the problem through." The answer appears so directly and immediately available to inspection that it seems absurd to suggest, for example, that knowledge of topological properties of figures is relevant to the elongating square example or that tacit knowledge of the formal properties of the relation "to the right of" (that it is irreflexive, antisymmetric, transitive, connected, acyclic, etc.) is involved in the array of letters example. Such considerations have suggested to people that various intrinsic properties of imaginal representations are fixed by the underlying medium and that we exploit these fixed functional capacities when we reason imagistically. I believe that this intuition is the primary motivation for the widespread interest in analog processes.

Now in general these are not implausible views. One should, however, be cautious in what one assumes to be an intrinsic function that is *instantiated* by the underlying biological structure, as opposed to one that is *computed* from tacit knowledge by the application of rules to symbolically represented beliefs, goals, and so on. In the previous section (as well as in Pylyshyn, 1980b) I have attempted to provide some necessary (though not sufficient) conditions for a function's being instantiated in this sense. The condition that I have found to be particularly useful in clarifying this distinction, especially in the case of deciding how to interpret observations such as those sketched above, is the one I called the *cognitive impenetrability criterion*. Recall that a function was said to be cognitively impenetrable if it could not be altered in a way that exhibits a coherent relation to the meaning of its inputs. For example, although a function might still count as being cognitively impenetrable if it varied with such things as practice or arousal level or ingestion of drugs, it would not be viewed as cognitively impenetrable if it changed in rationally explainable ways as a function of such things as whether a subject believes that the visually presented stimulus depicts a heavy object (and hence visualizes it as moving very slowly) or whether the subject views it as consisting of one or two figures, or as depicting an old woman or a young lady (in the well-known illusion), and as a consequence behaves in a way appropriate to that reading of the stimulus. I argued that cognitively penetrable phenomena such as the latter would have to be explained in terms of a cognitive rule-governed process, acting upon semantically interpreted representations and involving such activity as logical inferences, problem solving, guessing, associative recall, and so on, rather than in terms of the sort of natural laws that explain the behavior of analog process.

Now many functions that appear at first to be biologically instantiated, and therefore alterable only in certain highly constrained law-governed respects, could turn out on closer inspection to be arbitrarily alterable in logically coherent way by changes in subject's beliefs and goals (i.e., they could turn out to be cognitively penetrable) and therefore to require a cognitive process account (based on appeal to tacit knowledge and rules). The tremendous flexibility of human cognition, especially in respect to the more central processes involved in thinking and common-sense reasoning, may very well not admit of many highly constrained (nonprogrammable) functions. It may illuminate the nature of the appeals to tacit knowledge if we consider some additional everyday examples. For instance, imagine holding in your two hands, and then simultaneously dropping, a large and a small object or two identically shaped objects of different weights. Which object in your image hits the ground first? Imagine turning a large heavy flywheel by hand. Now imagine applying the same torque to a small aluminum pulley. Which one completes one revolution in your image first? Imagine a transparent yellow filter and a transparent blue filter side by side. Now imagine slowly superimposing the two filters. What color do you see in your image through the superimposed filters? Form a clear and stable image of your favorite familiar scene. Can you now imagine it as a photographic negative, or as being out of focus, or in mirror image inversion, or upside down? Imagine a transparent plastic bag containing a colored fluid, being held open with four parallel rods at right angles to the mouth of the bag, and in

to view phen
as providing
medium (or,
surface displa
are more resi
that we coulc
ing through
shapes in difi
one of them
orientations?

I believe th
a natural inte
through is pi
(1978), whicl
in terms of pi
of the repres
tion itself (i.
however, leac
processes op(
value. This ii
terms of proj
of the struc
pressing a pr
main begs th
mechanism l
domain excep
resentation ii
must be stat(
representatio
in the theory

Consider t
Kosslyn et a
of operation
to be explan:
images are tr
intermediate

such a way that the cross section of the bag is a square. Now imagine the four rods being moved apart so that, with the plastic bag still tight around them, the rods now give the bag a rectangular cross section. As you imagine this happening, does the fluid in the bag rise, fall, or stay at the same level (in other words, how does volume vary with changes of cross-sectional shape, perimeter remaining constant)? Imagine a glass half full of sugar and another nearly full of water. Imagine the sugar being poured into the glass with water in it. Examine your image to see the extent to which the resulting height of water rises (if at all).

These examples, it seems to me, are not in principle different from the ones in the first list I presented. For many people these imaginings also unfold naturally and effortlessly, without any need to reason through what would happen. Yet it seems clearer in these cases that whatever happens as the sequence unfolds under one's "mind's eye" is a function of what principles one believes govern the events in question. In fact, most people tend to get several of these examples wrong. Clearly the laws of dynamics or optics and the principles of geometry that determine the relation, say, between the perimeter and the area of a figure are not intrinsic (built in) to the representational media or to the functional mechanisms of the mind. Not only must one have tacit knowledge of them, but the way in which the imaginal events unfold naturally can usually be influenced with considerable freedom simply by informing the subject of the appropriate principle. Thus what seems to be a natural and autonomous unfolding process is cognitively penetrable—that is, it is under the control of an intellectual process, with all that this implies concerning the intervention of inferences and "reasoning through." As Harman (1973) has argued, our intuitions concerning when there are or are not inferences taking place must give way before the logical necessity to posit such processes. The mind, it seems, is faster than even the mind's eye.

Another particularly intriguing demonstration, by Ian Howard, shows that even in the case of a simple task involving the recognition of physically possible events, knowledge of physical

principl
such kn
why im;
Howard
graduate
photogr;
surface
angles r
presentai
photogra
who fail
horizont;
surface
thus sho
What wa:
mental i
revealed
test (i.e.,
failed to
ulate the
who mad
principle.
areas suc
obtainabl
evidence
that tacit
for exam
phenomei

Once ex
that tacit
prising. I
formation
and henc
imaginal
guishable
of their p

of distortion will be proportional to the size of the transformational step" (p. 542). Shepard (1975) also cites such principles in discussing his image tranformation results.

In each case these principles only make sense if terms such as *size* or *small steps* refer to the *represented* domain. In other words, the intended interpretation of the first of the above principles would have to be something like the following: Representations are transformed in such a way that successive representations correspond to small differences in the scene being depicted. However, what we need is a statement that refers only to the structure of the representation and its accessing process. We need to be able to say something like, "Representations are transformed in small structural steps or degrees," where *small* is relative to a metric defined over the formal structure of the representation and process. For example, relative to a binary representation of numbers and a machine with a bit-shifting operation, the formal (or syntactic) transformation from a representation of the number 137 to a representation of the number 274 is smaller than the transformation from a representation of 137 to a representation of 140 (since the former requires only one shift operation), even though it clearly corresponds to a larger (semantic) transformation in the represented domain of abstract numbers. It is thus important to distinguish between the intrinsic syntactic domain and the extrinsic semantic domain when speaking (typically ambiguously) about transformations of representations. Not only are the two domains logically distinct, but, as we have seen, they involve two quite different similarity metrics and their behavior is governed by quite different principles.

Cognitive principles such as those invoked by Kosslyn et al. (1979), Shepard (1975), and Anderson (1978) would only be theoretically substantive (i.e., explanatory) if they specified (a) how it was possible to have formal operations that had the desired semantic generalization as their consequence—that is, how one could arrange a formal representation and operations upon it so that small steps in the formal representations corresponded to small steps in the represented domain—and (b) why these particular operations, rather than some other ones that could also accomplish the task, should be used (this is the issue of making the underlying theory principled, or restricting its degrees of freedom by reducing the number of free parameters in it). Simply asserting that representations do, as a matter of fact, have this property (because, for example, they are said to "depict" rather than merely "represent"; cf. Kosslyn et al., 1979) is not enough. One reason that it is not enough is that such a property is simply stipulated in order to conform to the data at hand: It is a free empirical parameter. Another reason is that, as with our earlier cases, there are two distinct options available to account for how this can happen. They correspond to our options 1 and 2: We can appeal either to tacit knowledge or to intrinsic properties of a representational medium. In other words, we can make the account principled by relating the process either to the rationality of the method adopted, given the organism's goals and tacit knowledge, or to the causal relations that hold among physical properties of the representational medium.

Before examining in greater detail the proposal that many imagery phenomena, including specifically those dealing with mental scanning, should be explained in terms of tacit knowledge, we need to touch on two additional points, since they frequently muddy the discussion. For this reason we shall make a brief digression.

Constraints of Habit and the Executive Retreat

The first point is that we must distinguish here, as we do in other areas of theory evaluation, between what typically or frequently or habitually happens and what *must* happen because of some lawful regularity. Insofar as the origin of visual imagery no doubt lies in visual experience, and insofar as we frequently see things happen in certain ways, this could easily influence the way in which we typically imagine certain kinds of events. For example, since our visual experiences are primarily with common, middle-sized objects, certain typical speeds of acceleration, deceleration, and trajectory shapes are much more common than others.

If this sort of experience did influence our tendency to most frequently imagine movements in certain ways, it would clearly not be something attributable to the nature of the mechanism or to properties of the representational medium.

Examples of habitual modes of processing determined by the nature of our experience rather than by our fixed functional capacities are frequent in many areas of cognition. For example, when we learn to read, the teacher monitors our performance auditorily. Consequently, we first learn to read out loud and later to suppress the actual sound. As a result, many of us continue to read by converting written text into a phonetic form prior to further analysis. But there is good reason to believe that this stage of processing is not a necessary one (e.g., Forster, 1976). In fact, there is a plausible view that this habitual mode of processing is responsible for the slow reading speed that some of us suffer from and that we can be trained to abandon.

Although knowing the habitual modes of processing is useful if one is interested in describing the typical, or in accounting for variance, or in developing practical tools (say for education), providing an explanation of behavior requires that we understand the nature of the underlying mechanism (or medium). This, in turn, requires that we empirically establish how imaginal processing is constrained, or which of its functions are independent of particular beliefs or goals (i.e., we must discover the cognitively impenetrable properties of imaginal processing). Thus it becomes important to ask which particular characteristics (if any) the use of imagery forces on us, rather than to report the strategies that tend to go along with the use of imagery. For example, rather than asking whether, in using imagery, subjects *typically* take more time to locate (or otherwise focus their attention on) objects represented as more distant or to report the presence of features in an image that they describe as smaller, we should ask whether subjects *must* do so, whenever the image mode of representation is being used. A variety of experimental findings—e.g., Kosslyn et al. (1979); Bannon (unpublished); Spoehr and Williams (unpublished)—have demonstrated that, left to their own devices, people habitually solve certain kinds of problems (typically ones involving metrical or geometrical properties) by visualizing some physically possible event taking place (e.g., they imagine themselves witnessing the stimulus changing in certain characteristic ways). Yet no one, to my knowledge, has tried to set up an experimental situation in which subjects were discouraged from carrying out the task by this habitual means to determine whether they were constrained to do so by some cognitive mechanism or medium. Later in this paper I shall report several studies carried out with this goal in mind.

The second point that needs clearing up concerns the grain of truth in Anderson's (1978) claim that the form of representation cannot be determined unequivocally by appeal to behavioral data alone. Anderson's argument is that for any model using some particular form of representation, one can always conjure up another behaviorally indistinguishable model that uses a different form of representation simply by making compensatory changes in the accessing process. As I tried to show (Pylyshyn, 1979b), this cannot be done in general without considerable loss in explanatory power. One of the considerations that led Anderson to the indeterminism view is the apparent unresolvability of the so-called imaginal versus propositional representation debate. No sooner does one side produce what they take to be a damaging result than the other side finds a way to compensate for this by adjusting the process that accesses the representation while leaving fixed the assumed properties of the representation itself. In my view, the lesson to be learned from this observation is simply that in adjudicating such a debate, as in determining the correct interpretation of any empirical phenomenon, one should not appeal solely to data (for even adding neurophysiological and any other class of data does not solve the problem, since no finite amount of data alone can ever uniquely determine a theory), but one should also consider the explanatory power of the model—that is, how well it captures important generalizations, how constrained it is (i.e., how many free parameters it has), how general it is, and so on. Anderson's views on this criterion notwithstanding, the issue is not fraught with vagueness and subjectivity. Although it clearly is not simple to apply in practice, the notion of explanatory power is crucial to the conduct of scientific inquiry, inasmuch as we need to distinguish between such predictive devices as curve fitting or statistical extrapolations and genuine cases of law-like explanatory principles. I shall have more to say about the issue of predictive versus explanatory adequacy in the concluding section.

These remarks are intended as an introduction to the most common rejoinder made to arguments (such as those based on the informal examples considered above, as well as experimental observations of cognitive penetrability) that we should attribute the properties and behavior of images to tacit knowledge rather than to intrinsic properties of an imaginal medium. This rejoinder consists of the counterproposal that we retain the analogue medium but simply modify the processes that generate, transform, and interpret the representation and thus enable the analogical model to account for such findings. For example, my objections to certain particular analog models of image processing, which are based on demonstrations that certain imaginal processes are cognitively penetrable, can often be sidestepped by merely adding an additional layer of executive process that varies the generation and transformation of images in response to cognitive factors. Sometimes this sort of executive overlay can be made to produce the desired behavior in an imagery model, but rarely can this be done without adding various ad hoc contrivances and consequently losing explanatory power.

Consider, for the sake of a concrete example, the case of the phenomenon called "mental rotation." I claimed (Pylyshyn, 1979a) that the operation of mentally rotating a whole image is not one of the functions that is instantiated by the knowledge-independent functional capacities of the brain and hence should not be explained by appealing to properties of some analog medium. My conclusion in this case was based on the empirical finding that the slope of the relationship between the relative orientations of two figures and the time it takes to carry out certain comparisons between them (such as deciding whether they are identical)—which is generally taken as the behavioral measure of rate of mental rotation—depends on various cognitive factors such as figural complexity and the difficulty of the actual postrotation comparison task. In these studies the difficulty of the comparison task was varied by requiring subjects to decide whether one figure was embedded in the other and then varying the "goodness" or gestalt value of the embedding (see Pylyshyn, 1979a, for details). One counterargument to my conclusion suggested by Kosslyn et al. (1979)—and one, incidentally, that I considered in my original paper—is that these findings are compatible with a holistic analogue view because an executive process might have determined, on the basis of some property of the stimulus or probe figure, what rate of rotation to use and set this as the value of a parameter to the rotation function. A number of responses might be made to this suggestion.

First, although nothing in principle prevents one from making rotation rate a parameter of the analog, such a proposal weakens the explanatory power of the model considerably, for any behavioral property, not just rate of rotation, could be made a parameter (including, for example, the form of the function relating reaction time to orientation). The more such parameters there are, the more the model becomes an exercise in curve fitting. Because these parameters are not constrained a priori, each contributes to the degrees of freedom available for fitting the observed data and hence detracts from the explanatory power of the model. This is another way of saying that unless we have some independent means of theoretically assigning a rotation rate to each stimulus, such a parametric feature of the model will be completely ad hoc. Thus there is considerable incentive to try to account for the comparison times in some principled way, either on the basis of some intrinsic property of the representational medium or else in terms of some aggregate characteristic of the cognitive process itself (such as, for example, the number of basic operations carried out in each condition).

It is this very consideration that leads me to agree with Kosslyn et al. (1979) when, in discussing the relative merits of the analogue

view of mental rotation—as opposed to the alternative propositional account proposed by Anderson (1978), in which a parameter
describing the orientation of a figure is incrimentally recom-
puted—they state, "Thus the question now becomes: Is incremental
transformation an equally motivated assumption in both theories,
or is it integral to one and added on as an afterthought in the
other?" (p. 545). From this point of view, the analog proposal
is clearly less ad hoc, since it posits a universal constraint that is
associated with the medium itself (not with that phenomenon
alone) and that is therefore not a free empirical parameter. However, it should be noted that this account is only principled when
it refers to the intrinsic analogue medium model of rotation, not
to the symbol-structure (or matrix) view I discussed earlier. In the
latter case the principles (e.g., rotation proceeds by application of
transformations that correspond to small distances) appeal to properties of the represented domain, rather than to intrinsic properties of the representation, precisely as does Anderson's ad hoc
incrimental parameter adjustment proposal. In both cases no principle based on some independently determined property of the
representation or of the structure of the process is given for why
this should be so. On the other hand, the trouble with the principled analog view is that it appears to be false as it stands, as
I argued in Pylyshyn (1979a).

Despite the fact that there is strong incentive to account for observed properties, such as rotation rate, in the principled ways suggested above, it could still turn out that the best we can do at the
present time is to appeal to something like a rotation rate parameter.
In fact, as I have argued (Pylyshyn, 1980b), there will necessarily be
some primitive functions that are themselves not explainable in
terms of symbol manipulation processes. These constitute what I
called the "functional architecture" of the mind. There is no a
priori reason why a one-argument version of the operator ROTATE
(speed) cannot be such a process. In such a model, the speed parameter would be viewed as being adjusted by some physical means (e.g.,
a digital-to-analog converter) on the basis of a cognitive analysis of
the stimulus and the subject's beliefs and goals. The question of

whether this is the correct story is ultimately an impirical one, just as was the original question of whether ROTATE is an instantiated analogue function (i.e., an intrinsic property of the medium, or what I have called Alternative 2). What has to be done in that case is to expose this new proposal to empirical tests such as those that asses cognitive penetrability. Of course, as I pointed out, each such retreat from the original holistic analogue hypothesis brings us closer to Alternative 1 (the tacit knowledge explanation), as more of the determinants of the phenomena are put into the class of logical analyses and inferences.

Finally it should be pointed out that the particular proposal for parametrizing rotation rate does not, in any case, apply to the experimental results I reported. In these studies the slope of the reaction time versus angle curve was shown to be a function not merely of properties of the stimulus figure or the comparison figure but of the difficulty of the comparison task itself (i.e., the task of deciding whether the probe was an embedded subfigure of the stimulus). The holistic analog model assumes that the comparison phase can only be carried out after the stimulus figure has been rotated into the appropriate (independently determined) orientation (indeed, that is the very phase of the process that is responsible for the linear relation between angle and time). In fact Kosslyn et al. (1979) appear to implicitly accept this particular order of events when they propose the alternative that "people may choose in advance slower rates for 'worse' probes" (p. 546). The trouble with this alternative, however, is that we found rotation rate to be not only a function of the nature of the stimulus and of the probe but also of the relation between them, specifically of how well the probe fits as an embedded part of the stimulus. Since this particular feature of the comparison phase cannot be known in advance of rotation, it could not possibly be used as a basis for setting a rate parameter.

Now I have no doubt that one could come up with some kind of executive process that utilized a holistic analogue and yet exhibited different rates of apparent rotation for the different conditions, as observed. However the fact that one could design such an executive would itself be of little interest. It would require some strong independent motivation for going to such lengths in order to retain the analog rotation components. As I suggested earlier, the main attraction of the analog model is that it is both principled (i.e., it posits a universal property of mind) and constrained. It is constrained because it permits only one way to transform an image of a figure in one orientation into an image of a figure in another orientation, in contrast with the unlimited number of ways in which an arbitrary symbol structure can in principle be transformed. This constraint would have constituted a powerful explanatory principle. But now as we locate more and more of the explanatory burden in the executive process, there remains less and less reason to retain the ROTATE analogue operation, although, as I stated above, we will always need to posit some knowledge-independent functional properties or capacities (i.e., *analogue* in my sense).

Having thus outlined two general methodological considerations that need to be kept in mind when interpreting empirical findings bearing on the contrast between the intrinsic property of the medium view and the tacit knowledge view, I am ready to consider the specific case of the mental scanning phenomena in some detail.

Tacit Knowledge and Mental Scanning

In examining what takes place in studies such as those discussed by Kosslyn et al. (1979), it is critical to note the difference between the following two tasks:

1a. Solve a particular problem by using a certain prescribed form of representation, or a certain medium or mechanism.

1b. Attempt to recreate as accurately as possible the sequence of perceptual events that would occur if you were actually observing a certain real event happening.

The reason this difference is critical is that quite different criteria of success apply in these two cases. For example, solving a problem by using a certain representational format does not entail that various incidental properties of a known situation even be considered, let alone simulated. On the other hand, this is precisely what is required of someone solving Task 1b. In this case failure to duplicate such conditions as the speed with which an event occurs would constitute a failure to carry out that task correctly. Take the case of imagining. The task of imagining that something is the case, or of considering an imagined situation in order to answer questions about it, does not entail (as part of the specification of the task itself) that it take any particular length of time. On the other hand, the task of imagining that an event is actually happening before your very eyes does entail, for a successful realization of this task, that you consider as many as possible of the characteristics of the event, even if they are irrelevant to the discrimination task itself, and that you attempt to place them into the correct time relationships.

For instance, in discussing how he imaged his music, Mozart claimed (see Mozart's letter reproduced in Ghiselin, 1952), "Nor do I hear in my imagination, the parts *successively*, but I hear them, as it were, all at once" (p. 45). He felt that he could hear a whole symphony in his imagination all at once and apprehend its structure and beauty. Clearly he had in mind a task that is best described in terms of 1a. Even the word *hear*, taken in the sense of having an auditorylike imaginal experience, need not entail anything about the duration of that experience. We can be reasonably sure that Mozart did not intend the sense of *imagining* implied by 1b, simply because if what he claimed to be doing was imagining witnessing the real event of, say, sitting in the Odeon Conservatoire in Munich and hearing his Symphony Number 40 in G Minor being played with impeccable precision by the resident orchestra under the veteran Kapellmeister, and if he had been imagining that it was actually happening before him in real time and in complete detail—including the minutest flourishes of the horns and the trills of the flute and oboe, all in the correct temporal relations and durations—then he would have taken very close to 22 minutes for this task. If he had not taken that long to imagine it, this would only signify that he had not quite been doing what he had alleged, that is, he had not been imagining witnessing the actual real event in which every note was being played at its proper duration, or else we might conclude that what he had in fact been imagining was not a good performance of his symphony. In other words, if it takes n sec to witness a certain event, then an accurate mental simulation of the act of witnessing that same event should also take n sec, simply because how well the latter task is performed is by definition dependent on how accurately it mimics various properties of the former task. On the other hand, the same need not apply merely to the act of imagining that the event *has* a certain set of properties, that is, imagining a situation to be the case but without the added requirements as specified in the 1b version of the task. These are not empirical assertions about how people imagine and think: They are simply claims about the existence of two distinct natural interpretations of the specification of a certain task.

Applying this to the particular case of mental scanning, one must be careful to distinguish between the following two tasks that subjects might set themselves:

2a. Using mental image and focusing your attention on a certain object in that image, decide as quickly as possible whether a second named object is present elsewhere in that image.

2b. Imagine yourself in a certain real situation in which you are viewing a certain scene and are focusing directly on some particular object in that scene. Now imagine that you are looking for (or scanning toward, or glancing up at, or seeing a speck moving across the scene toward, etc.) a second named object in the scene. When you succeed in imagining yourself finding (and seeing) the object (or when you see the speck arrive at the object), press this button.

The relevant differences between Tasks 2a and 2b should be obvious. As in the previous examples, the criteria of successful completion of the task are different in the two cases. In particular, Task 2b includes, as part of its specification, such requirements as that subjects should attempt to imagine various intermediate states (corresponding to ones that they believe would be passed through in actually carrying out the corresponding real task) and that they spend more time visualizing those episodes that they believe (or infer) would take more time in the corresponding real task. The latter conditions are clearly not part of the specification of Task 2a, as there is nothing about Task 2a that requires that such incidental features of the visual task be considered in answering the question. In the words of Newell and Simon (1972), the two tasks have quite different "task demands."

To show that subjects are actually carrying out Task 2b in the various studies reported by Kosslyn (and therefore that the proper explanation of these findings should appeal to subjects' tacit knowledge of the depicted situation rather than to properties of their imaginal medium), I shall attempt to establish several independent points. First, it is independently plausible that the methods used in experiments reported in the literature should be inviting subjects to carry out Task 2b rather than Task 2a. Second, the arguments against experimental demand effects raised by Kosslyn et al. (1979) do not bear on the above proposal. Third, this alternative view has considerable generality and can account for a variety of imaginal phenomena. And fourth, there is independent experimental evidence showing that subjects can indeed be led to carry out Task 2a rather than Task 2b, and when they do, the increase in reaction time with increase in imagined distance disappears.

Task Demands of Scanning Experiments

With respect to the first point, all published studies that I am aware of in which larger image distances led to longer reaction times used instructions that quite explicitly required subjects to imagine witnessing the occurrence of a real physical event. In most scanning experiments subjects are asked to imagine a spot moving from one point to another, although in a few (e.g., in Kosslyn, 1973; Kosslyn, Ball, and Reiser, 1978, Experiment 4) they were asked to imagine shifting their attention or their glance from one imagined object to another in the same imagined scene. In each case, what subjects were required to imagine was a real physical event (since terms like *move* and *shift* refer to physical processes) about the duration of which they would clearly have some reasonable tacit knowledge. For example, they would know implicitly that it takes a moving object longer to move through a greater distance, that it takes longer to shift one's attention through greater distances (both tranversely and in depth), and so on. Although subjects may or may not be able to state these regularities, they plainly do have that tacit knowledge, as evidenced by the critical precision necessary to make realistic motion pictures by splicing pan and zoom sequences. (The exact time relationships needed to make such sequences appear realistic, especially in the case of splicing together takes of slower and more deliberate movements of actors and of points of view, seem to depend on one's prior interpretation of the actions. Hence the process involved in detecting poor film editing, like the process of imagining realistic scenarios, would seem to be knowledge dependent and therefore cognitively penetrable.)

The Arguments Against Demand Characteristics

Kosslyn et al. (1979) appear to recognize some of the force of the tacit knowledge position, but in responding to it they concern themselves only with the possibility that "experimental demand characteristics," or unintentional influences due to the experimental setting and subjects' expectations, might have been responsible for the outcome of the experiments. Although recent results by Richman, Mitchell, and Reznick (1979) and Mitchell and Richman (1980) inicate that phenomena such as those found in mental scanning experiments can be brought about by experimental demand factors, it has not yet been established that this is in fact the correct explanation for all such results. Kosslyn et al. have argued that it is unlikely that demand factors could explain all their results. On the other hand, neither have they provided any definitive control studies to rule out this alternative (the "pseudo-experiment" described by Kosslyn et al. is inadequate in this respect, inasmuch as simply asking subjects what they expect is the best way to invite acquiescence effects, as opposed to genuine expectations or other types of demand biases).

However, whether the case for experimental demand effects

will stand up to empirical tests or whether the Kosslyn et al. counterarguments are correct is not relevant to the present proposal. There is a major difference between the contaminating effects of experimental demands, or subjects' expectations of the outcome or their desire to please, and the entirely legitimate task demands, or requirements placed on the solution process by the specifications of the task itself. In the latter case what is at issue is not a contamination of results but simply a case of subjects solving the task as they interpret it (or as they choose to interpret it, for one reason or another) by bringing to bear everything that they know about a class of physical events, which they take to be the ones that they are to imagine witnessing. If they take the task to be the one characterized in Task 2b, then they will naturally attempt to reproduce a temporal sequence of representations corresponding to the sequence they believe would arise from actually viewing the event of scanning across a scene (or seeing a spot move across the scene). Thus, beginning with the representation corresponding to "imagining seeing the initial point of focus," the process would continue until a representation was arrived at which corresponded to "imagining seeing the named point." Of course, according to this way of viewing what is going on, there is no need to assume that the process halts as a *result* of a certain imagined state's being reached, or when a certain visual predicate is satisfied. It could just as plausibly stop when some independent psychophysical mechanism had generated a time interval corresponding to an estimate of expected duration (we know such mechanisms exist, since subjects can generate time intervals corresponding to known magnitides with even greater reliability than they can estimate them; cf. Fraisse, 1963). In other words, it could just as easily be independently estimated time intervals that drive the imagined state changes.

For the purpose of this account of the scanning results, we need assume little or nothing about intrinsic constraints on the process or even about the content of the sequence of representations that are generated. Such a sequence could, for example, simply consist of a sequence of beliefs such as that the spot is *now here* and *now* it is *there*—where the locative demonstratives are pointers into the symbolic representation being constructed and updated. Though the sequence is almost certainly more complex than this, there is no need to assume that it is constrained by any special property of the representational medium, as opposed to simply being governed by what subjects believe or infer about some likely intermediate stages of the event being imagined and about the relative times at which they would occur. Now such beliefs and inferences could obviously depend on anything that the subject might tacitly know or believe concerning what usually happens in the corresponding perceptual situations. Thus the sequence could in one case depend on tacit knowledge of the dynamics of physical objects, in another on tacit knowledge of some aspects of eye movements or of what happens when one has to glance up or refocus on a more distant object, or even on tacit knowledge of how long it takes to notice or to recognize certain kinds of visual patterns (e.g., it might even take subjects longer to imagine trying to see something in dim light or against a camouflage background for this reason). Thus none of the examples and contrary evidence that Kosslyn et al. (1979) cite against one or another of the alternative "experimental demand" explanations is to the point here, since the exact domain of knowledge being appealed to can vary from case to case, as is to be expected if imagining is viewed as a species of common-sense reasoning, as opposed to a process that has access to a special sort of representational medium with extraordinary functional properties (e.g., being characterized by Euclidean axioms).

Sometimes experiments involving superimposing images on actual visual stimuli have been cited against the demand characteristics view (e.g., Kosslyn et al., 1979). However, such experiments differ from studies of imaginal thinking in several important respects that make them largely irrelevant to the present discussion. When a subject is instructed to view a display and then to imagine a stationary or a moving pattern superimposed on it (as in the studies by Hays, 1973; Finke, 1979; Shulman, Remington, and McLean, 1979; and those mentioned in Shepard, 1978), there is no need to posit an internal medium of representation to explain the stable, *geometrical* relationships that hold among features of the resulting construction. The perceived background itself is all we need in this case. For example, when a subject thinks of an imaginary spot as being *here* and then *there* (as in the discussion above), the locative terms can in this case be bound to places in a perceptual construction that are under direct stimulus control and that are generally veridical with respect to relative spatial locations. This is essentially equivalent to binding the internal symbols to the actual places in the stimulus, which, being in the actual stimulus, will maintain their locations relative to one another regardless of subjects' beliefs about space or about what they are viewing (assuming only that perception is free from major time-varying distortions). In fact, Pylyshyn, Elcock, Marmor, and Sander (1978) have developed a model of how indexical binding of internal symbols to primitive perceptual features can be carried out within a limited-resource computational system and how such bindings can be used by the motor system to enable it to, say, point to the bound features.

Thus in such superposition cases if, for instance, the subject imagines a spot moving from perceived location A to perceived location B, then all that is required to ensure that the spot crosses some location C is (a) that the successive locations where the point is imagined to be actually correspond to a certain path on the stimulus (i.e., that the successive mental locatives in fact refer to a certain sequence of adjacent places on the stimulus) and (b) that place C actually be on that path, somewhere between A and B. In the pure imagery case, by contrast, the corresponding notions of *path, lying on*, and *between* are not available in the same literal sense (i.e., there are only representations of paths). In other words, subjects must not only imagine the spot to be moving with respect to an imagined background but they must have tacit knowledge of such things as that if C lies between A and B, then going from A to B requires passing through C. Another way to put this is to say that the geometrical properties of the layout that is being viewed (e.g., the relative locations of features in it) remain fixed because of the way the world being viewed is (in this case, rigid), and different geometrical characteristics of the layout can simply be "noticed" or "perceived" by the viewer, including the relative position of a place being attended to (i.e., a place that is bound to an internal locative indexical symbol). On the other hand, what remains fixed and what can be noticed in a purely constructed image depends either on intrinsic properties of some medium of representation or on subjects' tacit knowledge about the behavior of the sorts of things they are imagining and their ability to draw inferences from such knowledge—exactly the dichotomy we are examining. This issue is closely connected with the general problem of reasoning about actions, which in artificial intelligence research raises a technical problem called the "frame problem." The relevance of such issues to the imagery controversy is discussed in Pylyshyn (1978, 1980b).

The Generality of the Tacit Knowledge View

With respect to the generality of explanations based on appeal to tacit knowledge, one could point to a variety of findings that fall nicely within this explanatory framework. For instance, the list of illustrative examples presented in the last section shows clearly that in order to imagine the episode of seeing certain physical events, one needs to have access to tacit knowledge about physical regularities. In some of these cases one might even say that one needed an implicit theory, since a variety of related generalizations must be brought to bear in order to correctly predict what some imagined process would do (e.g., the sugar solution or the color filter case). In other cases simply the knowledge (or recollection) that certain things typically happen in certain ways and that they take certain relative amounts of time will suffice.

Several of Kosslyn's findings, allegedly revealing properties of the "mind's eye," might also be explainable on this basis—including the finding (Kosslyn, 1975) that it takes longer to report properties of objects when the objects are imagined as being small. Consider that the usual way to inspect an object is to take up a viewing position at some convenient distance from the object which depends on its size (and in certain cases on other things as well; e.g., consider imagining a deadly snake or a raging fire). So long as we have a reasonably good idea of the object's true size we would imagine viewing it at the appropriate distance. Now if someone instructed me to imagine some object as especially small, I might perhaps think of myself as being further away or as seeing it through, say, the wrong end of a telescope. In any case if I were then asked to do something, such as report some of its properties, and if the instructions were to imagine that I could *actually see* the property I was reporting (which was the case in the experiments reported), or even if I simply chose to make that my task for some obscure reason, I would naturally try to imagine the occurrence of some real sequence of events in which I went from seeing the object as small to seeing it as big enough so I could easily discern certain details (i.e., I would very likely take the instructions as meaning that I should carry out Task 1b). In that case I would probably imagine something that was in fact a plausible visual event, such as a zooming-in sequence (and indeed this is what many of Kosslyn's subjects reported). If that were the case then we would naturally expect the time relations to be as actually observed.

Although the above story may sound quite a bit like the one Kosslyn (1975) himself gives, there is one difference that is crucial from a theoretical standpoint. In this version of the account, no appeals need to be made to knowledge-independent functional properties of a medium, and especially to properties of a *geometrical* sort. The representational medium, although it no doubt has some relevant intrinsic properties that restrict how things can be represented, plays no role in accounting for any of the particular phenomena we have been examining. These phenomena are seen as arising from (a) subjects' tacit knowledge of how things typically happen in reality and (b) their ability to carry out such psychophysical tasks as to generate time intervals corresponding to inferred durations of certain possible physical events. This is not to deny the importance of different forms of representation, of the nature of such inferential capacities as alluded to above, or of the nature of the underlying mechanisms. It is simply to suggest that the particular findings we have been discussing do not necessarily tell us anything about such matters.

Although we intuitively feel that the visual image modality (or format, or medium) severely constrains both the form and the content of potential representations, it is no easy matter to say exactly what these constraints are (and the informal examples given earlier should cast at least some suspicions on the validity of such intuitions in general). It seems clear, for example, that we cannot image any arbitrary object whose properties we can describe, and this does give credence to the view that images are more constrained than descriptions. Although it is doubtlessly true that imagery is in some sense not as flexible as discursive symbol systems (such as language), it is crucial to know the nature of this constraint before we can say whether it is a constraint imposed by the medium or merely a habitual way of doing things or of interpreting the task demands, or whether it might even be a limitation attributable to the absence of certain knowledge or a failure to draw certain inferences. Once again I would argue that we cannot say a priori whether certain constraints implicated in the use of imagery ought to be attributed to the functional character of the biological medium of representation (the analogue view) or to the subject's possession and use (either voluntarily or habitually) of certain tacit knowledge.

Consider the following proposals made by Kosslyn et al. (1979) concerning the nature of the constraints on imagery. The authors clearly take such constraints to be given by the intrinsic nature of the representational medium. They suggest that something they call the "surface display" (a reference to their cathode ray tube protomodel) gives imagery certain fixed characteristics. For example, they state,

> We predict that this component will not allow cognitive penetration: that a person's knowledge, beliefs, intentions, and so on

will not alter the spatial structure that we believe the display has. Thus we predict that a person cannot at will make his surface display four-dimensional, or non-Euclidean.   [p. 549]

Now it does seem to be obviously true that one cannot image a four-dimensional or non-Euclidean space. Yet the very oddness of the supposition that we might be able to do so should make us suspicious as to the reason for this.

To see why little can be concluded from this fact, consider the following. Suppose a subject insisted that he or she could imagine a non-Euclidean space. Suppose further that mental scanning experiments were consistent with this claim (e.g., scan time conformed to, say, a city block metric). Would we believe that what the subject really did was to

> *simulate* such properties in imagery by filling in the surface display with patterns of a certain sort in the same way that projections of non-Euclidean surfaces can be depicted on two-dimensional Euclidean paper?   [Kosslyn et al., 1979, p. 547]

Of course we would conclude the latter. But the reason for doing so is exactly the reason we gave earlier for discounting one possible interpretation of what Mozart might have meant when he claimed to be able to imagine a whole symphony instantaneously. That reason, you will recall, had to do entirely with the implications of one particular sense of the phrase *imagine a symphony*— namely that the Task 2b sense demands that certain conditions be fulfilled. If we transpose this to the case of the spatial property of visual imagery, we can see that this is also the reason why the notion of imagining four-dimensional space in the sense of Task 2b is incoherent. The point is sufficiently central that it merits a brief elaboration.

Let us first distinguish, as I have been insisting we should, the sense of imagining (call it *imagine$_t$X*) that means to *think of X* or to consider the hypothetical situation that X is the case (or mentally construct a symbolic model or a mental description of a possible world in which X is the case) from the sense of imagining (call this one *to imagine$_s$ X*) that means to image that you are *seeing* X or to imagine yourself observing the actual event X happening. Then the reason for the inadmissibility of four-dimensional or non-Euclidean imaginal space becomes clear, as does its irrelevance to the question of what the properties of an imaginal medium are. The reason we cannot imagine$_s$ such spaces is that they are not the sorts of things that could be seen. Our inability to imagine$_s$ such things has nothing to do with intrinsic properties of a surface display, but with a lack of a certain sort of knowledge: We do not know what it would be like to see such a thing. We have no idea, for example, what kind of configuration of light and dark contours there would have to be, what sorts of visual features would need to appear, and so on. Presumably congenitally color-blind people cannot imagine$_s$ a colored scene for similar reasons. In this case it would hardly seem appropriate to attribute this failure to something's being wrong with their surface display. On the other hand, we do know, in nonvisual (i.e., nonoptical) terms, what a non-Euclidean space is like, and we can imagine$_t$ there being such a space in reality (certainly Einstein did) and thus solve problems about it. Perhaps, given sufficient familiarity with the facts of such spaces, we could even produce mental scanning results in conformity with non-Euclidean geometries. There have frequently been reports of people who claimed to have an intuitive grasp of four-dimensional space in the sense that they could do such things as mentally rotate a four-dimensional tesseract and imagine$_s$ its three-dimensional projection from a new four-dimensional orientation (for example, Hinton, 1906, has an interesting discussion of what is involved). If this were true, then they might be able to do a four-dimensional version of the Shepard mental rotation task.

Of course if we drop all this talk about the geometry of the display and consider the general point regarding the common conceptual constraints imposed on vision and imagery, there can be no argument: Something is responsible for the way we cognize the world. Whatever it is probably also explains both the way we see it and the way we image it. But that is as far as we can go. From this we can no more draw conclusions about the geometry, topology, or other structural property of a representational medium than we can draw conclusions about the structure of a language by considering the structure of things that can be described in that language. There is no reason to believe that the relation is anything but conventional—which is precisely what the formalist (or computational) version of functionalism claims (see Fodor, 1980).

Incidentally, the distinction between the two senses of imagine discussed above also clarifies why various empirical findings involving imagery might tend to occur together. For example, there is a brief report in the authors' response section of Kosslyn et al. (1979) of a study by Kosslyn, Jolicoeur, and Fliegel showing that when stimuli are sorted according to whether subjects tend to visualize them in reporting certain of their properties (i.e., whether subjects typically imagine$_s$ them in such tasks), then it is only those stimulus-property pairs that are classified as mental image evokers that yield the characteristic reaction time functions in mental scanning experiments. But that is hardly surprising, since anything that leads certain stimuli to be habitually processed in the imagine$_s$ mode will tend to exhibit all sorts of other characteristics associated with imagine$_s$ processing—including the scanning time results and such phenomena as the "visual angle of the mind's eye" or the relation between latency and imagined size of objects (see the summary in Kosslyn et al., 1979). Of course nobody knows which features of a stimulus or task tend to elicit the imagine$_s$ habit or why some stimuli should do so more than others, but that is not a problem that distinguishes the analogue from the tacit knowledge views.

Some Empirical Evidence

Finally I shall consider some provisional evidence suggesting that subjects can be induced to use their visual image to carry out a task such as 2a that does not entail imagining oneself seeing a natural sequence of events happening. Recall that the question was whether mental scanning effects (i.e., the linear relation between time and distance) should be viewed as evidence for an intrinsic property of a representational medium or as evidence for such things as what tacit knowledge (of geometry and dynamics) people have and what they take the task to be. If the former were the correct interpretation, then it must not merely be the case that people usually take more time for retrieving information about more distant objects in an imagined scene. That could arise, as we have already noted, merely from some habitual or preferred way of imagining or a preferred interpretation of the task demands. If the phenomenon is due to an intrinsic property of the imaginal medium, then it must be a necessary consequence of using this medium; that is, the linear (or at least monotonic) relation between time and represented distance must hold whenever information is being accessed through the medium of imagery.

As it happens, there exists a strong preference for interpreting tasks involving doing something imaginally as tasks of type 1b— that is, as requiring one to imagine$_s$ an actual physically realizable event happening over time. In most of the mental scanning cases, it is the event of moving one's attention from place to place or of witnessing something moving between two points. It could also involve imagining such episodes as drawing or extrapolating a line and watching its progression (which may be what was involved, for example, in Spoehr and Williams (unpublished). But the question remains: Must a subject imagine such a physically realizable event in order to access information from an image, or more precisely, in order to produce an answer which the subject claims is based on examining the image?

A number of studies have been carried out in our laboratory which suggest that conditions can be set up so that a subject uses an image to access information, yet does so without having to imagine the occurrence of some particular real life temporal event (i.e., the subject can be induced to imagine$_t$ rather than imagine$_s$). I will mention only two of these studies for purposes of illustration. The design of the experiments follows very closely that of experiments reported in Kosslyn, Ball, and Reiser (1978; see Bannon, unpublished, for more details). Subjects had to memorize a map containing approximately seven visually distinct places (e.g., a church, a castle, a beach) up to the criterion of being able to reproduce it with the relative location of places within 6 mm of the correct location. Then they were asked to image the map in front of them and to focus their attention on a particular named place, while keeping the rest of the map in view in their mind's eye. We then investigated various conditions in which they were given different instructions for what to do next, all of which (a) emphasized that the task was to be carried out exclusively by consulting their image and (b) required them to notice, on cue, a second named place on the map and to make some discriminatory response with respect to that place as quickly and as accurately as possible.

So far this description of the method is compatible with the Kosslyn et al. (1978) experiments. Indeed, when we instructed subjects to imagine a speck moving from the place of initial focus to the second named place, we obtained the same kind of strongly linear relation between distance and reaction time as did Kosslyn et al. When, however, the instructions specified merely that subjects should give the compass bearing of the second place—that is, to say whether the second place was N, NE, E, SE, and so forth of the first, there was no relation between distance and reaction time. (In this experiment subjects were first given practice in the use of the compass direction responses and were instructed to be as fast and accurate as possible within the resolution of the eight available catagories. In postexperiment interviews, subjects reported that they carried out the task by consulting their image, as they had been instructed.)

This result suggests that it is possible to arrange a situation in which subjects use their images to retrieve information and yet do not feel compelled to imagine the occurrence of an event that would be described as scanning their attention between the two points (i.e., to imagine$_s$). Although this result was suggestive, it lacked controls for a number of alternative explanations. In particular, since a subject must in any case know the bearing of a second place on the map before scanning to it (even in Kosslyn's experiments), one might wish to claim, for independent reasons, that in this experiment the relative bearing of pairs of points on the map was retrieved from a symbolic, as opposed to imaginal, representation, in spite of subjects' insistence that they did use their image in making their judgements. Although this tends to weaken the imagery story somewhat, since it allows a crucial spatial property to be represented off the display (and so raises the question, Why not represent other spatial properties this way?) and because it discounts subjects' reports of how they were carrying out the task in this case while accepting such reports in other comparable situations, it is nonetheless one possible avenue of retreat.

Consequently, a second instructional condition was investigated, aimed at making it more plausible that subjects had to consult their image in order to make the response, and to make it more compelling that they must have been focused on the second place and mentally seeing both the original and the second place at the time of the response. The only change in the instructions that was made for this purpose was to explicitly require subjects to focus on the second place after they heard its name (e.g., *church*) and, using it as the origin, give the orientation of the first place (the place initially focused on) relative to the second. Thus the instructions strongly emphasized the necessity of focusing on the second place and of actually seeing both places before making the orientation judgment. Subjects were not told how to get to the second place from the first, but only to keep the image before their "mind's eye" and to use this image to read off the correct answer. In addition, for reasons to be mentioned shortly, the identical experiment was run (using a different group of subjects) entirely in the visual modality, so instead of having to image the map, subjects could actually examine the map in front of them. Eight subjects were run in the image condition and eight in the vision one. Each subject was given 84 trials, thus providing four times for each of the 21 interpoint distances.

What we found was that in the visual condition, there was a significant correlation between response time (measured from the presentation of the name of the second place) and the distance between places, whereas no such relation held in the imaginal condition. In doing the analysis, distances were grouped into small, medium, and large, and a linear regression was carried out on the grouped data. In the visual condition there was a significant correlation between distance and reaction time ($r = .50$, $p < .05$). In the imaginal condition there was no significant correlation ($r = -.03$, ns). The mean reaction time in the visual condition was 2.60 sec and in the imaginal condition was 2.90 sec. Such results indicate quite clearly that even though the linear relation between distance and time (the scanning phenomenon) is a frequent concomitant of imaging a transition between seeing two places on an image, it is not a necessary consequence of using the visual imagery modality and consequently that it is not due to an intrinsic (hence knowledge- and goal-independent) functional property of the representational medium for visual images.

Yet perhaps not suprisingly, results such as these can be accommodated without too much trouble by the Kosslyn et al. model. That model has been conveniently provided with the option of "blinking" its way to a second location—or of regenerating a new image from symbolic information. In that case it would clearly be able to respond in fixed time, regardless of the distance between places. Several remarks can be made concerning this alternative.

First, the existence of both scan and blink transforms can be used simply to ensure that no empirical data could falsify the assumption of an intrinsic medium of representation. Whether or not this is the case depends on what, if any, additional constraints are placed on the use of these transforms. Kosslyn et al. (1979) do suggest that people will use whichever transform is most efficient. Thus they ought to scan through short distances but blink over longer ones. This, however, presupposes that they know in advance how far away they will have to move over the image—and hence that distance information is available for arbitrary pairs of places without consulting the image and without requiring scanning. Clearly this assumption is inconsistent with the original assumption regarding how spatial information is accessed from images. We shall return to this point briefly in the concluding section, when we consider where the predictive power of such imagery models comes from.

Second, if the correct explanation for our results is that subjects used the blink transformation and hence generated new images instead of using their initial ones to locate the second place (as they were instructed to do, and as they reported having done), then we should be able to see the effect of this in the overall response times. Since it took our subjects 1 or 2 sec to generate the initial image, it is very unlikely that they were regenerating a completely new image and making the required orientation judgment in the 2.9 sec it took for them to respond. Perhaps they were only regenerating the two critical places within the existing outline in their image. But even that seems implausible for the following reason. The average reaction time to make orientation judgments in the visual condition, where no image had to be generated, was only 300 msec shorter than the average time to make the judgment in the imagery condition. This indicates that if an image had to be regenerated in the imagery condition, as assumed by the blink transformation explanation, it would have taken less than 300 msec to regenerate such an image. Since, according to Kosslyn, Reiser, Farrah, and Fliegel (unpublished), it usually takes several seconds to generate even simple images—and never less than 1 sec even for images containing only one simple part—there is insufficient time to both regenerate parts of an image and make an orientation judgment in the total 2.9 sec it took subjects to respond. Hence subjects could not have been using a blink transformation to regenerate their image in that case.

These experiments demonstrate that, at least in the one situation investigated, images can be examined without the putative constraints of the surface display postulated by Kosslyn and others. It is also reasonable to expect that other systematic relations between reaction time and image properties may disappear when appropriate instructions are given that are designed to encourage subjects to interpret the task as in 1a instead of 1b. For example, if subjects could be induced to generate what they considered small but highly detailed and clear images, then the effect of image size on time to report the presence of features (e.g., Kosslyn, 1975) might disappear as well. There is even some evidence that this might be the case from one of Kosslyn's own studies. In one of the studies reported in Kosslyn et al. (Note 3), the time to retrieve information from images was found to be independent of this size of the image. From the description of this experiment, it seems that a critical difference between it and the earlier ones (Kosslyn, 1975), in which an effect of image size was found, is that in this case subjects had time to study the actual objects, with instructions to practice generating equally clear images of each of them, and were also tested with these same instructions (which I assume encouraged them to entertain equally detailed images at all sizes). Thus it seems that it is possible, when subjects are encouraged to have detailed information readily available, for subjects to put as fine a grain of detail as they wish into their imaginal constructions (though presumably the total amount of information in the image is still limited along some dimension, even if not the dimension of resolution). Unlike the case of real vision, however, such imaginal vision need not be limited by problems of grain or resolution or any other difficulty associated with making visual discriminations. Of course, as we have already noted, subjects can exhibit some of the behavioral characteristics associated with such limitations (e.g., taking longer to recall fine details), but that may very well be because they know what real vision is like and are simulating the relevant behavior as best they can, rather than because of the intrinsic nature of the imaginal medium.

Conclusions: What Is the Theoretical Claim?

It has often been said that imagery models, such as that of Kosslyn and Shwartz (1977) or Shepard (1975), contribute to scientific progress because they make correct predictions and because they motivate further research. Although I would not want to deny this claim, it is important to ask what it is about such imagery models that carries the predictive force. It is my view that there is only one empirical hypothesis responsible for the predictive success of the whole range of imagistic models and that nearly everything else about such models consists of free empirical parameters added ad hoc to accommodate particular experimental results. The one empirical hypothesis is just this: *When people imagine a scene or an event, what goes on in their minds is in many ways similar to what goes on when they observe the corresponding event actually happening.*

It is to the credit of both Shepard (1978) and Paivio (1977) that they recognize the central contribution of the perceptual metaphor. For example Shepard (1978) states,

> Most basically, what I am arguing for here is the notion that the internal process that represents the transformation of an external object, just as much as the internal process that represents the object itself, is in large part the same whether the transformation, or the object, is merely imagined or actually perceived.
>
> [p. 135]

Paivio (1977) has been even more direct in recognizing and approving of the metaphorical nature of this class of models when he asserts,

> The criteria for a psychological model should be what the mind can do, so why not begin with a psychological metaphor in which we try to extend our present knowledge about perception and behavior to the inner world of memory and thought. . . . The perceptual metaphor . . . holds the mirror up to nature and makes human competence itself the model of mind.   [p. 71]

One difficulty with metaphorical explanation in general is that by leaving open the question of what the similarities are between the primary and secondary objects of the metaphor, it remains flexible enough to encompass most eventualities. Of course this open-endedness is also what gives metaphors their heuristic and motivational value and is what provides the feeling of having captured a system of regularities. But in the case of the perceptual metaphor for imagery, this sort of capturing of regularities is, to a large extent, illusory, because it is parasitic upon our informal commonsense knowledge of psychology and our tacit knowledge of the natural world. For example, I have argued that the reason I imagine things happening more or less the way that they actually do happen in the world is not because my brain or my cognitive endowments are structured to somehow correspond to nature but simply because I know how things generally happen—because I have been told, or have induced, what some of the general principles are. In other words, I have a tacit physical theory which is good enough to predict most ordinary everyday natural events correctly most of the time. Now the claim that our imagery unfolds the same way as our perceptual process trades on this tacit knowledge in an even more insidious way, because it does so in the name of scientific explanation.

The story goes like this. The claim that imagery is (in some ways) like perception has predictive value because it enables us to predict that, say, it will take longer to mentally scan longer distances, to report the visual characteristics of smaller imagined objects, to rotate images through larger angles, to mentally compare more similar images, and so on. It does this because we know that these generalizations hold in the corresponding visual cases. But notice that the reason we can make such predictions is not that we have a corresponding theory of the visual cases. It is simply that our tacit commonsense knowledge is sufficiently accurate to provide us with the correct expectations in such cases. An accurate analogy would be to give, as a theory of Mary's behavior, the statement that Mary is a lot like Susan, whom we know very well. This would enable us to perhaps make very accurate predictions of Mary's behavior, but it would scarcely qualify as an adequate explanation of why she behaves as she does. Another parallel, even closer in spirit to the metaphorical explanation of imagery, would be if we gave as the explanation of why it takes longer to rotate a real object through a greater angle that this is the way we typically perceive it happen, or if we explained why it takes more time to visually compare two objects of similar size than two objects of very different sizes by saying that this is what happens in the mental comparison case. In both these cases we would be able to make the correct predictions as long as we were informally well enough acquainted with the second of each of these pairs of situations. Furthermore, in both cases there would be some nontrivial empirical claim involved. For instance, in these cases it would be the claim that perception is generally veridical or that what we see generally corresponds to what we know to be the case. Although these are real empirical claims, no one takes them to have the theoretical significance that is attributed to corresponding theories of imagery, even though both may in fact have the same underlying basis.

Of course some models of imagery appear to go beyond such mere metaphors. For example, Kosslyn and Shwartz (1977) actually have a computer model of imagery that accounts for a very wide range of experimental findings. However, as we suggested in referring to its use of the blink transformation, unless the model incorporated a greater number of principled constraints, it is much too easy for it to accommodate any finding. It can do this because the model is, in fact, just a simulation of some largely commonsense ideas about what happens when we image. That is why the principles it appeals to are invariably stated in terms of properties of the represented domain (e.g., a principle such as *images must be transformed through small angles* clearly refers to what is being represented, since images themselves do not actually have orientations, as opposed to representing them). Yet this is how we often explain things in informal, everyday terms. We say that we imagine things in a certain way, because that is the way they really are. As I have already remarked, a theory of the underlying process should account for how imagery can come to have this character, not use this very property as an explanatory principle.

Another consequence of the model's being a simulation of commonsense views is that anything that could be stated informally as a description of what happens in the mind's eye can easily and naturally be accommodated in the model. For example, in arguing against the expectation or demand explanation of their scanning results, Kosslyn et al. (1979) cite one subject who said that he or she thought objects close together would take longer to image because it would be harder to see them or tell them apart. This is exactly the sort of process that could very easily be accommodated by the model. All that has to be done is to make the grain of the surface display whatever size is required to produce this effect. There is nothing to prevent this sort of tuning of the model to fit each situation. Such properties therefore have the status of free parameters, and unfortunately there is no limit to how many such parameters may be implicit in the model. Similarly, in our experiment (in which subjects judged the compass bearing of one place relative to a second) we found a negative correlation for some of the subjects between reaction time and distance between focal points on the imagined map. The computer model would have little difficulty accommodating that result if it turned out to be a general finding. In fact it is hard to think of any result which could not be naturally accommodated—including, as Kosslyn et al. (1980) themselves suggest, the possibility of representing non-Euclidean space. What is crucial is not merely that such results could be accommodated, but that this could be done without violating any fundamental design criteria of the model and without threatening any basic principle of its operation—without, for example, violating any constraints imposed by the hypothesized surface display. What this amounts to is that the really crucial aspects of the model have the status of free parameters rather than structural constants.

Now to some extent Kosslyn appears to recognize this flexibility in his model. In the last section of Kosslyn et al. (1979), the authors insist that the model ought to be evaluated on the basis of its heuristic value. I agree with that proposal. The ad hoc quality characteristic of early stages of some scientific modeling may well be unavoidable. However we should make every effort to be realistic and rid ourselves of all the attending illusions. One of the illusions that goes with this way of thinking about imagery is that there is an essential core of the model that is not merely heuristic but is highly principled and highly constrained. That core is contained in the postulated properties of the surface display (or in the "cathode ray tube proto-model"). This immutable core involves the assumption that there is an internal display medium with intrinsic geometrical (or geometry-analogue) properties. For example, Pinker (1980) claims that the "array structure" captures a set of generalizations about images. But without knowing which properties of the array structure are doing the work, and whether such properties can be altered by changes in what the subject believes, this sort of capturing of generalizations may be no better than merely listing them. We need to know what it is about the intrinsic character of arrays that requires them to have the properties that Pinker suggests (e.g., "that they represent shape, size, and locations implicitly in an integral fashion, that they are bounded in size and grain, that they preserve interpoint distances" p. 148). If there is nothing apart from stipulation that requires arrays to have these properties, then each of these properties is precisely a free parameter.

For example, if the facts supported the conclusion that size, shape, and orientation were naturally factored apart in one's mental representation (as I believe they do), or that grain size is nonhomogeneous and varies as a function of what the subject believes the referent situation to be like (e.g., how brightly lit, how detailed in its design, how important different features are to the task at hand), does anybody believe for one moment that this would undermine the claim that an array structure was being used? Clearly all that it would require is some minor adjustment in the system (e.g., making resolution depend on additional features of the image, allowing the cognitive process to access an orientation parameter in memory and so on). But if that is the case, then it is apparent that claiming an array structure places no constraints on the sorts of phenomena that can be accommodated—that is, that properties of this structure are *free empirical parameters*. Thus, although one may have the impression that there is a highly constraining core assumption that is crucial to the predictive success of the model, the way this impression is maintained is simply by giving the rest of the system enough degrees of freedom to overcome any effort to empirically reject that core assumption. So, whereas the intuitive appeal of the system continues to hang on the unsupported view that properties of imagery are determined by the intrinsic properties of an internal display medium, its predictive power may in fact come entirely from a single empirical hypothesis of imagery theory (viz., the perception metaphor).

The phenomenon of having the real appeal of a theoretical system come from a simplified (and strictly false) view of the system while its predictions come from more complex (and more ad hoc) aspects is commonplace in science. In fact, even the initial success of the Copernican world view might be attributable to such a characteristic. Copernicus published his epoch-making proposal, *de Revolutionibus*, in two volumes. The first volume showed how the solar-centered system could in principle elegantly handle certain aspects of stellar and planetary motions (involving reverse movements) without the necessity of such ad hoc devices as epicycles. In the second volume Copernicus worked out the details of his system for the more comprehensive case. That required reintroducing the ad hoc mechanisms of epicycles. In fact, Copernicus's system only did away with the five major Ptolomaic epicycles and retained all the complexity associated with the larger number of minor ones needed to make the theory fit the observations. Of course in time his system was vindicated because the discovery of the general principle of gavitation made it possible to subsume the otherwise ad hoc mechanisms under a universal law and hence to remove that degree of freedom from the theory.

The lesson for imagery is clear enough. In order for a theory of imagery to be principled it is necessary to locate the knowledge-independent functional properties correctly. We must be critical in laying a foundation of cognitively impenctrable functions to serve as the basic architecture of a formal model. The reason is not simply that in this way we can get to the most primitive level of explanation: It is rather that we can only get a principled and constrained (and therefore not ad hoc) model if we first fix those properties which arc the basic functional capacities of the system. This does not mean, of course, that we must look to biology to provide us with a solution (though we can use help from all quarters), because the fixed functional capacities can be inferred behaviorally and specified functionally, as they are when the architecture of computers is specified. But it does mean that unless we set ourselves the goal of establishing the correct functional architecture or medium in order to properly constrain our models in the first place, we could well find ourselves in the position of having as many free parameters as we have independent observations.

THE MEDIUM AND THE MESSAGE IN MENTAL IMAGERY

A Theory

8

Stephen M. Kosslyn

In the *Theaetetus* Plato likened memory representations to impressions on a wax tablet, perhaps thereby becoming the first theorist to distinguish between representations (the different possible impressions) and the medium in which they occur (the wax tablet). The distinction between a representation and a medium has proven important in the study of visual mental imagery. Although no serious researcher today maintains that images are actual pictures in the head, some still find it reasonable to posit quasi-pictorial representations that are supported by a medium that mimics a coordinate space. On this view, images are not languagelike "symbolic" representations but bear a nonarbitrary correspondence to the thing being represented. Partly because of the primitive origins of this idea, many people seem wary of it. But the idea that images are a special kind of representation that depicts information and occurs in a spatial medium is not patently ridiculous, and in fact can be developed in a very coherent way that violates neither philosophical nor empirical considerations. In this article I will sketch out one way this is being done and will show that none of the criticisms of this approach to understanding mental imagery, recent (especially see Pylyshyn, 1979a, 1980, 1981) or traditional (see Kosslyn and Pomerantz, 1977), are penetrating or incisive. Further, I will also show that none of the data that purportedly speak against this approach is in fact damaging. Finally, I will consider the relative merits of two kinds of accounts of imagery data: those based on processing of depictive images and those based on appeal to the influence of demand characteristics, task demands, and use of tacit knowledge.

Background Assumptions

Before one begins to theorize one should have a reasonably clear conception of both the domain of the theory and the form the theory should take. In addition, I have found it useful and important to distinguish between the theory proper and two sorts of models, specific and general.

THE DOMAIN OF THE THEORY

The goal of this article is to describe a theory of how information is represented in, and accessed from, visual mental images. For example, when asked to count the number of windows in their living room, most people report mentally picturing the walls, scanning over them, and "looking" for windows. The present theory is intended to provide accounts of this "mental picturing" process, of "looking" at images, and of transforming images in various ways. In addition, the theory also specifies when images will be used spontaneously in the retrieval of information from memory (as in the foregoing example).

THE FORM OF A COGNITIVE THEORY OF IMAGERY

A cognitive account of imagery is a theory about the *functional capacities* of the brain—the things it can do—that are invoked during imagery. There are numerous ways to describe the range and kinds of functional capacities involved in any given domain of processing, but most theorists have found it useful to describe these capacities in terms of structures and processes. Let us distinguish between two kinds of structures, *data structures* and *media,* and two general kinds of processes, *comparisons* and *transformations.*

Data structures. Data structures are the information-bearing representations in any processing system. They can be specified by reference to three properties, their *format, content,* and *organization.* The format is determined by (a) the nature of the "marks" used in the representation (such as ink, magnetic fluxes, or sound waves) and (b) the way these marks are interpreted (the mark *A* could be taken as a token of a letter of the alphabet or a picture of a particular pattern). The format specifies whether a representation is composed of primitive elements and relations and, if so, specifies their nature. The content is the information stored in a given data structure. Any given content can be represented using any number of formats. For example, the information in the previous sentence could be stored on a magnetic tape, on a page, as a series of dots and dashes etched on metal, and so on. The organization is the way elementary representations can be combined. The format of a representation constrains the possible organizations but does not determine them. For example, propositional representations can be ordered into various kinds of lists and networks.

Media. A medium does not carry information in its own right. Rather, a medium is a structure that supports particular kinds of data structures. This page, a TV screen, and even the air are media —supporting ink, glowing phosphor, and sound patterns, respectively. Media can be specified by reference to their *formatting* and *accessibility.* The formatting places restrictions on what sorts of data structures can be supported by a medium. A short-term store, for example, might have five "slots" that take "verbal chunks"— but not visual images or abstract propositions. The accessibility characteristics dictate how processes can access data structures within a medium. The slots of a short-term store, for example, might be accessible only in a given sequence.

Note that all of the properties of the media and the data structures are by necessity defined in the context of a particular processing system. Even though structures have an independent existence, and their nature imposes constraints on the kinds of processes that can be used (see Hayes-Roth, 1979; Keenan and

Moore, 1979; Pylyshyn, 1979c), structures attain their functional properties only vis-à-vis the operation of particular processes. For example, if items on a list can be retrieved only in one order on one day and another order on the next day, the functional order of the list has changed—even though the data structure has not.

Comparison processes. These procedures compare two data structures or parts thereof and return a match/mismatch decision or a measure of the degree of similarity (defined over a specific metric) between the representations.

Transformation processes. There are two very general classes of transformation processes, *alterations* and *productions*. Alteration transformations operate to alter a given data structure by changing its contents (e.g., by adding or deleting an item on a list) or reorganizing it (e.g., by reordering items on a list). Production transformations, in contrast, leave the initial data structure intact but use it as an impetus either to replace or to supplement it with a new data structure. This new data structure may differ from the initial one in its format (as when a pattern is described), in content (as when an initial image is replaced by one with more details), and/or in organization (as when a list is replaced by a new one with the same items but in a different order). It is difficult for me to conceive of how an alteration transformation can itself change the format of a data structure, and this may prove to be a critical distinction between the two classes (see chapter 5 of Kosslyn, 1980).

The reader should note that the actual expression of the theory may not preserve the individual functional capacities as distinct terms. It may turn out that a more perspicuous statement of the theory can be made mathematically by grouping various capacities together at more abstract levels. I make no commitment as to the form of such an ultimate abstract expression but only claim that it will express lawful relations among the kinds of cognitive entities described above. The job for empirical research programs at this time, as I see it, is to isolate and develop the clearest possible characterization of the individual functional capacities and their interrelations.

SPECIFIC MODELS AND GENERAL MODELS

One way to begin to formulate a cognitive theory is to develop a model of the presumed functional capacities. Models differ from theories in at least two ways. First, models have three sorts of components: those that are theory-relevant, those that are not theory-relevant (e.g., in the case of a computer model, those aspects that are a consequence of the particular hardware being used), and those that are theory-neutral (that cannot be assigned to either of the other two classes with certainty; see Hesse, 1963; Kosslyn, Pinker, Smith, and Shwartz, 1979). Second, models contain an element of "as if" that is not present in a theory proper. That is, a model is assumed to be under a description, or under a certain interpretation, that leads one to draw points of similarity between it and the modeled domain. A theory proper is unambiguous and not in need of such interpretation.

It is useful to distinguish two basic kinds of models, *specific* and *general.* Specific models are designed to account for performance in a particular task (see Clark & Chase, 1972; Sternberg, 1966, for examples), whereas general ones embody the entire set of principles (assumptions about functional capacities and their interrelations) that should account for performance in all the tasks in a given domain (Anderson & Bower, 1973, and Newell and Simon, 1972, were developing general models; in physics, Bohr's atom was a general model). One problem with attempting to develop isolated specific models for particular tasks is that it is difficult to be sure that any theoretical claims that emerge from developing them will be consistent with claims derived from other specific models. In a general model, since all the proposed functional capacities are available to be used in performing any task, one is forced to define precisely the input conditions and output characteristics of each process and is forced to be consistent across tasks. If the rules of combination are specified precisely enough (and these are implicit in the input and output specifications of each process; the output from one usually will serve as the input to another), then a given particular input configuration will evoke only one sequence of operations, providing a specific model of how a particular task is accomplished. Thus, I assume that although a given task logically could be accomplished in more than one way and in fact may be done differently on different occasions (such as when one is tired versus rested), on any given occasion the total input configuration and state of the system at the time will uniquely determine the way a task is performed.

The general model of image representation and processing we have developed takes the form of a computer simulation (see Kosslyn, 1980; Kosslyn and Shwartz, 1977, 1978). Each process is represented as a subroutine or set of subroutines, and each structure has been implemented as well (as described below). There are numerous virtues in building a general model of the sort we have been developing, but two stand out: First, if one tries to motivate the decisions necessary to model an entire domain in a consistent, precise way, one will be inspired to collect new and interesting data to select among plausible alternative ways of building the model. Second, the model allows one to formulate precise accounts for performance in numerous specific tasks, and these accounts are self-consistent. Thus one can test the theory as a whole by generating predictions about what should happen in particular tasks, as we in fact have done (see Kosslyn, 1980). On our view, then, the main reason to formulate a model for a particular task is to test the underlying assumptions of the theory that dictated that specific model. It is simply too easy to explain performance in any given task in isolation for this exercise to be very useful (as should be evident later in this article); it is only when one is trying to provide accounts for all the tasks in a domain that one seems to learn very much.

Overview of the Theory

The following review outlines the most central claims of the Kosslyn and Shwartz (1977, 1978; Kosslyn, 1980) theory of mental image representation and processing, which will be described in terms of the kinds of structures and processes discussed in the previous section. Properties of the general model embodying the theory will also be described occasionally to clarify the theoretical claims; unless otherwise noted, only the theory-relevant properties of our simulation will be mentioned (see Kosslyn, 1980, for a more detailed treatment). Although a few of the criticisms of this type of theory—and our particular theory per se—will be addressed in this section when relevant, a more thorough defense will be deferred until after the theory as a whole is sketched out.

STRUCTURES

On our view, images have two major components. The "surface representation" is a quasi-pictorial representation that occurs in a spatial medium: this representation depicts an object or scene and underlies the experience of imagery. The "deep representation" is the information in long-term memory that is used to generate a surface representation.

THE SURFACE REPRESENTATION

The properties of the surface image are in part a consequence of the properties of the medium in which it occurs, which we call the *visual buffer*. The visual buffer is implemented as an array in our computer simulation (the *surface matrix*); a surface image is represented by a configuration of points in this array that depicts an object or objects.*

1. The Medium

Formatting. (a) the visual buffer functions as if it were a coordinate space. This "space" is not an actual physical one but is rather a functional space defined by the way processes access the structure. The functional relations of the loci in the visual buffer

---

*The fact that the array used to simulate the visual buffer is square is a good example of a property of the model that was not intended to be theory relevant. We never have claimed that the visual buffer is a strict Cartesian space with anisotropic properties resulting from a rigid organization into rows and columns. It is an empirical question whether this incidental feature of the model should be taken seriously or not; it is not a priori obvious, at least to me, that the spatial medium must be isotropic.

need not be determined by actual physical relations any more than the functional relations of cells in an array in a computer need be determined by the physical relations among the parts of core memory. That is, the processes that operate on an image access the medium in such a way that local regions are separated from each other by different numbers of locations (i.e., differences in the number of just-noticeable differences in position in the coordinate space). We posit that the organization of the visual buffer is innately determined and fixed. Information is represented by selectively activating local regions of the space. (b) The visual buffer has a limited extent and specific shape, as measured empirically (see Finke and Kosslyn, 1980; Kosslyn, 1978), and hence can support only representations depicting a limited visual arc. This makes sense if this medium is also used in perceptual processing; if so, then it presumably only needed to evolve to represent input from the limited arc subtended by the eyes.

Accessibility. (a) The visual buffer has a grain, resulting in a limited resolution. Thus, portions of subjectively smaller images (i.e., those which seem to subtend a smaller angle) are more difficult to classify because subtle variations in contour are obscured (see Kosslyn, 1975, 1976a; an initial attempt at measuring the resolution of the medium is described in Pennington and Kosslyn). (b) The resolution is highest at the center of the visual buffer and decreases toward the periphery (see Finke and Kosslyn, 1980; Kosslyn, 1978). Importantly, although grain is not homogeneous throughout the medium, at any given location it is presumed to be fixed. (c) Representations within the visual buffer are transient and begin to decay as soon as they are activated. This property results in the medium's having a capacity defined by the speed with which parts can be generated and the speed with which they fade; if too many parts are imaged, the ones activated initially will no longer be available by the time the later ones have been imaged. This property was posited in order to explain my finding (Kosslyn, 1975) that images of objects in complex scenes were more degraded than images of objects in simple contexts.

2. The Data Structure

Format. The surface image *depicts* an object or scene. The primary characteristic of representations in this format is that every portion of the representation must correspond to a portion of the object such that the relative interportion distances on the object are preserved by the distances among the corresponding portions of the representation (cf. Shepard, 1975). Three implications of this characterization are that (a) size, shape, orientation, and location information are not independent in this format—in order to depict one, values on the other dimensions must be specified; (b) any part of a depictive representation is a representation of a part of the represented object; and (c) the symbols used in a depiction (such as points in an array) cannot be arbitrarily assigned their roles in the representation (i.e., a given point must represent a given portion of the object or scene once the mapping function from image to object is established; on our view this function is innately determined and fixed by the human visual system). None of these properties are shared by discursive propositional (or "symbolic") representations (see chapter 3 of Kosslyn, 1980, for a detailed development of these points).

Thus, surface images consist of regions of activation in the visual buffer that correspond to regions of depicted objects, with distances among the regions on an object (as seen from a particular point of view) being preserved by distances among the regions used to represent it in the medium. Importantly, *distance* in the medium can be defined without reference to actual physical distance but merely in terms of the number of locations intervening between any two locations.

It is important to note that when terms such as *distance* and *orientation* are used to refer to surface images, they are being used in a technical way, referring to functional relations among regions in the visual buffer. Increased distance, for example, will be represented by increased numbers of locations in the visual buffer. Thus, although there is no physical distance or orientation in a depictive representation in the visual buffer, the corresponding states can sensibly be interpreted by using these terms. Contrary to what Pylyshyn (1981) asserts, we have not committed an erroneous "slip of scope" by talking about properties of the image rather than properties of the imaged object. In perception one can talk about properties of the "optical array" (such as those noticed by painters who use perspective) and of the objects themselves; whereas the size of an object does not change with distance, its "size" in the optical array (angle subtended) does. Similarly, in imagery we can speak of properties of the image itself by reference to the position, location, area occluded, and so on in the visual buffer (the analogue spatial medium). In this case it makes no difference what the image is an image of; the "subjective size" is independent of the actual size of the object. And in point of fact, a number of processes—such as scanning (see Kosslyn, Ball, and Reiser, 1978)—depend on the subjective size, not on the actual size of objects.

Content. Images depict appearances of objects seen from a particular point of view (and hence are *viewer-centered*, to use the term of Marr and Nishihara, 1978). Images may represent the actual objects depicted, or images of objects may be used to represent other information (as occurs, for example, if one represents the relative intelligences of three people by imaging a line with three dots on it, a dot for each person; see Huttenlocher, 1968). Note that the content is determined not just by the image itself but also by how the interpretive processes "read" the image. We are specifying the way a system of representations and processes operates in which the properties of the components are to some degree mutually interdependent.

Organization. Individual images may be organized into a single composite representing a detailed rendition of a single object or a scene. Because parts of images are theorized to be generated sequentially, and parts begin to fade as soon as they are imaged, different parts of the image will be at different levels of activation. Level of activation ("fade phase") will dictate an organization of the surface image because points at the same level will be grouped together according to the Gestalt Law of Common Fate.

THE UNDERLYING DEEP REPRESENTATIONS

Our findings suggest that there are two types of representations in long-term memory that can be used to generate images, which we call *literal* and *propositional*. Literal information consists of encodings of how something looked, not what it looked like; an image can be generated merely by activating an underlying literal encoding. Propositional information describes an object, scene, or aspect thereof and can be used to juxtapose depictive representations in different spatial relations in the visual buffer.

THE LITERAL ENCODINGS

1. The medium

Formatting. The long-term memory medium does not function as if it were a coordinate space. Rather, it stores information in nonspatial units analogous to the files stored on a computer. In our computer simulation model, files store lists of coordinates specifying where points should be placed in the surface matrix to depict the represented object or objects (but we do not theorize that images are sets of dots or that underlying literal encodings are sets of coordinate pairs; these implementation details are not meant to be theory-relevant). The units are identified by name.

Accessibility. The units are accessed by name; the extent of the represented object along a given dimension can be computed without first generating a surface image; and the representation can be sampled a portion at a time. (These last two properties were posited in order to explain how parts of objects can be imaged at the appropriate size on a foundation part; for details see chapters 5 and 9, Kosslyn, 1980).

2. The data structure

Format. We have not as yet made any strong claims about the precise format of the underlying literal encodings.

Content. The underlying literal encodings have the same content as the surface images they can produce.

Organization. Every object is represented by a "skeletal encoding," which represents the global shape or central part. In addition to the skeletal encoding, objects may be represented by additional encodings of local regions or parts. (See chapters 4, 6, and 7 of Kosslyn, 1980, for data that bear on these claims.) Multiple encodings are linked by propositional relations that specify where a part belongs relative to another part or the skeleton. (This property seemed necessary to explain the flexibility with which images may be reorganized and combined in accordance with a new description; see chapters 4 and 6 of Kosslyn, 1980.)

THE PROPOSITIONAL ENCODINGS

1. The medium

Formatting. The medium is structured to contain ordered lists of propositions, and the lists are named.

Accessibility. Lists are accessed by name, and are searched serially, starting from the "top." (This assumption allowed us to explain the effects of association strength on property-verification times and led to some interesting predictions about image generation; see chapter 7, Kosslyn, 1980.)

2. The data structure

Format. The entries in these lists are in a propositional format. Propositions are abstract languagelike discursive representations, corresponding roughly to simple active declarative statements. Kosslyn (1980) presents a more detailed and formal treatment of propositional representation, but this general characterization is sufficient for present purposes.

Content. Lists contain information about (a) parts an object has (included in order to explain how detailed images can be generated and in order to model question-answering processes); (b) the location of a part on an object (necessary in order to integrate separate encodings into a single image); (c) the size category of a part or object (necessary in order to adjust the size scale so that a part or object will be optimally resolved); (d) an abstract description of a part or object's appearance (required for the interpretive processes to identify the pattern of points depicting a part or object); (e) the name of the object's supercordinate category (included for inference procedures used during question answering); and (f) the name of literal encodings of the appearance of the object (necessary in order to integrate multiple encodings into a single image).

Organization. Pointers in lists indicate which other list or lists to look up in sequence, resulting in lists' being organized hierarchically or in any graph structure.

PROCESSES

The imagery theory at present provides accounts for four classes of imagery processing: those involved in image generation, inspection, or transformation, and those that determine when imagery will be used spontaneously when people retrieve information from long-term memory. We have also begun to extend the theory to answer questions about how images are encoded as mnemonic devices and the role of imagery in reasoning. Space limitations preclude a detailed description of the processing components we posit or of how they are invoked when one is performing a specific task (see Kosslyn, 1980). In brief, the major processing components are as follows.

1. Image generation

Image generation occurs when a surface image (which is quasi-pictorial) is formed in the visual buffer on the basis of information stored in long-term memory. Image generation is accomplished by four processing components, which we call PICTURE, FIND, PUT, and IMAGE. The PICTURE process converts information encoded in an underlying literal encoding into a surface image (in the model, it prints points in the cells of the surface matrix specified by the coordinate pairs stored in the underlying literal file). The PICTURE process can map the underlying representation into the visual buffer at different sizes and locations, depending on the values of the size and location parameters given it. (This property was motivated by our finding that people can voluntarily form images of objects at different sizes and locations; see chapter 4 of Kosslyn, 1980.) The FIND process looks up a description of an object or part and searches the visual buffer for a spatial configuration that depicts that object or part. This process is used when multiple literal encodings are amalgamated to form a single image in the visual buffer; in this case the FIND process locates the "foundation part" where a new part should be added to previously imaged material. The PUT process performs a variety of functions necessary to image a part at the correct location on an image, including looking up the location relation in the list of propositions associated with an object and adjusting the size of the to-be-imaged part. The IMAGE process coordinates the other processing components and, in so doing, determines whether an image will be detailed (i.e., include parts stored in separate literal encodings) or undetailed (i.e., be constructed solely on the basis of the skeletal encoding). The IMAGE process is invoked by a command to form an image of a given object, either detailed or not, at some specified size and location (or at a default size and location). All of the processes used in image generation are production transformations except FIND, which is a comparison process.

2. Image inspection

Image inspection occurs when one is asked a question such as, "Which is higher off the ground, the tip of a racing horse's tail or its rear knees?" and one "looks at" an image of the horse with the "mind's eye." The process of "looking" is explained by reference to a number of distinct processing components, notably LOOKFOR (a production transformation). The LOOKFOR process retrieves the description of a sought part or object, looks up its size, employs the RESOLUTION process (a production transformation) to determine if the image is at the correct scale, adjusts the scale if need be by invoking the ZOOM or PAN process (alteration transformations), scans to the correct location, if necessary, by using the SCAN process (also an alteration transformation), and then employs FIND to search for the sought part. If the sought part is not found, the PUT process is used to elaborate the image further by generating images of parts that belong in the relevant region, and then FIND is used to inspect the image again. Note that because the FIND process is used in both image inspection and image generation, we should discover effects of the ease of executing this process in both kinds of tasks. And sure enough, less discriminable parts are not only more difficult to "see" during image inspection but are more difficult to locate as foundation parts (i.e., places where additional parts will be placed) during image construction (see chapters 4 and 6 in Kosslyn, 1980).

3. Image transformation

According to our theory there are two classes of transformations and two modes of performing these transformations.

Classes of transformations: Field-general and region-bounded. Field-general (FG) transformations alter the entire contents of the medium, of the visual buffer, without respect to what is actually represented. Region-bounded (RB) transformations first delineate a region in the visual buffer and then operate only within the confines of that region. Virtually every FG transform has an RB analogue. For example, "zooming in" is FG but "growth" is RB. According to our theory the number of objects manipulated should affect processing time only for RB transformations, because each object is manipulated separately here (but not in the FG case). Pinker and Kosslyn (1978) present some data that support this distinction (although this was not realized at the time the experiment was conducted; see Kosslyn et al., 1979).

Modes of transformation: Shifts and blinks. The bulk of the data on image transformations suggest that images are transformed incrementally, passing through intermediate points along a trajectory as the orientation, size, or location is altered (see chapter 8, Kosslyn, 1980). This property is a hallmark of *shift* transformations, which operate by translating the locations of individual portions of the data structure to new locations in the visual buffer (and it remains an empirical question how to define *portion*). Because the system is inherently noisy (as are all physical systems), if portions are moved too far, they become too scrambled to be realigned by "cleanup routines." Thus, the limits of the cleanup routines force the processor to translate points in a series of relatively small increments. This results in greater transformations requiring more operations and hence more time. Note that this account hinges on the amount of distortion increasing as points are translated greater "distances;" if this were not true then portions could be "moved" the entire "distance" in one increment. The idea of increases in distortion with larger step sizes makes sense if the transformation process makes use of an analogue adder and multiplier in which the bigger the value, the larger the range of error. Further, because scanning is treated as another form of image transformation (in which a SCAN process shifts the data structure through the visual buffer, so that different parts fall in the center of the medium and hence are most sharply in focus), the same principles apply to it as to other forms of image transformation (such as rotation). The ZOOM and PAN processes dilate and contract the image, respectively, and the ROTATE process alters the orientation of the image. All "sizes" and "orientations" are, of course, defined relative to the visual buffer. SCAN, ZOOM, and PAN are field-general and ROTATE is region-bounded.

We did not initially plan on positing a second mode of image transformation. However, we were stuck with the possibility of *blink* transformations, given our prior claims that surface images can be generated (from the underlying deep representations) at optional sizes and locations and that images fade over time. Given these assumptions, we were forced to assume that people can transform images by letting an initial image fade and then generating another image of the object at a new size or location (and hence the contents or organization of an image can be changed via a production transformation as well as via an alteration transformation). In this case the transformation is discontinuous; images do not pass through intermediate states of transformation. The reason shift transformations are the default, we claim, is that they generally are less effortful (i.e., fewer and less complex operations are required to manipulate an existing image than to generate a new one from the underlying representations). But in the case of shift transformations, effort increases with the extent of the transformation (because more iterations are required)—but not so with blink transformations. Thus, there will come a point when it is "cheaper" to abandon the initial image and generate a new one. We have in fact collected data supporting this claim (see chapter 8, Kosslyn, 1980).

But how do people know which mode of transformation will be more efficient before using one? In scanning, for example, it is possible that people can decide which transformation to use on the basis of an initial estimate of the distance to be scanned, which can be computed in any number of ways, for example by using the underlying propositional representations of location (which we needed to posit in order to explain how parts can be placed at the correct location on an image during the generation process). In addition to explaining data, the distinction between a shift and a blink transformation has led us to make a number of predictions, some of which are not intuitively obvious (see Kosslyn, 1980).

4. Spontaneous use of imagery in fact retrieval

Imagery is likely to be used in fact retrieval if the fact is about a visible property of an object a person has seen and it has not been considered frequently in the past. According to our theory, image encodings are accessed in parallel with propositional ones. Thus, the more overlearned the propositional information is (and hence the higher the entry on an object's propositional list, according to our theory), the more likely it is that a propositional encoding will be looked up or deduced before image processing is complete (i.e., before an image can be generated and inspected). Thus, imagery will often be used in retrieving information about objects learned "incidentally," as occurs when one retrieves from memory the number of windows in a room or considers the shape of a dog's ears. In addition, images—by the very nature of the format—make explicit information about relative shapes, relative positions of objects or parts thereof, and the appearances of objects and parts as seen from a particular point of view. Thus, when these sorts of information are required in order to make a judgment, imagery will often be used. However, because most objects are categorized, at least roughly, along these kinds of dimensions in a presumably propositional format (which may be well learned and hence likely to be accessed prior to image processing), imagery is most likely to be used when relatively subtle comparisons along these dimensions are required (and the to-be-compared objects fall in the same propositionally encoded category, preventing such category information from being used to make a judgment). For example, imagery should be used if one is asked to decide which is larger, a hamster or a mouse (both presumably are categorized as "small"), but should not be used in deciding which is larger, an elephant or a rabbit (which presumably fall in different categories). These principles are derived from results presented in Kosslyn, Murphy, Bemesderfer, and Feinstein (1977), Kosslyn and Jolicoeur (1980), and Kosslyn (1980, chapter 9).

CRITICISMS OF THE THEORY

Pylyshyn (1979a, 1980, 1981) offers numerous specific criticisms of our theory. These criticisms are of two sorts, purported deficiencies of our theory itself and the relative virtues of an alternative theory.

SPECIFIC CRITICISMS OF THE KOSSLYN AND SHWARTZ THEORY

The five most important criticisms of our theory are discussed below.

Ad Hoc Theories

Pylyshyn seems to subscribe to the view that if the properties of theoretical entities are not constrained a priori, they are equivalent to "free empirical parameters" that are merely stipulated ad hoc in order to explain data. The broad form of virtually any theory is guided by a wide range of considerations (e.g., shared mechanisms with perception, a clear mechanism for ontogenesis, and possible instantiation in the brain, in our case—see Kosslyn, 1980, chapters 5 and 10 and Kosslyn and Shwartz, 1978). But where are the specific claims of a theory supposed to come from, if not from an attempt to explain data in a perspicuous fashion? It is true that the data that provided the motivation to adopt a specific theoretical position are explained ad hoc by that part of the theory, but this does not mean that the theory is ad hoc: when new data are explained, and these new data are not similar to the old data that provided the initial motivation for formulating the theory, this explanation is clearly not ad hoc. Importantly, once we characterize a property we do not casually revise our theory simply to explain additional data.

Parameters and free parameters

Pylyshyn also decries the number of components specified by the theory, suggesting that we are in danger of having an unlimited number of free parameters. We must distinguish between number of parameters and number of free parameters. It simply is not true that we are in danger of having as many free parameters as we have components, as should be evident even in the brief description of the theory offered above. The parameters (properties of the theory) are not left vague enough to adjust whenever the whim comes over us. Properties of the medium, the data structures, and the processing components we posit place genuine constraints on the kinds of explanations we can formulate. For example, an important feature of the theory is our assumption that the medium does have a fixed grain (which we have begun to measure; see Pennington and Kosslyn) that places an upper bound on the degree of resolution with which one can image a given object. That is, one can image an object at less than optimal resolution—just as one can draw, paint, or represent an object on photographic film with less than optimal resolution—but one cannot image at greater resolution than the medium will allow. The degree to which the theory is in fact well specified should be apparent in the efforts necessary to provide detailed accounts for some of the data reviewed in Kosslyn (1980).

Pylyshyn especially decries the fact that we theorize that the generation and transformation processes are flexible. Pylyshyn may be bothered by two things: missing details of the theory and optional procedures (e.g., an image can be generated with or without details). With regard to the first worry, indeed, we have not presented a complete theory. Many properties of the theory are currently open. The alternative would be to simply make up properties on the basis of our intuitions, which strikes us as overly optimistic at best and a meaningless exercise in fantasy at worst. With regard to the second complaint, we do in fact posit that some of the process components are flexible and alter their operation depending on the input. We see no reason why this need not be true—even though it makes things less convenient for the theorist.

The source of predictive power

Pylyshyn has claimed that the predictive power of our theory is deceptive. One criticism is that our imagery theory is really just a restatement of common sense analogies to perception. First of all, it should be apparent even from the brief overview offered above that our theory is not based on a simple analogy to perception. Rather, we have tried to specify the nature of the mental structures and processes that are used in mental image representation and processing per se. Further, the predictions of the theory do not hinge on common sense knowledge of perception of the world. Predictions from the field-general/region-bounded distinction, between transformations that operate over the visual buffer as a whole (regardless of its contents) and ones that operate only within a bounded region, are not intuitive. Nor is the claim that parts are often inserted into an image only at the time of inspection, and hence the association strength between an object and part should affect times in the same way in image inspection and image generation. (This prediction rests on claims about when and how ordered lists of propositions are searched: see chapters 5 and 7, Kosslyn, 1980.) Nor are the predictions about when imagery should be spontaneously used when people answer questions (see Kosslyn and Jolicoeur, 1980), and so on.

Pylyshyn has denied that our theory has genuine explanatory or predictive power on other grounds. He claims—and suggests that we are ready to admit—that much of our model's explanatory and predictive capacity derives from our original cathode ray tube metaphor of imagery (which merely likened images to spatial displays on a CRT screen that could be classified as depicting instances of a category and were generated from more abstract underlying representations). This simply is not true. The explanatory and predictive power of the theory and general model are drawn from the explicit claims we have made about the nature of internal structures and processes, which are not simple reworkings of the minimal assumptions that underlay the initial metaphor. Scanning is a case in point: In the original CRT metaphor (see Kosslyn, 1975), scanning was considered as shifting the point of focus across the image, whereas in the current theory, scanning is considered as a kind of image transformation in which the data structure is shifted across the visual buffer, with different portions falling in the most highly resolved, center region. The current theory allows us to explain why scanning times increase linearly at the same rate when one scans across the visible portions of the image as when one scans to a part that initially had "overflowed" the medium (see chapters 5 and 8 of Kosslyn, 1980). In addition, the theory predicts similarities between scanning and other image transformations (e.g., size scaling) that would never have been predicted on the basis of the CRT metaphor; for example, consider the properties of "blink scans," to be discussed shortly. The second half of Kosslyn's (1980) book presents numerous examples of explanations and predictions that clearly rest on more than the minimal assumptions underlying the original CRT metaphor.

Cognitive penetration

Cognitive penetration occurs when one's knowledge, beliefs, goals, or other cognitive states alter performance in a "semantically systematic" way (see Pylyshyn, 1981), as occurs when one's knowledge of the laws of color mixing influences how colors appear in an image when they are mixed.* Cognitive penetration

---

*The actual technical definition of *cognitive penetration* is considerably more subtle than this one. The added subtlety is necessary for Pylyshyn to avoid classifying various noncognitive phenomena as cognitive by this criterion. For example, blood flow in the brain is affected by one's beliefs about stimuli one is viewing (because some stimuli can excite one, affecting heart rate and blood vessel dilation). But no one would want to classify blood flow as a cogis important insofar as it demonstrates that properties of structures or processes are not fixed. We have claimed that the properties of the visual buffer are innately determined and that they should not be subject to cognitive penetration. As outlined below, one cannot take the existence of cognitive penetration in imagery tasks as evidence that this claim is incorrect.

Tasks and components. It has long been acknowledged in cognitive psychology that performance of any given task involves numerous processing components. Not only are there distinct stages of processing, such as those used in encoding, in central processing of the encoded information, and in generation of responses, but each stage involves an interplay of structures and processes (see Anderson, 1978; Sternberg, 1969). Unlike the "additive factors" methodology developed by Sternberg (1969), which is designed to allow one to identify the effects of given variables with distinct processing stages, the cognitive penetrability criterion applies to tasks taken as a whole: Cognitive penetration demonstrates that the operation of at least one component of processing in a given task is systematically altered by the meaning of an input, but it does not serve to specify which component has been affected. If the effects of cognitive penetration are localized to processes that access a fixed analogue spatial medium, then the mere existence of cognitive pentration does not show that properties of this medium play no role in information processing—even if for some tasks one does not necessarily have to invoke these properties to provide one possible account for the data. Whether or not the properties of the medium constrain performance in any given task is an empirical question. At the present juncture it is important to note that the existence of nonanalogue components in a given set of processes in no way bears on the truth or falsity of the claim that one component is an analogue spatial medium which supports mental images that depict an object or scene.

---

nitive process. It is not clear to me, however, that even Pylyshyn's more complex and subtle technical definition of cognitive penetration necessarily excludes cases like this.

The necessary and the typical. All parties agree that a cognitive theory ought to specify the constraints imposed on processing by a particular structure recruited during processing. This is to be distinguished from the characteristics of processing in a habitual or typical way. However, in order to know what behavioral consequences *must* be incumbent on processing a given structure, one needs to know more than just the properties of the structure itself: One also needs to know the properties of the process. It is important to realize that representations in an analogue medium need not be operated on solely by analogue processes. For example, we theorize that the visual buffer is accessed both by analogue processes, such as those involved in performing shift transformations, and by nonanalogue processes, such as those involved in classifying a spatial pattern as a depiction of a particular object or part. Depending on which sort of process is accessing the medium, a given property of the medium may or may not be evident during task performance. For example, the distance between two images in the most resolved region of the visual buffer should affect the time to move them together but should not affect how vividly they appear when inspected. Thus, it is critical that we realize that the only way to discover the properties of any structure is to observe how numerous different processes operate on it and at the same time observe how these processes operate on different structures, trying to abstract out which characteristics of the behavior are a consequence of properties of the structure and which are a consequence of properties of the processes.

The necessity of prior knowledge. It seems clear that at least some imagery phenomena, such as imaging what color results when one mixes red and green, require a prior knowledge of the principles involved. However, Pylyshyn wants to maintain that most imagery phenomena depend on one's prior knowledge and offers an argument with the following structure: First, he presents two lists of imagery phenomena, ones that do not seem to exhibit the effects of cognitive penetration (i.e., the effects of prior knowledge altering the image to achieve the correct result) and ones that do. Next, he claims that there is no principled way of distinguishing between the two sets of phenomena. Therefore, we are to conclude that it is more plausible to assume that all are a consequence of nonanalogue processes. Consider the following two responses to this argument:

First, the lack of a ready principle does not mean there will not be one eventually. For example, most of the cases Pylyshyn cites that do not seem to require the influence of prior knowledge seem to depend on purely spatial properties of arrays containing relatively few units, whereas the others do not. The examples that cannot be characterized this way, namely, dropping an object and watching it fall and throwing a ball and watching it bounce, do not seem autonomous in the same way as do the other examples (e.g., a dot imaged in a square remains in the square while its sides are expanded). And in fact these two examples seem misclassified to me, both seeming to depend on one's knowledge of physical law as opposed to geometrical properties of the image representation per se.

Second, the plausibility argument can cut either way: At least some of the examples Pylyshyn cites do not seem to depend on prior knowledge (e.g., the dot in the expanding square), and are plausibly interpreted as revealing properties of an analogue spatial medium. Given that even one phenomenon leads one to posit an analogue spatial medium, it then makes sense to make use of the putative properties of this medium in providing straightforward accounts for other data. Whether or not these accounts are correct is, of course, an empirical question.

Cognitive penetration and mental rotation. Pylyshyn has offered the results of two experiments he reported earlier (Pylyshyn, 1979b) as evidence that the analogue account of mental rotation is wrong. We must be careful here because Pylyshyn is using the term *analogue* to include the entire operation: Encoding, rotation, and comparison processes are all considered part of a single analogue process. I am not certain who in fact subscribes to this position, but even if one were to maintain such a view, Pylyshyn's results are not a cause for concern. In these experiments subjects saw two stimuli simultaneously, one a geometric figure (containing internal lines dividing it into subpatterns) and the other possibly a part of the figure. The part was presented at different angular disparities from the orientation of the figure. The subject was asked to decide whether the part was a component of the figure, rotating the figure into congruence with the part if necessary. As is usual with this sort of experiment, decision times increased with the amount of rotation required to compare the stimuli. The main result of interest here, however, is the rate of increase in time with the amount of rotation: The amount of time required with greater amounts of rotation increased more sharply when the part was not a "good" (in the Gestalt sense) subpattern. That is, "bad" parts were apparently rotated at a slower rate. Pylyshyn argues that because subjects' knowledge of part goodness affected rotation, rotation is not an analogue process. Given that the goodness of a part was apparent only after it was located in a figure, it is not clear how any model could account for such clairvoyant behavior—which leads me to suspect that subjects did not simply rotate figures (at different rates) until part of the figure matched or did not match the probe part.

In fact, Pylyshyn's (1979b) results may not have anything to do with "goodness" per se: Because Pylyshyn used different patterns for his "good" and "bad" parts (instead of constructing sets of figures such that the same pattern could serve in both conditions), we cannot know whether this result is due to peculiarities of the individual patterns per se or to the relationship between the pattern and the figure in which it was embedded. But in any case, Pylyshyn's results may simply reflect task-specific strategies that have nothing to do with mental rotation as it occurs when stimuli are not presented simultaneously (as in the experiments reported by Cooper and Shepard, 1973) and hence are not available for successive visual comparisons. For example, they may reflect, as Pylyshyn himself notes, a "piecemeal rotate and compare" (p. 27) process. Perhaps the subjects did not encode the entire figure into a mental image but encoded only parts that they hoped would help in performing the task. If they guessed wrong, they fixated again on the figure and re-parsed it, encoding different parts into the image. In this case, when the test part corresponded to a "bad" part of the figure (one that violated natural parsing procedures), subjects would have to encode the figure many times and rotate it each time. Thus, the effects of angular disparity would be more pronounced for "bad" parts (and the difference in slopes would reflect the number of times the figure was re-parsed to find the "bad" part). If this account is correct, then this result says nothing about how entire figures are rotated or how the rotation procedure itself operates but merely speaks to specific strategies subjects adopt when performing this particular task.

Another possibility is that these results are due to a visual comparison process, where subjects never rotate a mental image—even of a part. On this account, the results simply indicate that the detection task becomes increasingly difficult for "bad" parts when the subpattern is rotated further. A third possibility is that even if subjects did encode the entire figure and then mentally rotated it into congruence with the part, the results may be due to the image's becoming increasingly degraded with more rotation because it has had more time to fade. If so, "good" parts may still be relatively easily detectable at amounts of degradation that make it difficult to detect "bad" parts (see my discussion of Reed's, 1974, findings in chapter 7 of Kosslyn, 1980), resulting in detection times for "bad" parts that increase more sharply with increasing amounts of rotation. In short, then, one can draw no general conclusions about mental rotation from Pylyshyn's results.

Pylyshyn claims that attempts to modify his "holistic analogue view" bring one closer to the nonanalogue position. The issue is, however, whether one can best explain the data without positing an analogue spatial medium. It simply is not clear why the contribution of this medium to the transformation stage is in any way detracted from by recognition that there are other stages used in performing any given task. There is nothing inherent in the position that the imagery representation system includes an analogue medium that even suggests that Pylyshyn's holistic analogue processing view (which includes many assumptions about process as well as structure) need be necessary or true.

The new data

On Pylyshyn's mistaken view of our theory, scanning should always occur when images are inspected, and hence he takes his failure to find scanning in one situation as a disconfirmation of the theory. However, in point of fact our theory leads us to expect scanning to be required only if a to-be-classified part of the imaged object is depicted so far toward the periphery that it is too blurred to be easily categorized (recall that acuity decreases toward the periphery of the visual buffer; see Finke and Kosslyn, 1980; Kosslyn, 1978). For example, if one is focused on the tail of an imaged German Shepherd dog one will not be able to "see" the ears sharply enough to categorize their shape (round or pointed?) without scanning. (But even here scanning will be required only if the initial image is in fact used in performing the task, as I will explain shortly.)

Not only do Pylyshyn's results fail to disconfirm the theory, but the theory does not even have to strain to explain them. In fact, the results can be explained in numerous ways (and further experimentation is required to distinguish among these possibilities): One ready account of Pylyshyn's finding that subjects could judge relative orientation of imaged objects without scanning among them rests on the fact that one can "see" more than a single location in an image at the same time. Image inspection is not like viewing an object through a small hole in a piece of cardboard that must be moved around to infer a general shape. Thus, subjects conceivably could have performed the Pylyshyn task without having to scan, if they did in fact use an image. The size of the image is critical here, however, but it is impossible to estimate it, given the available description of the materials and procedure used in the new experiments. (Note that even if the stimulus configuration subtended too large a visual angle, the subjects may have formed their images at a smaller size unless carefully instructed not to do so—cf. Kosslyn et al., 1978.)

Another counterexplanation of Pylyshyn's findings is as follows: In our theory we had to explain how people could scan from one location to another along a direct path. There were two basic options. First, we could have posited that people "see" the target position in the image and use this feedback to guide their scanning. Second, we could have posited that an abstract representation of position is encoded, allowing one to compute the direction to scan. The first alternative seems ruled out by our finding that people can scan a given distance to an overflowed part of an image as easily as to a visible part of an image (see Kosslyn, 1978; Kosslyn et al., 1978). Further, when explaining how people generate images, we found it necessary to include relative location as an implicit part of the description of a part of an object. Thus, in our model each location on a map would be associated with a rough location specification. Hence, one can in fact perform Pylyshyn's task without recourse to an image, and Pylyshyn's results may simply indicate that his subjects did not in fact use imagery in performing the task. One way to distinguish between this notion and the first account offered above is to ask subjects to "zoom in" on the initial focus location, so that the rest of the image seems to overflow (as was done in the third experiment reported in Kosslyn, et al., 1978). If the task is no more difficult here, it would seem that subjects were not consulting the initial image in the condition where the entire array was visible at once.

Pylyshyn is disturbed by this last counterexplanation, which rests on use of an abstract form of spatial encoding. He worries that this undercuts the reasons for positing an analogue spatial medium in the first place. The point here is that we are dealing with a system that has many properties, some of which will be useful in performing some tasks and some of which will be useful in others. We did not simply introduce this abstract form of spatial representation to explain Pylyshyn's data, but needed it for entirely different reasons. And given that we did posit it, one can then ask under what conditions it will be useful.

Finally, what about the "blink" alternative explanation that Pylyshyn himself considered? We did not initially plan on building this property into our theory. However, as is discussed in the section on image transformations, we were stuck with the possibility of blink transformations, given our claims about image generation and the nature of the visual buffer (i.e., that it is a temporary store). Thus, we expect that subjects can image a transformed object in two ways: by shifting portions of it through the visual buffer or by letting the initial image fade and generating a new image of the object that is transformed in some way. If a blink transformation is used, the magnitude of the transform should not affect the time necessary to carry it out. And in fact, blink scans are equally easy over different distances (see chapter 8, Kosslyn, 1980). Pylyshyn argues that the amount of time required to generate images rules out a blink-transformation account of his data. This is an error. Pylyshyn used as his estimate of generation time the entire time subjects required to respond that they had generated an image after encoding a stimulus. This time includes encoding and response components of no interest here, since in a blink transform subjects already know which image to generate.

A better estimate of generation time is not the intercept but the slope, that is, the amount of time to generate an image of each additional part placed on an image. Interestingly, this time varies from about 50 to 150 msec for images of line drawings (see chapter 4, Kosslyn, 1980). Thus, even if time is required to adjust the values of the parameters used by the PICTURE process, and if the initial image requires some time to fade before the new one can be generated, the 300 additional msec in Pylyshyn's imagery condition may be enough to permit us to invoke a blink transform in explaining the data. In fact, times to perform blink scans and shift scans (where distance affects scan time) converge after relatively small distances are shift scanned (see chapter 8, Kosslyn, 1980). But this is really not to the point: Because different processing components are involved in performing the perceptual and imagery tasks, we cannot use the data from the perceptual task as a baseline for the imagery task. For example, eye movement control and execution add time in the perceptual condition but not the imagery one. Presumably, aspects of imagery processing add time in that condition relative to the perceptual one (e.g., the image may be less sharp than the percept and hence more difficult to inspect, but we have no way of knowing if the extra processing in the two tasks neatly cancelled each other out. (In fact, this seems very unlikely.) Thus, we simply cannot use the difference in times in Pylyshyn's two conditions to place contraints on the possible imagery processes. In addition, it is in general very dangerous to use estimates of absolute times obtained in different experiments in the way Pylyshyn uses them, given the vagaries of different apparatuses, different subject populations, different experimenters, and so on. Finally, we cannot interpret the finding that distance affected time in the perceptual condition without knowing how well the locations were learned beforehand, how large the visual angle was at which the array was viewed, and the details of the instructions and procedure in general.

In short, then, Pylyshyn's new experiments were not so conceived that the predicted outcomes can serve to distinguish among the alternative positions.

THE TACIT KNOWLEDGE ACCOUNTS

Pylyshyn (1979a, 1980, 1981) offers alternative accounts of the data from imagery experiments that rest on three major claims: First, the implicit task demands inherent in the instructions and the tasks themselves lead subjects to recreate as accurately as possible the perceptual events that would occur if they were actually observing the analogous situation. Second, subjects draw on their tacit knowledge of physics and the nature of the human perceptual system to decide how to behave in an experiment. Third, the subjects have the psychophysical skills necessary to produce the appropriate responses, for example by timing the interval between the onset of the stimulus and their pressing a key. There is one additional assumption that is critical for Pylyshyn's argument: The means by which tacit knowledge is invoked and used must not involve a spatial medium. That is, the issue at the heart of the differences in the alternative accounts centers on the existence of "depictive" representational structures in human memory, and thus a demonstration of the effects of tacit knowledge is relevant only if it can also be shown that this knowledge is not represented in a depictive form at some stage during the necessary processing. It would not be surprising if task demands and tacit knowledge sometimes affected imagery processing, given the long-standing claim that imagery can serve as a "dry run" simulation of the analogous physical events; if imagery were not able to be influenced by ideas, it would have only limited use in many forms of reasoning, such as those involved in the "thought experiments" reported by many distinguished scientists (see Shepard, 1978). Because Pylyshyn emphasizes the first two assumptions noted above in making his argument, it will behoove us to consider them in more detail.

Task demands

Pylyshyn's argument depends on the notion that the instructions and the very nature of our tasks always led subjects to imagine what would happen in the analogous real event. However, this assumption fails to explain a number of our findings. Consider three examples: First, Kosslyn, Jolicoeur, and Fliegel (described in Kosslyn et al., 1979) performed a study in which subjects were asked to image an object and mentally "stare" at one end of it. Shortly thereafter, the name of a property was presented, and subjects were to judge the appropriateness of the property for the object as quickly as possible. It was stressed that the subject need not use the image in making the judgment. Interestingly, the distance from the point of focus to the property affected verification time only for properties that a separate group of subjects had rated to require imagery to verify (e.g., for a honeybee, "dark head"). No effects of distance were found for properties previously rated not to require imagery, even though the two kinds of items were randomly intermixed (and in fact the subjects had no idea that there were two different kinds of items). Pylyshyn's claim that some unspecified features of the task selectively evoke the "imagery habit" is merely an assertion of faith in the truth of his theory. This claim is tantamount to saying the results are explained by task demands because they must be explained by task demands—which is hardly a satisfactory account of the data.

Second, in another experiment, similar effects of the subjective size of parts of an image were obtained with first graders, fourth graders, and adults (see Kosslyn, 1976b). Further, in this experiment subjects began by evaluating a set of items without being asked to use imagery. But after this verification task, the subjects were simply asked whether they had spontaneously tended to "look for" the named properties on images. When data from the first graders were analyzed in terms of which strategy was reported, I found effects of the size of properties only for those subjects who claimed to use imagery spontaneously. The result cannot be interpreted in terms of implicit demands in the instructions, since imagery was never mentioned at all.

Third, Finke and Kosslyn (1980) asked subjects to image pairs of dots moving toward the periphery and to indicate when the two dots were no longer distinct in the image. We also included a control group that was shown the stimuli and told the instructions we gave our experimental subjects. These people were asked to try to guess what our real subjects did and were explicitly asked not to use imagery in making these judgments. Interestingly, although these control subjects were able to guess that dots placed further apart would be "visible" at greater distances toward the periphery, they did not guess that distances increased less rapidly as dot separation increased. Further, the imagery field we measured was 1.83 times larger than that estimated by the control subjects. In general, the actual magnitudes estimated by the control subjects were consistently incorrect and were almost twice as variable as the corresponding data from the experimental subjects. Thus, although task demands may have evoked tacit knowledge about the general aspects of the imagery field, it did not make available all of the subtle properties that affect imagery processing. Finke (1980) presents numerous examples along these lines, all of which put strain on the kind of account advocated by Pylyshyn.

Tacit knowledge of perception

According to the tacit knowledge position, the imagery data are produced when subjects consider (without making use of analogue images) what something would look like if they were actually seeing it as it typically appears. I have three responses to this claim.

First, this position fails to provide accounts for the discoveries that imagery and perception share certain very counterintuitive properties, properties that people have never had the opportunity to discover in perception and that many people do not initially believe and find surprising when convinced. These properties are only manifest in highly novel laboratory settings, which precludes the subject from developing tacit knowledge about them from prior experience. Finke (1980) provides a good review of many of these studies in a recent issue of this journal, and I will not duplicate his efforts here. In addition to the studies he reviews, however, we have recently demonstrated that the geometrical properties of images affect processing in a way that is difficult to explain by appeal to tacit knowledge of perception or the physical world: Nancy Pennington and I asked people to image alternating black and white striped gratings receding into the distance. We were interested in how far away the grating seemed at the point when the stripes blurred into a gray field. Interestingly, imaged vertical stripes seemed to blur at greater distances than oblique ones. This was true even if subjects began by seeing stripes at a given orientation and mentally rotated the stripes to a different orientation. None of our subjects were familiar with this "oblique effect" (which also occurs in perception and was found at the same magnitude in a separate group performing the perceptual analogue of the imagery experiment). In addition, the effects of different spatial frequencies (i.e., bar widths) were different in imagery and perception, which would not be expected if subjects were using tacit knowledge of perception to produce the expected results.

Second, the tacit knowledge view has considerable difficulty when properties of subjects' images differ from what they believe is typical about an object's appearance. For example, I found that the size (i.e., apparent angle subtended) at which images are spontaneously generated is different from that at which the objects are reportedly commonly seen (see Kosslyn, 1978). If subjects simply recall the typical perceived size of objects when asked to image them, this result makes no sense. If different factors constrain imaged size (such as the extent of an analogue spatial medium within which images are formed) and typical viewed size, the result is not surprising.

Third, it is not enough simply to say that we cannot imagine some things because we could never see them (such as a four-dimensional cube). We should try to specify what it is about the perceptual system and the world that limits the range of possible percepts and images. One possibility, not ruled out by any of Pylyshyn's arguments, is that an analogue medium (such as the visual buffer we posit or the medium that supports a "2½-D sketch" in the Marr and Nishihara, 1978, model of perceptual processing) is used in both perception and imagery, and properties of this medium are one source of constraints on both what we can see and what we can imagine.

EVALUATING THE THEORIES

Theories are often evaluated by applying a set of abstract criteria, such as precision, generality, falsifiability, parsimony, and heuristic value. Let us consider the tacit knowledge theory and compare it to the Kosslyn and Shwartz theory on each of these criteria.

Precision. The tacit knowledge position has not been worked out in sufficient detail to evaluate its precision. The only claim is that there is some set of representations and processes that allows one to "simulate" physical or perceptual events without using analogue representations. In fact, Pylyshyn has presented some general metaprinciples for a theory, not a theory itself. With regard to the general issue of free parameters, it is worth noting that the tacit knowledge accounts may represent the ultimate in unspecified theories. These accounts seem virtually unconstrained and have no clearly specified parameters, free or otherwise.

The Kosslyn and Shwartz theory, in contrast, is precise enough to be implemented in a running computer simulation model. This general model produces specific models for numerous tasks (see the second half of Kosslyn, 1980), and these models in some cases account for quantitative relations in the data as well as the qualitative trends. Our theory is clearly more precise than Pylyshyn's.

Generality. To the extent that the tacit knowledge view rests on subjects' knowledge of or beliefs about how things typically happen in reality, the view has considerable generality. Our theory covers the domains of image generation, inspection, transformation, and the role of imagery in fact retrieval. Pylyshyn seems to intend his theory to cover almost all known imagery phenomena, and thus Pylyshyn's theory would appear the more general. But not all imagery phenomena simply mirror the analogous perceptual phenomena, and hence the tacit knowledge story can only go so far. That is, to the extent that imagery exhibits properties that differ from the analogous perceptual or physical ones, Pylyshyn's theory loses generality. My finding that images are not typically generated at the apparent size at which subjects believe the objects are usually seen (see Kosslyn, 1978) is a case in point, as is Pinker's (1980b) finding that the effects of 2- and 3-D distances are different in image scanning and actual perceptual scanning.

Falsifiability. Pylyshyn (1981) claims that tacit knowledge "could obviously depend on *anything* the subject might tacitly know or believe concerning what usually happens in the corresponding perceptual situations." Moreover, "the exact domain of knowledge being appealed to can vary from case to case." Thus, one can never be sure one has controlled for the effects of tacit knowledge in an experiment, in Pylyshyn's view. In other words, whereas the demand characteristics account may be disprovable, Pylyshyn's account, resting on implicit task demands, is sheltered from such a rude fate.

Our theory makes numerous predictions, and these predictions are subject to empirical test (see the second half of Kosslyn, 1980, and Shwartz, 1979). Because we eschew altering the properties of our theory merely to explain data, if predictions are not borne out, the theory can be falsified. In short, our theory is clearly more "vulnerable," more easily falsified, than Pylyshyn's.

Parsimony. Parsimony is not a property that is inherent in a theory in and of itself (see Pinker, 1980a). Thus, one must compare two theories and decide which is the more parsimonious. Pylyshyn's theory appears more parsimonious than ours, but this is a consequence of his not filling in any details. Only when the tacit knowledge theory provides accounts at least as precise as ours can we then compare the two in terms of relative parsimony.

Heuristic value. The tacit knowledge account seems to have had little value thus far in producing new data (note that the results reported in Pylyshyn, 1981, are directed at undermining the analogue position, not supporting the tacit knowledge one per se). Further, mere demonstrations that tacit knowledge or task demands can affect image processing will neither demonstrate how they operate (which could involve manipulating images in a spatial medium) nor show that they usually underlie image processing. In contrast, the Kosslyn and Shwartz theory has proven to have a high degree of heuristic value. It has led us to collect data on a whole raft of imagery phenomena, data that all parties must now explain. The fact that Pylyshyn's theory has not led to important discoveries could simply reflect its relatively recent vintage, however, and thus it is premature to pass judgment on it with regard to this criterion.

Conclusions

Most of the criticisms of the Kosslyn and Shwartz theory were easily countered after the essentials of the theory were described, and Pylyshyn's recent alternative view did not prove incisive. Further, the data Pylyshyn introduced with an eye toward disproving an assumption of our theory were also found wanting. Not only was the prediction based on a confusion between the properties of structures and the properties of structure/process pairs, but the data themselves could be explained in multiple ways within the context of our imagery theory.

It is tempting to compare the present Pylyshyn critique with an earlier one (Pylyshyn, 1973) and to compare this reply with the one by Kosslyn and Pomerantz (1977). A number of points of similarity are apparent: First, both exchanges have been concerned with essentially the same issue (albeit approached in different ways), namely, whether image representations are different in kind from those underlying language processing. Second, both exchanges draw heavily on concepts drawn from outside psychology proper, from computer science, philosophy, and linguistics; the area of imagery representation now seems to have moved firmly into the domain of cognitive science.

More striking, however, are the dissimilarities between the present exchange and the earlier one: First, the earlier theorizing was at a much higher level of abstraction. In the present articles there is real movement toward development of explicit, detailed theories; we have proposed a detailed simulation model, and Pylyshyn is no longer merely asserting that processing is "propositional" but is offering some principles about how such processing would proceed. Second, in the earlier debate there were few data that bore directly on the nature of the imagery representation and processing system. We now have an abundance of data that place real constraints on theories (see Kosslyn & Shwartz, in press), and all parties are now concerned both with explaining the existing data and with collecting new data that speak to the issues. This is a very healthy sign, it seems to me. Third, there has been some real convergence in the alternative theories themselves. Both classes of accounts focus on imagery as a means whereby internal simulations can be conducted, and the main issue could be regarded as one concerning how far to carry this notion. Pylyshyn wants the spatial analogue medium itself to be merely simulated, whereas we want it to be an innately determined fixed structure that supports "depictive" data structures.

What, then, should we make of the apparent widespread dissatisfaction in the field that the so-called imagery–proposition debate has not yet been resolved? Some have even taken the view that the debate is in principle not capable of resolution (Anderson, 1978). Given the complexity of the issues involved, it seems overly optimistic to expect a speedy solution to such a knotty problem. It is a mistake to think that theoretical issues in other fields have typically been resolved much more quickly. For example, it took about

30 years for physicists to resolve the issue of whether cathode rays were electromagnetic waves or trains of electrified particles (see D. L. Anderson, 1964), and it is not clear that we have any right to expect a speedier resolution to the present dispute. At the present juncture the best we can do is to continue to work out the empirical implications of the respective positions and to continue to collect new data that support one view while putting strain on others.

ACKNOWLEDGMENTS

Chapter 1, "Icons and Images." From *Psychology* (Boston, Little Brown), pp. 422–436. Reprinted by permission of the publisher and the authors.

Chapter 2, "The Nature of Images and the Introspective Trap." From *Content and Consciousness* (London, Routledge and Kegan Paul, 1969), pp. 132–141. Reprinted by permission of Routledge and Kegan Paul, Humanities Press, and the author.

Chapter 3, "Imagistic Representation." From *The Language of Thought* (New York, Crowell 1975), pp. 177–195. Reprinted by permission of Harper and Row and the author. Notes and figures have been renumbered for this edition.

Chapter 4, "Two Approaches to Mental Images." From *Brainstorms: Philosophical Essays on Mind and Psychology* (the MIT Press/Bradford Books, 1979), pp. 176–189. Reprinted by permission of the publisher and the author.

Chapter 5, "Imagery—There's More to It Than Meets the Eye." First given as an invited talk at the Philosophy of Science meeting, Toronto, 1980 and will appear in the proceedings of that meeting. Philosophy of Science Association 1980. Vol. 2. P. Asquith and R. Giere, editors. I wish to thank Margaret Atherton for her comments and criticism. After sketching out this paper I came across Kolers and Smythe (1979). There is a good deal in common between us, and their paper has a more thorough set of references to positions and claims alluded to herein.

Chapter 6, "On the Demystification of Mental Imagery." From *The Behavioral and Brain Sciences* (Cambridge University Press, 1979), Vol. 2, pp. 535–

548. Reprinted by permission of the publisher and the authors. What is reprinted here is mainly a revised version of section 1.

Chapter 7, "The Imagery Debate." This paper was written while the author was a fellow at the Center for Cognitive Science at MIT and at the Center for Advanced Study in the Behavioral Sciences at Stanford. The support of both these institutions is gratefully acknowledged, as well as the assistance provided by the Alfred P. Sloan Foundation and by a leave fellowship from the Social Science and Humanities Research Council of Canada. I would also like to thank Ned Block, Jerry Fodor, and Bob Moore for their helpful comments.

Chapter 8, "The Medium and the Message in Mental Imagery." I wish to thank Ned Block, Sharon Fliegel, Alexander George, Reid Hastie, Edward E. Smith, George E. Smith, and Lucia Vaina for insightful comments and illuminating criticisms of an earlier draft of this article. Work reported herein was supported by National Science Foundation Grant BNS 79-12418.

REFERENCES

The numbers in square brackets following each entry indicate the chapters in which the references are cited.

[Introduction]	Block	[5]	Schwartz
[1]	Brown and Herrnstein	[6]	Kosslyn et al.
[2]	Dennett	[7]	Pylyshyn
[3]	Fodor	[8]	Kosslyn
[4]	Dennett		

Abelson, R. P. (1968). "Simulation of Social Behavior." In Lindzey and Aronson, 1968. [6]

Alpern, M. (1953). "Metacontrast," *Journal of the Optical Society of America,* 43 (1953), 648–657. [1]

Anderson, J.R. (1964). *The Discovery of the Electron,* New York: Van Nostrand. [8]

——. (1976). *Language, Memory and Thought,* Hillsdale, N.J.: Erlbaum Associates. [6]

——. (1978). "Arguments Concerning Representations for Mental Imagery," *Psychological Review,* 85 (1978), 249–277. [5] [6] [7] [8]

——. (in press). "Further Arguments Concerning Mental Imagery: A Response to Hayes-Roth and Pylyshyn," *Psychological Review.* [6]

Anderson, J. R., and Bower, G. H. (1973). *Human Associative Memory,* New York: V. H. Winston & Sons. [6] [8]

Arbib, M. (1972). *The Metaphorical Brain,* New York: Wiley. [7]

Arieti, S. (1955). *Interpretation of Schizophrenia,* New York: Bruner-Mazel. [6]

Armstrong, D. M. (1971). *Belief, Truth and Knowledge,* Cambridge, Eng.: Cambridge University Press. [4]

Asch, S. E. (1956). "Studies of Independence and Conformity: A Minority of One against a Unanimous Majority," *Psychological Monographs* 70 (whole issue). [6]

Ashton, R.; McFarland, K.; Walsh, F.; and White, K. (1978). "Imagery Ability and the Identification of Hands: A Chronometric Analysis," *Acta Psychologica,* 42 (1978), 253–262. [6]

Attneave, F. (1968). "Triangles as Ambiguous Figures," *American Journal of Psychology*, 81 (1968), 447-453. [6]

——. (1974). "How Do You Know?" *American Psychologist*, 29 (1974), 493-499. [7]

Averback, E., and Coriell, A. S. (1961). "Short-term Memory in Vision," *Bell Systems Technical Journal*, 40 (1961), 309-328. [1]

Baddeley, A., and Long, J., eds. (in press). *Attention and Performance IX*, Hillsdale, N.J.: Erlbaum. [6]

Bahill, A. T., and Stark, L. (1979). "The Trajectories of Saccadic Eye Movements," *Scientific American*, 240 (1979), 108-117. [6]

Barlow, H. B. (1961). "Possible Principles Underlying the Transformations of Sensory Messages." In Rosenblith, 1961. [2]

Baylor, G. W. (1971). A Treatise on the Mind's Eye. Unpublished Ph.D. thesis, Carnegie-Mellon University. [6]

Beech, J. R. (1979). A Chronometric Study of the Scanning of Visual Representations. Unpublished Ph.D. thesis, The New University of Ulster, Northern Ireland. [6]

Beech, J. R., and Allport, D. A. (1978). "Visualization of Compound Scenes," *Perception*, 7 (1978), 129-138. [6]

Black, M. (1972). "How Do Pictures Represent?" In Mandelbaum, 1972. [5]

Block, N., ed. (1981). *Readings in Philosophy of Psychology*, Vol. 2, Cambridge: Harvard University Press. [Intr.] [4] [6] [7] [8]

Boggess, L. C. (1978). Computational Interpretation of English Spacial Prepositions. Unpublished Ph.D. thesis, University of Illinois. [6]

Bower, G. H. (1970). "Analysis of a Mnemonic Device," *American Scientist*, 58 (1970), 496-510. [6]

——. (1978). "Representing Knowledge Development." In Siegler, 1978. [6]

Bridgeman, B. (1971). "Metacontrast and Lateral Inhibition," *Psychological Review*, 78 (1971), 528-539. [6]

——. (1978). "Distributed Sensory Coding Applied to Simulations of Iconic Storage and Metacontrast," *Bulletin of Mathematical Biology*, 40 (1978), 605-623. [6]

Broadbent, D. E. (1958). *Perception and Communication*, New York: Pergamon. [1]

Brooks, L. R. (1967). "The Suppression of Visualization in Reading," *Quarterly Journal of Experimental Psychology*, 19 (1967), 288-299. [6]

——. (1968). "Spatial and Verbal Components of the Act of Recall," *Canadian Journal of Psychology*, 22 (1968), 349-368. [3] [6]

Brown, R. (1958). *Words and Things*, New York: Free Press. [3]

Bruner, J. S. (1957). "On Perceptual Readiness," *Psychological Review*, 64 (1957), 123-152. [3]

Bruner, J. S.; Goodnow, J. J.; and Austin, G. A. (1956). *A Study of Thinking*, New York: Wiley; paperback Wiley Science Editions, 1962. [3]

Bruner, J. S.; Olver, R. R.; and Greenfield, P. M. (1966). *Studies in Cognitive Growth*, New York: Wiley. [3]

Bundesen, C., and Larsen, A. (1975). "Visual Transformation of Size," *Journal of Experimental Psychology: Human Perception and Performance*, 1 (1975), 214-220. [6]

Chase, W. G., ed. (1973). *Visual Information Processing*, New York: Academic Press. [1] [3] [4] [6] [7]

Cherry, E. C. (1953). "Some Experiments on the Recognition of Speech with One and with Two Ears," *Journal of the Acoustics Society of America*, 25 (1953), 975-979. [1]

Chomsky, N. (1980). "Rules and Representations," *The Behavioral and Brain Sciences*, 3, No. 1 (1980), 1-62. [7]

Clark, H. H. (1969). "Linguistic Processes in Deductive Reasoning," *Psychological Review,* 76 (1969), 387–404. [6]

Clark, H. H., and Chase, W. G. (1972). "On the Process of Comparing Sentences against Pictures," *Cognitive Psychology,* 3 (1972), 472–517. [8]

Conrad, C. (1972). "Cognitive Economy in Semantic Theory," *Journal of Experimental Psychology,* 92 (1972), 149–154. [6]

Cooper, L. A. (1975). "Mental Rotation of Random Two-Dimensional Shapes," *Cognitive Psychology,* 7 (1975), 20–43. [6]

Cooper, L. A., and Podgorny, P. (1976). "Mental Transformations and Visual Comparison Processes: Effects of Complexity and Similarity," *Journal of Experimental Psychology: Human Perception and Performance,* 2 (1976), 503–514. [6]

——. (1975). "Mental Transformations in the Identification of Left and Right Hands," *Journal of Experimental Psychology: Human Perception and Performance,* 1 (1975), 48–56. [6]

Cooper, L. A., and Shepard, R. N. (1973). "Chronometric Studies of the Rotation of Mental Images." In Chase, 1973. [1] [3] [4] [6] [8]

Crowder, R. G., and Morton, J. (1969). "Precategorical Acoustic Storage (PAS)," *Perception Psychophysics,* 5 (1969), 365–373. [1]

Dennett, Daniel C. (1979). "On the Absence of Phenomenology." In Tapscott and Gustafson, eds., *Body, Mind, and Method: Essays in Honor of Virgil Aldrich,* Dordrecht: Reidal. [4]

——. (1968). "Geach and Intentional Identity," *Journal of Philosophy,* 6, No. 5 (1968), 335–341. [4]

——. (1969). *Content and Consciousness,* New York: Humanities Press. [3] [4]

——. (1979). *Brainstorms,* Montgomery, Vt.: Bradford Books. [6]

DiVesta, F. J.; Ingersoll, G.; and Sunshine, P. (1971). "A Factor Analysis of Imagery Tests," *Journal of Verbal Learning and Verbal Behavior,* 10 (1971), 471–479. [6]

Eriksen, C. W., and Spencer, T. (1969). "Rate of Information Processing in Visual Perception: Some Results and Methodological Considerations," *Journal of Experimental Psychology Monographs,* 79, No. 2, Pt. 2. [1]

Estes, W. K., ed. (1978). *Handbook of Learning and Cognitive Processes,* Vol. 5, Hillsdale, N.J.: Erlbaum Associates. [6]

Farley, A. M. (1974). VIPS: A Visual Imagery and Perception System; The Result of Protocol Analysis. Unpublished Ph.D. thesis, Carnegie-Mellon University. [6]

Favreau, O. E., and Corballis, M. C. (1976). "Negative Aftereffects in Visual Perception," *Scientific American* 235 (1976), 42–48. [Intr.]

Field, H. (1977). "Logic, Meaning and Conceptual Role," *Journal of Philosophy,* 74 (1977), 379–409. [Intr.]

Finke, R. A. (1979). "The Functional Equivalence of Mental Images and Errors of Movement," *Cognitive Psychology,* 11 (1979), 235–264. [6] [7]

——. (1980). "Levels of Equivalence in Imagery and Perception," *Psychological Review,* 87 (1980), 113–139. [Intr.] [6] [8]

Finke, R. A., and Kosslyn, S. M. (1980). "Mental Imagery Acuity in the Peripheral Visual Field," *Journal of Experimental Psychology: Human Perception and Performance,* 6 (1980), 126–139. [6] [8]

Finke, R. A., and Schmidt, M. J. (1977). "Orientation-specific Color Aftereffects Following Imagination," *Journal of Experimental Psychology: Human Perception and Performance,* 3 (1977), 599–606. [Intr.] [6]

——. (1978). "The Quantitative Measure of Pattern Representation in Images Using

Orientation-specific Color Aftereffects," *Perception and Psychophysics,* 23 (1978), 515–520. [Intr.]

Fodor, J. A. (1968a). "The Appeal to Tacit Knowledge in Psychological Explanation," *Journal of Philosophy,* 65 (1968), 627–640. [7]

——. (1968b). *Psychological Explanation: An Introduction to the Philosophy of Psychology,* New York: Random House. [6]

——. (1975). *The Language of Thought,* New York: Thomas Y. Crowell. [7]

——. (1980). "Methodological Solipsism Considered as a Research Strategy for Cognitive Psychology," *The Behavioral and Brain Sciences,* 3, No. 1 (1980), 63–110. [6] [7]

Fodor, J. D.; Fodor, J. A.; and Garrett, M. F. (1975). "The Psychological Unreality of Semantic Representations," *Linguistic Theory,* 4 (1975), 515–531. [6]

Fodor, J. A., and Katz, J. J., eds. (1964). *The Structure of Language: Readings in the Philosophy of Language,* Englewood Cliffs, N.J.: Prentice-Hall. [3]

Forster, K. I. (1976). "Accessing the Mental Lexicon." In Wales and Walker, 1976. [7]

Foss, B. M., ed. (1978). *Psychology Survey,* No. 1, London: Allen and Unwin. [6]

Fraisse, P. (1963). *The Psychology of Time,* New York: Harper and Row. [7]

Freud, S. (1958). *The Interpretation of Dreams,* London: Hogarth Press. [6]

Friedman, A. (1978). "Memorial Comparisons without the Mind's Eye," *Journal of Verbal Learning and Verbal Behavior,* 17 (1978), 427–444. [6]

Galton, F. (1883). *Inquiries into Human Faculty and Development,* London: Dent, 1905. [6]

Ghiselin, B. (1952). *The Creative Process,* New York: New American Library. [7]

Gibson, J. J. (1966). *The Senses Considered as Perceptual Systems,* Boston: Houghton Mifflin. [6]

Gombrich, E. H. (1960). *Art and Illusion,* New York: Pantheon Books. [5]

Goodman, N. (1968). *Languages of Art,* Indianapolis: Bobbs-Merrill. [5] [6]

Green, D. M., and Luce, R. D. (1973). "Speed-Accuracy Tradeoff in Auditory Detection." In Kornblum, 1973. [6]

Gregg, L. W., ed. (1972). *Cognition in Learning and Memory,* New York: John Wiley. [6]

Gunderson, K., ed. (1975). *Minnesota Studies in Philosophy of Science,* Vol. 7, Minneapolis: University of Minnesota Press. [Intr.]

Haber, R. N. (1966). "Nature of the Effect of Set on Perception," *Psychological Review,* 73 (1966), 335–351. [3]

——. (1970). "How We Remember What We See," *Scientific American* 222 (1970), 104–112. [6]

Halle, M., and Stevens, K. N. (1964). "Speech Recognition: A Model and A Program for Research." In Fodor and Katz, 1964. [3]

Hannay, A. (1971). *Mental Images: A Defence,* Atlantic Highlands, N.J.: Humanities. [4] [6]

Hanson, A. R., and Riseman, E. M., eds. (1978). *Computer Vision Systems,* New York: Academic Press. [6]

Harman, G. (1973). *Thought,* Princeton, N.J.: Princeton University Press. [7]

——. (1975). "Language, Thought, and Communication." In Gunderson, 1975. [Intr.]

Haugeland, J. "The Nature and Plausibility of Cognitivism," *The Behavioral and Brain Sciences,* 2 (1978), 215–260. [7]

Hays, J. R. (1973). "On the Function of Visual Imagery in Elementary Mathematics." In Chase, 1973. [7]

Hayes-Roth, F. (1977). "Critique of Turvey's 'Contrasting Orientations to the Theory of Visual Information Processing,'" *Psychological Review,* 84 (1977), 531–535. [6]

——. (1979). "Distinguishing Theories of Representation: A Critique of Anderson's 'Arguments Concerning Mental Imagery,' " *Psychological Review,* 86 (1979), 376–392. [6] [8]

Hebb, D. O. (1968). "Concerning Imagery," *Psychological Review,* 75 (1968), 466–477. [6] [7]

Hesse, M. B. (1963). *Models and Analogies in Science,* London: Sheed and Ward. [6] [8]

Hinton, C. H. (1906). *The Fourth Dimension,* London: George Allen & Unwin. [7]

Hinton, G. E. (1979). "Some Demonstrations of the Effects of Structural Descriptions in Mental Imagery," *Cognitive Science,* . [6]

Hirst, W. (1976). Memory for Proofs. Unpublished Ph.D. thesis, Cornell University. [6]

Howard, I. P. (1978). "Recognition and Knowledge of the Water-Level Principle," *Perception,* 7 (1978), 151–160. [7]

Hubel, D. H., and Wiesel, T. N. (1962). "Receptive Fields, Binocular Interaction and Functional Architecture in the Cat's Visual Cortex," *Journal of Physiology,* 160 (1962), 106–154. [6]

Hume, D. (1960). *A Treatise of Human Nature,* Vol. 1, London: Dent. (Originally published 1739.) [3]

Hunter, I. M. L. (1962). "An Exceptional Talent for Calculative Thinking," *British Journal of Psychology,* 53 (1962), 243–258. [6]

——. (1977). "Imagery, Comprehension and Mnemonics," *Journal of Mental Imagery,* 1 (1977), 65–72. [6]

Husserl, Edmund (1931). *Ideas,* trans. W. R. Bryce Gibson, London: Allen and Unwin. [4]

Huttenlocher, Janellen (1968). "Construction Spatial Images: A Strategy in Reasoning," *Psychological Review,* 75 (1968), 550–560. [5] [6] [8]

Johnson-Laird, P. N. (1979a). Formal Semantics and the Psychology of Meaning. Paper presented at the Symposium on Formal Semantics and Natural Language, University of Texas at Austin. [6]

——. (1979b). Mental Models in Cognitive Science. Paper presented at the La Jolla Conference on Cognitive Science. [6]

Jonides, J.; Kahn, R.; and Rozin, P. (1975). "Imagery Instructions Improve Memory in Blind Subjects," *Bulletin of the Psychonomic Society,* 5 (1975), 424–426. [6]

Just, M. A., and Carpenter, P. A. (1976). "Eye Fixations and Cognitive Processes," *Cognitive Psychology,* 8 (1976), 441–480. [6]

Kahneman, D. (1968). "Method Findings, and Theory in Studies of Visual Masking," *Psychological Bulletin,* 70 (1968), 404–425. [1]

Kandinsky, W. (1947). *Point and Line to Plane,* New York: The Guggenheim Foundation. [6]

Kant, I. (1953). *Critique of Pure Reason,* trans. N. K. Smith, New York: Macmillan. (Originally published 1781.) [3]

Keenan, J. M. (1978). "Psychological Issues Concerning Implication: Comments on 'Psychology of Pragmatic Implication: Information Processing between the Lines,' by Harris and Monaco," *Journal of Experimental Psychology: General,* 107 (1978), 23–27. [6]

Keenan, J. M., and Moore, R. E. (1979). "Memory for Images of Concealed Objects: A Reexamination of Neisser and Kerr," *Journal of Experimental Psychology: Human Learning and Memory,* 5 (1979), 374–385. [6] [8]

Kintsch, W. (1974). *The Representation of Meaning in Memory,* Hillsdale, N.J.: Erlbaum Associates. [6]

Kolers, P. A. (1962). "Intensity and Contour Effects in Visual Masking," *Vision Research,* 2 (1962), 277-294. [1]

Kolers, P. A., and Smythe, W. E. (1979). "Images, Symbols and Skills," *Canadian Journal of Psychology,* 33, No. 3 (1979), 158-184. [Intr.] [5] [6]

Kornblum, S., ed. (1973). *Attention and Performance IV,* New York: Academic Press. [6]

Kosslyn, S. M. (1973). "Scanning Visual Images: Some Structural Implications," *Perception and Psychophysics,* 14 (1973), 90-94. [6] [7]

———. (1974). Constructing Visual Images. Unpublished Ph.D. thesis, Stanford University. [6]

———. (1975). "Information Representation in Visual Images," *Cognitive Psychology,* 7 (1975), 341-370. [4] [6] [7] [8]

———. (1976a). "Can Imagery Be Distinguished from Other Forms of Internal Representation? Evidence from Studies of Information Retrieval Time," *Memory and Cognition,* 4 (1976), 291-297. [6] [8]

———. (1976b). "Using Imagery to Retrieve Semantic Information: A Developmental Study," *Child Development,* 47 (1976), 434-444. [6] [8]

———. (1978a). "Measuring the Visual Angle of the Mind's Eye," *Cognitive Psychology,* 10 (1978a), 356-389. [Intr.] [6] [8]

———. (1978b). "Imagery and Cognitive Development: A Teleological Approach." In Siegler, 1978. [6]

———. (1978b). *Imagery and internal representation.* In E. Rosch and B. B. Floyd (eds.), *Cognition and Categorization,* New Jersey: Erlbaum Associates. [6]

———. (1980). *Image and Mind,* Cambridge, Mass.: Harvard University Press. [Intr.] [6] [8]

Kosslyn, S. M. , and Alper, S. N. (1977). "On the Pictorial Properties of Visual Images: Effects of Image Size on Memory for Words," *Canadian Journal of Psychology,* 31 (1977), 32-40. [6]

Kosslyn, S. M.; Ball, T. M. : and Reiser, B. J. (1978). "Visual Images Preserve Metric Spatial Information: Evidence from Studies of Image Scanning," *Journal of Experimental Psychology: Human Perception and Performance,* 4 (1978), 47-60. [6] [7] [8]

Kosslyn, S. M., and Jolicoeur, P. (1980). "A Theory-based Approach to the Study of Individual Differences in Mental Imagery." In Snow et al., 1980. [6] [8]

Kosslyn, S. M.; Murphy, G. L.; Bemesderfer, M. E.; and Feinstein, K. J. (1977). "Category and Continuum in Mental Comparisons," *Journal of Experimental Psychology: General,* 106 (1977), 341-375. [6] [8]

Kosslyn, S. M.; Pinker, S.; Smith, G. E.; and Shwartz, S. P. (1979). "On the Demystification of Mental Imagery," *Behavioral and Brain Sciences,* 2 (1979) 535-581. [7] [8]

Kosslyn, S. M., and Pomerantz, J. R. (1977). "Imagery, Propositions, and the Form of Internal Representations," *Cognitive Psychology,* 9 (1977), 52-76; reprinted in Block, 1981. [Intr.] [6] [7] [8]

Kosslyn, S. M.; Reiser, B. J.; and Farah, M. Generating Visual Images (submitted for publication). [6]

Kosslyn, S. M., and Shwartz, S. P. (1977). "A Simulation of Visual Imagery," *Congitive Science.* 1 (1977), 265-295. [6] [7] [8]

——. (1978). "Visual Images as Spatial Representations in Active Memory." In Riseman and Hanson, 1978. [6] [8]

——. (in press). Empirical Constraints on Theories of Visual Mental Imagery. In Baddeley and Long, in press. [8]

Larsen, A., and Bundesen, C. (1978). "Size Scaling in Visual Pattern Recognition," *Journal of Experimental Psychology: Human Perception and Performance*, 4 (1978), 1–20. [6]

Lea, G. (1975). "Chronometric Analysis of the Method of Loci," *Journal of Experimental Psychology: Human Perception and Performance*, 1 (1975), 95–104. [6]

Lindzey, G., and Aronson, E., eds. (1968). *Handbook of Social Psychology*, Vol. 2, Reading, Mass.: Addison-Wesley. [6]

Luce, R. D., and Green, D. M. (1972). "A Neural Timing Theory for Response Times and the Psychophysics of Intensity," *Psychological Review*, 79 (1972), 14–57. [6]

Luria, A. R. (1968). *The Mind of a Mnemonist*, New York: Basic Books. [6]

McCulloch, W. S., and Pitts, W. H. (1943). "A Logical Calculus of the Ideas Immanent in Nervous Activity," *Bulletin of Mathematical Biophysics*, 5 (1943), 115–133. [6]

McKellar, P. (1963). "Differences of Mental Imagery," *The Mensa Correspondence*, 51 (1963), 1–5. [6]

McLeod, C. M.; Hunt, E. B.; and Mathews, N. N. (1978). "Individual Differences in the Verification of Sentence-Picture Relationships," *Journal of Verbal Learning and Verbal Behavior*, 17 (1978), 493–508. [6]

Mamor, G. S., and Zaback, L. A. (1976). "Mental Rotation by the Blind: Does Mental Rotation Depend on Visual Imagery?" *Journal of Experimental Psychology: Human Perception and Performance*, 29 (1976), 263–291. [6]

Mandelbaum, M., ed. (1972). *Art, Perception and Reality*, Baltimore: Johns Hopkins University Press. [5]

Marr, D. (1978). "Representing Visual Information." In Hanson and Riseman, 1978. [6]

Marr, D., and Nishihara, H. K. (1978a). "Representation and Recognition of the Spatial Organization of Three-Dimensional Shapes," *Proceedings of the Royal Society*, Series B, 200 (1978), 269–294. [6]

——. (1978b). "Visual Information Processing: Artificial Intelligence and the Sensorium of Sight," *Technological Review*, 81 (1978), 2–23. [8]

Marr, D., and Poggio, T. (1976) Cooperative Computation of Stereo Disparity. Cambridge, Mass. : M.I.T. AI Lab Memo 364. [6]

Mervis, C. B., and Rosch, E. (1981). "Categorization of Natural Objects." In Rosenzweig and Porter, 1981. [Intr.]

Miller, G. A.; Galanter, E.; and Pribram, K. (1960). *Plans and the Structure of Behavior*, New York: Holt, Rinehart and Winston. [6]

Minsky, M. L. (1975). "A Framework for Representing Knowledge." In Winston, 1975. [6]

——. (1977). Plain Talk about Neurodevelopmental Epistemology. Paper presented at the Fifth International Joint Conference on Artificial Intelligence, Cambridge, Mass. [6]

——. (1979). The Society of Mind. Cambridge, Mass.: M.I.T. AI Lab, unpublished manuscript. [6]

Mitchell, D. B., and Richman, C. L. (1980). "Confirmed Reservations: Mental Travel," *Journal of Experimental Psychology: Human Perception and Performance*, 6 (1980), 58–66. [6] [7]

Moran, T. P. (1973a). The Symbolic Nature of Visual Imagery. Paper presented at the

Third International Joint Conference on Artificial Intelligence, Stanford University. [6]
——. (1973b). The Symbolic Hypothesis: A Production System Model. Unpublished Ph.D. thesis, Carnegie-Mellon University. [6]

Moray, N. (1959). "Attention in Dichotic Listening: Affective Cues and the Influence of Instructions," *Quarterly Journal of Experimental Psychology,* 11 (1959), 56–60. [1]

——. (1970). *Attention: Selective Processes in Vision and Hearing,* New York: Academic Press. [1]

Morton, J. (1969). "Interaction of Information in Word Recognition," *Psychological Review,* 76 (1969), 165–178. [6]

Muntz, W. R. A., (1964). "Vision in Frogs," *Scientific American* 1964, pp. 110–119. [2]

Neisser, U. (1967). *Cognitive Psychology,* New York: Appleton. [1] [3]

——. (1976). *Cognition and Reality,* San Francisco: W. H. Freeman. [6]

——. (1978). "Anticipations, Images, and Introspection," *Cognition,* 6 (1978), 169–174. [6]

Newell, A., and Simon, H. A. (1972). *Human Problem Solving,* Englewood Cliffs, N.J.: Prentice-Hall. [3] [6] [7] [8]

——. (1976). "Computer Science as Empirical Inquiry," *Communications of the Association for Computing Machinery,* 19 (1976), 113–126. [7]

Nicholas, J. M., ed. (1977). *Images, Perception, and Knowledge,* Dordrech, Holland: Reidel. [7]

Norman, D. A. (1969). "Memory While Shadowing," *Quarterly Journal of Psychology,* 21 (1969), 85–93. [1]

Noy, P. (1973). "Symbolism and Mental Representation," *The Annals of Psychoanalysis,* 1 (1973), 125–158. [6]

Orne, M. T. (1962). "On the Social Psychology of the Psychology Experiment: With Special Reference to Demand Characteristics and Their Implications," *American Psychologist,* 17 (1962), 776–783. [6]

Paivio, A. (1971). *Imagery and Verbal Processes,* New York: Holt, Rinehart and Winston. [3] [4]

——. (1975a). "Perceptual Comparisons through the Mind's Eye," *Memory and Cognition,* 3 (1975), 635–648. [6]

——. (1975b). "Neomentalism," *Canadian Journal of Psychology,* 29 (1975), 263–291. [6]

——. (1977). "Images, Propositions, and Knowledge." In Nicholas, 1977. [7]

Palmer, S. E. (1978). "Fundamental Aspects of Cognitive Representation." In Rosch and Lloyd, 1978. [Intr.] [6] [7]

Penfield, W. (1958). *The Excitable Cortex in Conscious Man,* Springfield: Thomas. [2]

Penfield, W., and Roberts, L. (1959). *Speech and Brain Mechanisms,* Princeton, N.J.: Princeton University Press. [3]

Pennington, N., and Kosslyn, S. M. (in preparation). Measuring the Acuity of the Mind's Eye. [6]

Perky, C. W. (1910). "An Experimental Study of Imagination," *American Journal of Psychology,* 21 (1910), 422–452. [Intr.] [1] [3]

Pinker, S. (1979). The Representation of Three-dimensional Space in Mental Images. Unpublished Ph.D. thesis, Harvard University. [6]

——. (1980a). "Explanations in Theories of Language and Imagery," *Behavioral and Brain Sciences,* 3 (1980), 147–148. [7] [8]

——. (1980b). "Mental Imagery and the Third Dimension," *Journal of Experimental Psychology: General,* 109 (1980), 354–371. [6] [8]

Pinker, S., and Finke, R. A. (in press). Emergent Two-dimensional Patterns in Images

Rotated in Depth, *Journal of Experimental Psychology: Human Perception and Performance.* [6]

Pinker, S., and Kosslyn, S. M. (1978). "The Representation and Manipulation of Three-dimensional Space in Mental Images," *Journal of Mental Imagery*, 2 (1978), 69–84. [6] [8]

Podgorny, P., and Shepard, R. N. (1978). "Functional Representations Common to Visual Perception and Imagination," *Journal of Experimental Psychology: Human Perception and Performance*, 4 (1978), 21–35. [6]

Poulton, E. C. (1953). "Two-channel Listening," *Journal of Experimental Psychology*, 46 (1953), 91–96. [1]

Posner, M. I.; Boies, S. J.; Eichelman, W. H.; and Taylor, R. L. (1969). "Retention of Visual and Name Codes of Single Letters," *Journal of Experimental Psychology Monograph*, 79, No. 1, Pt. 2. [3]

Pylyshyn, Z. W. (1973). "What the Mind's Eye Tells the Mind's Brain: A Critique of Mental Imagery," *Psychological Bulletin*, 80 (1973), 1–24. [Intr.] [4] [6] [7] [8]

——. (1978a). Foundations of Cognitive Science. Presentation to the New Harvard Center for Cognitive Studies, Cambridge, Mass. [6]

——. (1978b). "Imagery and Artificial Intelligence," In Savage, 1978; reprinted in Block, 1981. [Intr.] [4] [7]

——. (1979a). "Imagery Theory: Not Mysterious—Just Wrong," *Behavioral and Brain Sciences*, 2 (1979), 561–563. [8]

——. (1979b). "The Rate of 'Mental Rotation' of Images: A Test of a Holistic Analogue Hypothesis," *Memory and Cognition*, 7 (1979), 19–28. [6] [7] [8]

——. (1979c). "Validating Computational Models: A Critique of Anderson's Indeterminacy of Representation Claim," *Psychological Review*, 86 (1979), 383–394. [6] [7] [8]

——. (1980a). "Cognitive Representation and the Process-Architecture Distinction," *Behavioral and Brain Sciences*, 3, No. 1 (1980), 154–169. [7]

——. (1980b). "Computation and Cognition: Issues in the Foundations of Cognitive Science," *Behavioral and Brain Sciences*, 3 (1980), 111–133. [6] [7] [8]

——. (1981). "The Imagery Debate: Analogue Media versus Tacit Knowledge," *Psychological Review*, 87 (1981),   . [6] [8]

Pylyshyn, Z. W.; Elcock, E. W.; Marmor, M.; and Sander, P. (1978). "Explorations in Perceptual-Motor Spaces." In *Proceedings of the Second International Conference of the Canadian Society for Computational Studies of Intelligence*, Toronto, Canada: University of Toronto, Department of Computer Science. [7]

Pribram, K. H. (1969). "The Neurophysiology of Remembering," *Scientific American*, 220 (1969), 73–86. [6]

——. (1971). *Languages of the Brain*, Englewood Cliffs, N.J.: Prentice-Hall. [3]

Putnam, H. (1973). "Reductionism and the Nature of Psychology," *Cognition*, 2 (1973), 131–141. [6]

Reed, S. K. (1974). "Structural Descriptions and the Limitations of Visual Images," *Memory and Cognition*, 2 (1974), 329–336. [6] [8]

Rey, G. (1981). "What Are Mental Images?" In Block, 1981. [Intr.]

Richardson, A. (1969). *Mental Imagery*, New York: Springer. [3]

Richman, C. L.; Mitchell, D. B.; and Reznick, J. S. (1979). "Mental Travel: Some Reservations," *Journal of Experimental Psychology: Human Perception and Performance*, 5 (1979), 13–18. [6] [7]

Riseman, E. M., and Hanson, A. R., eds. (1978). *Computer Vision Systems*, New York: Academic Press. [6] [8]

Rock, I. (1973). *Orientation and Form*, New York: Academic Press. [6]

Roe, A. (1951). "A Study of Imagery in Research Scientists," *Journal of Personality,* 19 (1951), 459–470. [6]

Rosch, E., and Lloyd, B., eds. (1978). *Cognition and Categorization,* Hillsdale, N.J.: Erlbaum Associates. [Intr.] [6] [7]

Rosenblith, W. A., ed. (1961). *Sensory Communication,* Cambridge: MIT Press. [2]

Rosenthal, R., and Rosnow, R. L., eds. (1969). *Artifact in Behavioral Research,* New York: Academic Press. [6]

Rosenzweig, M. R., and Porter, L. W., eds. (1981). *Annual Review of Psychology,* Vol. 32, . [Intr.]

Ryle, G. (1949). *The Concept of Mind,* London: Hutchinson & Co. [6]

Sarbin, T. (1972). "Imagining as Muted Role-taking: A Historical-Linguistic Analysis." In Sheehan, 1972. [6]

Savage, C. W., ed. (1978). *Perception and Cognition. Issues in the Foundations of Psychology,* Minnesota Studies in the Philosophy of Science, Vol. 9, Minneapolis: University of Minnesota Press. [Intr.] [7]

Schacht, Richard (1972). "Husserlian and Heideggerian Phenomenology," *Philosophical Studies,* 23 (1972), 293–314. [4]

Schank, R. C., and Abelson, R. P. (1977). *Scripts, Plans, Goals and Understanding: An Inquiry into Human Knowledge Structures,* Hillsdale, N.J.: Erlbaum Associates. [6]

Schwartz, Robert (1975). "Representation and Resemblance," *Philosophical Forum,* 7 (1975), 499–512. [5]

Segal, S. J., and Fusella, V. (1970). "Influence of Imaged Pictures and Sounds on Detection of Visual and Auditory Signals," *Journal of Experimental Psychology,* 83 (1970), 458–464. [6]

Segal, S. J., and Gordon, P. (1968). The Perky Effect Revisited: Paradoxical Thresholds or Signal Detection Error? Paper presented at the 39th Annual Meeting of the Eastern Psychological Association. [3]

Sekuler, R., and Nash, D. (1972). "Speed of Size Scaling in Human Vision," *Psychonomic Science,* 27 (1972), 93–94. [6]

Seuss, B. (1957). *The Cat in the Hat Comes Back,* New York: Random House. [6]

Sheehan, P. W. (1967). "A Shortened Form of Betts' Questionnaire upon Mental Imagery," *Journal of Clinical Psychology,* 23 (1967), 286–289. [6]

——, ed. (1972). *The Function and Nature of Imagery,* New York: Academic Press. [6]

——. (1978). "Mental Imagery." In Foss, 1978. [6]

Shepard, R. N. (1975). "Form, Formation, and Transformation of Internal Representations." In Solso, 1975. [7]

——. (1978). "The Mental Image," *American Psychologist,* 33 (1978), 123–137. [Intr.] [6] [7]

Shepard, R. N., and Chipman, S. (1970). "Second-order Isomorphism of Internal Representations: Shapes of States," *Cognitive Psychology,* 1 (1970), 1–17. [Intr.] [1]

Shepard, R. N., and Feng, C. (1972). "A Chronometric Study of Mental Paperfolding," *Cognitive Psychology,* 3 (1972), 228–243. [6]

Shepard, R. N., and Judd, S. A. (1976). "Perceptual Illusion of Rotation of Three-dimensional Objects," *Science,* 191 (1976), 952–954. [6]

Shepard, R. N., and Metzler, J. (1971). "Mental Rotation of Three-dimensional Objects," *Science,* 171 (1971), 701–703. [1] [4] [6]

Shepard, R. N., and Podgorny, P. (1978). "Cognitive Processes That Resemble Perceptual Processes." In Estes, 1978. [6]

Shiffrin, R. M.; Craig, J. C.; and Cohen, E. (1973). "On the Degree of Attention and

Capacity Limitation in Tactile Processing," *Perception Psychophysics,* 13 (1973), 328–336. [1]

Shiffrin, R. M., and Gardner, G. T. (1972). "Visual Processing Capacity and Attention Control," *Journal of Experimental Psychology,* 93 (1972), 72–82. [1]

Shiffrin, R. M., and Geisler, W. S. (1973). "Visual Recognition in a Theory of Information Processing." In Solso, 1973. [1]

Shulman, G. S.; Remington, R. W.; and McLean, J. P. (1979). "Moving Attention through Visual Space," *Journal of Experimental Psychology: Human Perception and Performance,* 5 (1979), 522–526. [6] [7]

Schwartz, S. P. (1979). Studies of Mental Image Rotation: Implications of a Computer Simulation Model of Visual Imagery. Unpublished Ph.D. thesis, Johns Hopkins University. [6]

Siegler, R. S., ed. (1978). *Children's Thinking: What Develops?* Hillsdale, N.J.: Erlbaum Associates. [6]

Simon, H. A. (1972). "What Is Visual Imagery? An Information Processing Interpretation." In Gregg, 1972. [6]

Simon H. A. (1969). "The Architecture of Complexity." In Simon, 1969. [6]

Simon, H. A., ed. (1969). *The Sciences of the Artificial,* Cambridge, Mass.: M.I.T. Press. [6]

Singer, G., and Sheehan, P. W. (1965). "The Effect of Demand Characteristics on the Figural After-effect with Real and Imagined Inducing Figures," *American Journal of Psychology,* 78 (1965), 96–101. [6]

Singer, W. (1979). "Temporal Aspects of Subcortical Contrast Processing," *Neurosciences Research Program Bulletin,* 15 (1979), 358–369. [6]

Smith, E. E., and Nielson, G. D. (1970). "Representation and Retrieval Processes in Short-term Memory: Recognition and Recall of Faces," *Journal of Experimental Psychology,* 85 (1970), 397–405. [6]

Smith, E. E.; Shoben, E. J.; and Rips, L. J. (1974). "Structure and Process in Semantic Memory: A Feature Model for Semantic Decisions," *Psychological Review,* 81 (1974), 214–241. [6]

Snow, R. E.; Federico, P. A.; and Montague, W. E., eds. (1980). *Aptitude, Learning, and Instruction: Cognitive Processes Analysis of Learning and Problem Solving,* Vol. 2, Hillsdale, N.J.: Erlbaum Associates. [6] [7]

Solso, R. L., ed. (1973). *Contemporary Issues in Cognitive Psychology: The Loyola Symposium,* Washington, D.C.: V. H. Winston & Sons. [1] [7]

Sperling, G. (1960). "The Information Available in Brief Visual Presentations," *Psychological Monographs,* 74 (1960), Whole No. 498. [1]

Spinelli, D. N., and Pribram, K. H. (1967). "Changes in Visual Recovery Functions and Unit Activity Produced by Frontal and Temporal Cortex Stimulation," *Electroencephalography and Clinical Neurophysiology,* 22 (1967), 143–149. [6]

Spinelli, D. N.; Pribram, K. H.; and Weingarten, M. (1965). "Centrifugal Optic Nerve Responses Evoked by Auditory and Somatic Stimulation," *Experimental Neurology,* 12 (1965), 303–319. [6]

Spinelli, D. N., and Weingarten, M. (1966). "Afferent and Efferent Activity in Single Units of the Cat's Optic Nerve," *Experimental Neurology,* 13 (1966), 347–361. [6]

Spoehr, K. T., and Williams, B. E. (1978). Retrieving Distance and Location Information from Mental Maps. Paper presented at the 19th annual meeting of the Psychonomic Society, San Antonio, Texas, November. [6]

Strawson, (1966). "Physical and Phenomenal Geometry," in *The Bounds of Sense,* London: Methuen. [4]

Stromeyer, C. F., and Psotka, J. (1970). "The Detailed Texture of Eidetic Images," *Nature*, 225 (1970), 346-349. [3]

Sussman, G. J. (1973). The FINDSPACE Problem. Cambridge, Mass.: M.I.T. AI Lab Memo 286. [6]

Sutherland, I. E. (1970). "Computer Displays," *Scientific American*, 222, No. 6 (1970), 56-81. [3]

Swets, J. A. (1963). "Central Factors in Auditory Frequency Selectivity," *Psychological Bulletin*, 60 (1963), 429-440. [1]

Tapscott, B. L., and Gustafson, D., eds. (1979). *Body, Mind and Method: Essays in Honor of Virgil Aldrich*, Dordrecht, Holland: Reidel. [4]

Treisman, A. M. (1964). "Selective Attention in Man," *British Medical Bulletin*, 20 (1964), 12-16. [1]

Treyens, J. C., and Brewer, W. F. (1978). The Effects of Expected Probability and Expected Saliency on Memory for Objects in a Room. Paper Presented at Annual Meeting of the MPA, Chicago. [6]

Wales, R. J., and Walker, E. (eds.) (1976). *New Approaches to Language Mechanisms*, Amsterdam: North-Holland. [7]

Waltz, D. L. (1979). Relating Images, Concepts, and Words. Proceedings of the NSF Workshop on the Representation of 3-D Objects, University of Pennsylvania, 1-29. [6]

Waltz, D. L., and Boggess, L. D. (1979). Visual Analog Representations for Natural Language Understanding, to appear in Proceedings of the Sixth International Joint Conference on Artificial Intelligence, Tokyo. [6]

Weber, R. J., and Harnish, R. (1974). "Visual Imagery for Words: The Hebb Test," *Journal of Experimental Psychology*, 102 (1974), 409-414. [6]

Weber, R. J.; Kelley, J.; and Little, S. (1972). "Is Visual Imagery Sequencing under Verbal Control?" *Journal of Experimental Psychology*, 96 (1972), 354-362. [6]

Weisstein, N. (1968). "A Rashevsky-Landahl Neural Net: Simulation of Metacontrast," *Psychological Review*, 75 (1968), 494-521. [1]

Wiener, N., and Schadé, J. P., eds. (1963). *Nerve, Brain and Memory Models. Progress in Brain Research*, Vol. 2, Amsterdam: Elsevier. [2]

Willis, J. (1621). *The Art of Memory as It Dependeth upon Places and Ideas*, London; facsimile, New York: Da Capo Press, 1973. [6]

Wilton, R. N. (1978). "Explaining Imaginal Inference by Operations in a Propositional Format," *Perception*, 7 (1978), 563-574. [6]

Winston, P. H., ed. (1975). *The Psychology of Computer Vision*, New York: McGraw Hill. [6]

Wittgenstein, L. (1953). *Philosophical Investigations*, trans. G. E. M. Anscombe, Oxford: Blackwell. [2] [3]

Wooldridge, Dean (1963). *The Machinery of the Brain*, New York: McGraw Hill. [2]

Yates, F. A. (1966). *The Art of Memory*, London: Routledge and Kegan Paul. [6]

Zopf, G. W. (1963). "Sensory Homeostasis." In Wiener and Schadé, 1963. [2]

INDEX

259